THE PENITENTE BROTHERHOOD

The

PENITENTE
BROTHERHOOD

*Patriarchy and Hispano-Catholicism
in New Mexico*

Michael P. Carroll

The Johns Hopkins University Press
Baltimore and London

This book has been brought to publication with the generous assistance of the J. B. Smallman Publication Fund administered by the Faculty of Social Science at the University of Western Ontario.

2 4 6 8 9 7 5 3 1

The Johns Hopkins University Press
2715 North Charles Street
Baltimore, Maryland 21218-4363
www.press.jhu.edu

Carroll, Michael P., 1944–
    The Penitente brotherhood : patriarchy and Hispano-
Catholicism in New Mexico / Michael P. Carroll.
    p.   cm.
Includes bibliographical references and index.
ISBN 0-8018-7055-0 (hardcover : alk. paper)
1. Hermanos Penitentes.   I. Title.
BX3653.U6 C37 2002
267'.242789—DC21
2001007989

A catalog record for this book is available from the British Library.

CONTENTS

LIST OF ILLUSTRATIONS

ACKNOWLEDGMENTS

Tony Mares, Robert Paul, and Robert Bunting all provided useful and thoughtful feedback on draft versions of particular chapters. A very early version of the argument in Chapter 7 was developed in a paper presented at the Symposium on the Psychohistory and Psychology of Religion held in Amsterdam in June 1999, and that paper was included in the proceedings of the Symposium (see Belzen 2001). The comments received from the participants in this symposium helped me to clarify some ambiguities in the original argument and are much appreciated. I owe a special debt to Thomas Steele; his close and always informed reading of various chapters has helped me to avoid some obvious mistakes. He may still disagree with much that is said, but this book is immeasurably better than it would have been without his critical comments. Finally, it may be obvious, but it always needs to be said: responsibility for the interpretations and arguments presented in this book is entirely my own.

The research in this book was made possible by a grant from the Social Sciences and Humanities Research Council of Canada (SSHRC). In an era of shrinking resources, SSHRC's continuing willingness to support scholarly investigation is something for which everyone in the Canadian academic community must be thankful. Publication of this book was also aided by a grant from the J. B. Smallman Publication Fund administered by the Faculty of Social Science of the University of Western Ontario.

For this book, as for everything I have done as an academic, I must thank my parents, Olga Ciarlanti and William Carroll. I have always known that they worked hard to provide me with the education I was able to get. Only over the last few years, however, as I have talked more with my mother about her life with my father (who, unfortunately, now suffers from the deterioration caused by Alzheimer's disease) have I truly come to realize the magnitude of the sacrifices they made and the stress that it caused at the time.

Finally, I must acknowledge my partner, Lori Campbell. She is, quite simply, the love of my life and the person who, more than anyone else, sustains me in all that I do.

THE PENITENTE BROTHERHOOD

INTRODUCTION

Juan de Oñate's Severed Foot and Other Good Stories

In 1598 a company of soldiers and colonists under the command of Don Juan de Oñate entered what is now New Mexico and established the first permanent Spanish settlements in the region. The first capital of this new colony was located a few miles to the north of the modern city of Española. Almost four hundred years later (in 1994), officials of Rio Arriba County decided to build the Oñate Monument and Visitor's Center near the site of that first capital. According to the center's promotional material, it was built to promote "the Hispanic heritage of the Española valley and Rio Arriba County"—and there is no reason to doubt that this *was* one of conscious goals that drove those promoting the center. Still, Española is a sprawling community known most of all for the low-rider autos that prowl its streets, and it has little to offer the hordes of mainly Anglo tourists who flock to New Mexico every year in search of Pueblo authenticity, the Santa Fe style, or the landscapes that inspired Georgia O'Keeffe. It thus seems likely that another reason for building the center was to siphon off some of the tourist-filled autos that would otherwise speed by along Route 68 as they make their mad dash from Santa Fe to Taos or vice versa.

The "monument" part of the Oñate Monument and Visitors Center is a magnificent bronze statue of Oñate on horseback set up in the outdoor courtyard just behind the center's main building. Sometime in early January 1998 somebody stole into that courtyard and used an electric saw to cut off Oñate's right foot. I say "sometime" because the electrified amputation appears not to have been noticed right away. Indeed, the center's staff were unaware of the amputation until contacted by an Albuquerque newspaper, which had received a communiqué from the group claiming responsibility for the deed (which tells us something, I think, about the number of visitors to the center). In any event, the communiqué received in Albuquerque

1

suggested that the action had been taken on behalf of "our brothers and sisters at Ácoma pueblo"—and *that* was supposed to explain the severed foot.

In January 1599 Acoma Pueblo had been attacked and subdued by Oñate's forces in reprisal for an earlier attack in which the inhabitants at Acoma had killed eleven Spanish soldiers. In a trial conducted the following month, most of those captured at Acoma were sentenced to various forms of servitude. Oñate, however, reserved a special punishment for all captured males over the age of twenty-five years: in addition to their being sentenced to twenty years of personal servitude, they were each to have one foot cut off. The vandalism done to Oñate's statue in 1998 was obviously calling attention to the punishment meted out to Acoma males four hundred years earlier.

The story of how and why the bronze Oñate came to have his foot severed in 1998, like so many other good stories, was dutifully reported in the *New York Times* (February 9, 1998). One of the things that made it a good story, at least from the perspective of the Anglo (English-speaking non-Hispanic) constituency on whom the *Times* relies, is that it involved the Pueblo Indians. After all, for more than a century now, New Mexico's Pueblo Indians have been constructed in Anglo popular culture as the bearers of an exotic and ancient culture that predisposes them to live in mystical harmony with the land they inhabit. As such, they are implicitly seen by many as a living reminder of what American society has lost in its drive for technological progress. Little wonder, then, that a story calling attention to the past wrongs done to such a noble people would appeal to modern audiences. Something else that made this story a good one, undoubtedly, was that the original injustice had been perpetuated by Spanish *conquistadores,* whom most Anglo-Americans undoubtedly see as foreigners (notwithstanding the fact that they settled permanently in what is now the United States almost a decade before the British established their first permanent settlement at Jamestown). It was, in short, an atrocities-against-the-Indians story that for once did not entail Anglo guilt.

Like so many other good stories, however, this one got even better in the retelling. Thus, suggested the *Times,* although Oñate had eventually been punished for his excesses at Acoma by the King of Spain, the "psychic wounds [occasioned by the amputations] remain fresh among the Acoma" mainly because "since 1598, the Acoma had passed from generation to generation the tale of how Juan de Oñate had punished the conquered Acomans by ordering his men to chop off the right feet of 24 captive warriors."

This psychic-wounds-kept-alive-by-a-continuously- operative-oral-tradition element neatly and concisely collapses past and present to create the timelessness that Anglo audiences like to associate with Pueblo culture. Just as importantly, this same element establishes an appealing contrast between traditional (Pueblo) cultures that rely on oral transmission to preserve their history, and modern (implicitly Anglo) cultures that, well, rely on newspapers like the *New York Times* to preserve their histories. Unfortunately, while the *Times's* retelling made better copy, it is a story that does not stand up to scrutiny. Consider the testimony offered by Simon Ortiz, a well-known New Mexican writer.

Ortiz tells us that while growing up at Acoma Pueblo he *never* heard about the attack on Acoma in 1599, *never* heard about the hundreds who died during that attack, *never* heard about the hundreds captured afterwards who were made slaves and servants, and *never* heard about the Acoma captives who had one foot cut off (Ortiz 1993, 152). He only learned about these things, he says, when he "read history as an adult"; and, he goes on to say, "I wondered why my Acoma people did not talk about it in our stories." It's a good question. Ortiz's own answer is that Spanish colonial authorities simply constructed a history that denied the truth of their atrocities and that the Pueblo peoples, at least until recently, accepted this sanitized version of history as their own. Ortiz, of course, is telling his own story here; and it's one that is well suited to the particular argument he is advancing in his article, which is that the same biases that pervaded early Spanish accounts of Pueblo history continue to structure the accounts of Pueblo history written by non-Pueblo authors.

Given the vestiges of unreconstructed positivism that still lurk in the dark corners of my scholarly soul even in this postmodern age, however, I have to point out that Ortiz's own story—like the *Times's* story—cannot be taken at face value. Spanish authorities did not erase references to the events at Acoma in January 1599. On the contrary, those events were well documented in a series of depositions taken both before and after the attack on Acoma and dutifully filed with Spanish government authorities. Those documents have been available to scholars for some time (see Hammond and Rey 1953, 425–79), which is precisely why the materials that Ortiz read as an adult were able to describe what happened at Acoma. If the horrors at Acoma in 1599 came to be erased from the memory of those living at Acoma in subsequent generations, it seems likely that this happened, not because Acomans uncritically accepted the vision of history written down by Spanish historians, but rather because the inhabitants at Acoma themselves did not pass on the memory of these events, or maybe—just maybe—because the oral transmission of tradition in traditional cultures isn't quite the efficient process that it's cracked up to be in the Anglo imagination.

In any event, the general lesson to be learned from the story of the bronze Oñate's amputated foot, I suggest, is this: anyone who writes anything about New Mexico does so against the backdrop of stories that are deeply ingrained in the popular imagination. This is not problematic for anyone (like the author of the *Times* article) who reaches conclusions that are consistent with these popular stories. It *is* a problem, however, for someone who writes on New Mexico and reaches conclusions that *subvert* the stories that have a hold on the popular imagination—which is precisely what I will be doing in this book. In my own defense, I can only say that the story I am about to tell is at least as consistent with the available historical evidence as the more familiar stories you may already have heard about New Mexico.

⊰⊱ Continuity or Discontinuity?

For the past two centuries, three things have most of all distinguished Hispano[1] Catholicism in New Mexico from the Catholicism of the Pueblo Indians, the Catholicism of the French clergy who were parachuted into New Mexico after the American annexation, and even from a more broadly defined Hispanic Catholicism practiced in Mexico and other areas of the Southwest. The first of these three things is the distinctive religious art of the *santero* tradition, which consists mainly of *bultos* (statues) and *retablos* (paintings on board) depicting different images of Christ, Mary, and the saints. The second is the sanctuary at Chimayó, which now attracts more pilgrims than any other Catholic sanctuary north of Mexico. The third is the Penitentes, the lay brotherhood that is the primary focus of this book.

It happens that each of these distinctive elements is associated with the last half-century or so of colonial rule in New Mexico. Thus, the *santero* tradition emerged in the late 1700s; the sanctuary at Chimayó was established around 1813; and, although the matter of Penitente origins is hotly contested (and we will be considering the various theories concerning Penitente origins in Chapter 1), the first documentary reference to the Penitentes only appears in 1833. On the face of it, then, it might seem that the late 1700s and early 1800s was a period of change and innovation as regards Hispano religiosity—and yet this is not the way most previous investigators have constructed this period. On the contrary, the historiographical emphasis in most existing studies of Hispano religiosity is on continuity with past traditions. Thus, studies of *santero* art routinely establish linkages between such art and image cults in the Catholic tradition generally; accounts of the sanctuary at Chimayó stress its similarity to an earlier sanctuary in Guatemala; and, as we shall see, all existing accounts of Penitente origins—though they may differ with regard to what particular organization was the precursor to the Penitentes—take it as obvious that the Penitentes were fueled by a tradition of Hispanic/Spanish piety that stretches

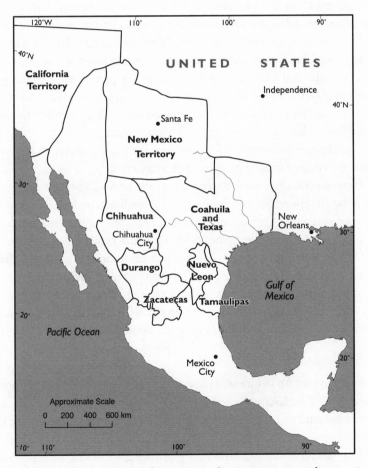

Mexico in the 1820s. Derived from Reséndez [1999, 671] with permission of the *Journal of American History.* Cartographic Section, Geography Department, University of Western Ontario.

back to the Middle Ages. William Wroth, who has written extensively on Hispano Catholicism, sums up what is still the prevailing consensus very succinctly: "In religious life, however, they [Hispano settlers] were not innovative, but rather were preservers of ancient traditions having roots in medieval and Renaissance Spain" (1988, 5).

I am not going to suggest that this prevailing historiographical emphasis on continuity is completely unsupported by the historical record. On the contrary, nothing emerges out of a social and cultural vacuum, so it will always be possible to say of any new phenomenon that it was to some extent shaped by, or modeled on, what went before. Thus, in the New Mexican case, the *santero* tradition undeniably *did* borrow some iconographical themes from earlier traditions of Catholic religious art; the sanctuary at Chimayó *was* to some extent modeled on a similar sanctuary in Guatemala; and (as will be made clear in Chapter 2) the Penitentes *do* share many elements in common with penitential *cofradías* that had existed previously in both Mexico and Spain. Even so, I will be arguing throughout this book that the prevailing historiographical emphasis on continuity has caused previous commentators to overlook some patterns that are central to any understanding of Hispano Catholicism.

More specifically, I will be arguing that this prevailing emphasis on continuity has led previous commentators to overlook the fact that in many ways the variant of Catholicism that emerged among the Hispano population of New Mexico during the early nineteenth century was qualitatively different both from the variants of popular Catholicism that flourished in Mexico and Spain (and other areas of the Catholic world) and from the Catholicism that their own Hispano ancestors had practiced previously in New Mexico itself. Establishing the truth of this ambitious statement is one of my primary goals of this book; explaining *why* it is true is the other.

❧ The Organization of This Book

Any account of Penitente religiosity must start with a description of the thing itself, so Chapter 1 reviews the history of the Penitentes and provides an account of the ceremonies and rituals that were central to the Penitente experience. It also reviews the various theories that have been offered to explain Penitente emergence. Although differing in many ways, these theories in the end rest on a common assumption: that Hispano Catholics were a deeply pious people, solidly attached to the sacramental rituals of the official church, notably including here the Mass, the Eucharist, and confession. In fact, there is much evidence, reviewed in the concluding section of the chapter, that this was not the case.

Chapter 2 reviews the available data relating to Hispano religiosity in the period before 1800. What emerges, first of all, is that Hispano settlers seem to have fallen far short of the standards that defined a "good Catholic" in the eyes of the Tridentine church. But the more important pattern that emerges in this chapter is that, Tridentine Catholicism aside, the Hispano experience in New Mexico before 1800 seems marked by the general *absence* of elements that in other parts of the Catholic world are the hallmarks of popular Catholicism. Apparitions of Mary, miraculous im-

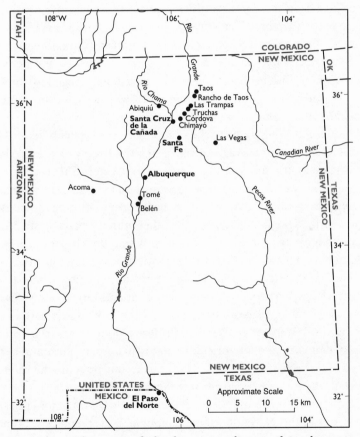

New Mexico, with some of the locations discussed in the text. Cartographic Section, Geography Department, University of Western Ontario.

ages, and pilgrimages to local sites that had been sacralized in some way—all of which were a routine part of the Catholic experience in Spain, colonial Mexico, and Italy—were simply not part of the Hispano experience in northern New Mexico.

Flagellation has always been central to Penitente ritual, and Chapter 3 looks at the history of flagellation in New Mexico. It turns out that there are *only three* documented instances of flagellation in pre-Penitente New Mexico. Although almost all previous commentators have pointed to these incidents as evidence that the Penitentes were the outgrowth of preexisting (and continuing) traditions, another interpretation is possible. Indeed, when these three incidents are viewed against the known history of flagellation and flagellant confraternities in the Catholic world generally, and Spain in particular, these incidents can be taken as providing evidence that the practice of public flagellation, though it probably did exist early in the history of the colony, had died out long before the Penitentes emerged in the early nineteenth century. The public flagellations staged by the Penitentes, in other words, were something relatively new, not the continuation of something old.

Chapter 4 is in many ways the theoretical core of the book. It starts by considering some puzzles concerning the iconography of Nuestro Padre Jesús Nazareno, the supernatural figure at the center of Penitente ritual. This leads to a consideration of two existing bodies of scholarship relating to New Mexico, one dealing with the changes set in motion by the Bourbon Reforms of the late 1700s, and the other with the pattern of communal/cooperative agriculture that prevailed within the Hispano communities of northern New Mexico until annexation. Taken together, these two bodies of literature lead to a fairly straightforward conclusion that has been unacknowledged in previous discussions. That conclusion is this: that the social changes taking place in late colonial New Mexico would have worked to erode the system of patriarchal authority upon which the communal/cooperative system of agriculture found in Hispano communities depended. This conclusion, I argue, helps us to understand why the Penitentes became so popular at precisely the time they did.

Chapter 5 looks carefully at the career of Padre Antonio José Martínez of Taos, one of the most important religious leaders in nineteenth-century New Mexico and someone who has long been recognized as being linked to the Penitentes. For his detractors, like the author Willa Cather, Martínez has always epitomized the clerical corruption that right-minded Catholic leaders like Bishop Lamy sought to eliminate; for his supporters, Martínez has always been a progressive nationalist leader in the tradition of Mexico's Miguel Hidalgo. The goal of this chapter, however, is to demonstrate that if we view Martínez's career through a lens fashioned by some recent theoretical developments in the study of the European Counter-Reformation, then there is a way of seeing Padre Martínez that has been overlooked by his detractors and his admirers alike. Very simply, such a lens allows us to see Padre Martínez as someone concerned with promoting Catholic Reform within a population that had never been particularly pious, and who, in the pursuit of this goal, used the very same methods that had been used centuries earlier by reformers like Carlo Borromeo, who had worked in the immediate aftermath of the Council of Trent.

Although the Penitentes were in many ways similar to traditional *cofradías* in Spain and Mexico (something that has been stressed in most existing accounts of Penitente history), they were also different. Chapter 6 explores the various organizational innovations that the Penitentes incorporated into the administrative structure of their local *moradas* and that made them different from traditional *cofradías*. What becomes apparent is that Penitente moradas were associated with organizational emphases that in other contexts have been identified as signifying the "rise of the modern." Recognizing this provides a basis for discussing the personality type that would have been fostered among Hispano males by Penitente membership, and, in turn, how the proliferation of this personality type would have interacted with other social processes—most notably those that were contributing to Hispano dispossession—in post-annexation New Mexico.

Chapter 7 confronts a puzzle: if Hispano Catholics were not particularly religious before 1800 (as I have claimed), then what explains the emotional intensity that quite obviously fueled Penitente practice? Although there can be no certain answer to such a question, this chapter uses a theory of religious ritual proposed by Robert Paul in another context to construct a possible answer. Quite apart from its ability to explain the emotional intensity associated with Penitente ritual, Paul's theory can also be used to explain several other patterns that have either been ignored or passed over quickly in most earlier commentaries on the Penitentes (e.g., why the *younger* brothers—the Brothers of Blood—are the ones most associated with punishment; why Doña Sebastiana images, which are found in all Penitente moradas, are called "Sebastiana"; why *sudario* means a prayer for the dead in New Mexico but nowhere else; and so on.)

In the Epilogue, I return to the matter of "privileged stories" in order to explore some issues relating to New Mexican historiography that pose a challenge to the notions of disinterested scholarship that have long prevailed in Western academic circles. In particular, I contrast the story that I am telling about the Penitentes with the stories preferred by Anglo audiences as well as with the stories preferred by Hispano audiences. I also consider some of the political implications (and there *are* political implications) of what I have done here.

ONE

Penitente Historiography and Its Problems

There are no documentary references to the *Hermandad de Nuestro Padre Jesús Nazareno* of New Mexico, more commonly known as the Penitentes, before 1833. In that year, however, the group seems to emerge in the documentary record as an ongoing and established concern only just come to the notice of ecclesiastical authorities. The first explicit reference to the Penitentes appears in a letter written in February 1833 by Antonio José Martínez,[1] parish priest at Taos, to José Antonio Zubiría, bishop of Durango (New Mexico being a part of the Diocese of Durango). In his letter (reproduced in Wroth 1991, 40), Martínez says that for the period of time he has had charge of his parish, a group of men belonging to a Brotherhood dedicated to the Blood of Christ has engaged in penitential activities, mainly on the Fridays of Lent, during all of Holy Week, and on the Fridays between Holy Week and Pentecost. In describing the nature of these activities, Martínez gives us our very first account of the rituals that would come to make the Penitentes so famous (or, for some, so infamous): wearing only white cotton trousers and a scarf that hides the lower part of their faces, these men drag heavy crosses, whip themselves with scourges, and lacerate their backs with sharp stones or flints until blood flows. Martínez also suggests that such activities cause the greatest scandal during Holy Week, when the Brothers perform these penitential activities while walking before the statues carried in procession, since on this occasion their behavior is witnessed by the attending crowds. Finally, Martínez says that he has stopped the public performance of these penitential activities, though the men are still permitted to engaged in penitential activities at night and in nonpublic areas. Padre Martínez, I might add, had been appointed pastor at Taos in 1826 and had assisted there for a brief period in early 1823 (Chávez 1981, 24–27). What his letter indicates, in other words, is that, at the very least, the Penitentes had been functioning at Taos since the early 1820s.

In his response, written from Chihuahua in April 1833 (reproduced in Wroth 1991, 50), Zubiría said that he approved of Martínez's prohibition, and he affirmed the view that the Brothers should be content to engage in penitential activity in the privacy of the church and even then only if such activity were done in moderation.

Bishop Zubiría made his first official visit to New Mexico a few months later; and during the course of that visitation, he again took note of the Brotherhood. In a letter written from Santa Cruz de la Cañada (reproduced in Weigle 1976a: 195–96), he says that a Brotherhood of Penitentes (*"una Hermandad de Penitentes"*) has existed in that villa for many years without episcopal authorization and has engaged in public penitential exercises that are both indiscreet and contrary to true Christian humility. While still endorsing the principle that moderate penitential activity done in private can be beneficial, Zubiría instructed all present and future priests at Santa Cruz not to permit the sort of public mortifications practiced by the Brothers. He also indicated that local priests should certainly not allow the construction of a special room where the instruments of mortification used by the Brothers could be stored and where the Brothers could hold their meetings. This suggests, of course, that the Brotherhood at Santa Cruz had just such a room, though whether this refers to a free-standing morada of the sort that would come to be associated with the Penitentes later in the century, or simply a special room attached to the local church, is unclear. In closing, Zubiría says that this letter should be shown to the local priest in any other part of the territory where a similar Brotherhood of Penitentes might be operating. Writing in October 1833 at the conclusion of his Visitation, Zubiría once again enjoined priests throughout the territory to suppress the Penitentes (see Weigle 1976a, 196–97).

It is difficult to know from these earliest references just how extensive the Penitentes were during the 1820s and 1830s. In the end, the only locations that can be associated with a functioning Penitente group with certainty are Taos and Santa Cruz de la Cañada. True, Zubiría clearly felt that Penitente groups *might* be operating elsewhere; hence, the instruction to show his letter to the local priest in any community where this might be the case. Even so, in his final letter he begins the paragraph that deals with the Penitentes by saying that "in order to end [a] great evil that could become worse in the future, I prohibit those brotherhoods of penitence, or better yet, brotherhoods of butchery (*hermandades de penitencia ó mas bien de carniceria),* that have been growing under the protection provided by an inappropriate tolerance" (Weigle 1976a, 196). The general tone here suggests, I think, that Zubiría felt he was confronting a movement that was in the process of gathering strength even as he spoke, not one that was well established and dispersed throughout the territory.

There are only a few references to the Penitentes between 1833 and the American annexation of New Mexico in 1846, and most of these are indirect. In 1845, for example, the parish priest at Santa Cruz wrote to the parish priest at Albuquerque reminding him of Bishop Zubiría's 1833 letter. Also in 1845, during the course of his second visitation, Bishop Zubiría himself ordered that his 1833 letter be read again throughout New Mexico. Weigle (1976a, 25) interprets both actions as suggesting that the Penitentes were spreading despite ecclesiastical opposition. Although this is possible, her interpretation here makes sense mainly because we know that the Penitentes became so important in the post-annexation period. Considered in isolation, without taking into account our knowledge of what the future would bring, these two incidents could be taken as indicating merely that a few Penitente groups continued to exist. Certainly, during the course of his second visitation in 1845, Zubiría nowhere singled out a specific Penitente group operating at some particular location for condemnation. Furthermore, as Weigle herself concedes (25), he made no reference whatsoever to the Penitentes during his third visitation in 1850.

In fact, between 1833 and 1846 we have only one certain report of Penitente activity from an eyewitness. That report appears in Josiah Gregg's *Commerce of the Prairies,* originally published in 1843. Writing of his experiences in New Mexico during the early 1830s, Gregg (1954, 181) tells us:

I once chanced to be in the town of Tomé on Good Friday, when
my attention was arrested by a man almost naked, bearing, in imitation of Simon, a huge cross upon his shoulders, which, though
constructed of the lightest wood, must have weighed over a hundred
pounds. The long end dragged upon the ground, as we have seen
it represented in sacred pictures, and about the middle swung a stone
of immense dimensions, appended there for the purpose of making
the task more laborious. Not far behind followed another equally
destitute of clothing, with his whole body wrapped in chains and
cords, which seemed buried in the muscles, and which so cramped
and confined him that he was scarcely able to keep pace with
the procession. The person who brought up the rear presented a still

more disgusting aspect. He walked along with a patient and composed step, while another followed close behind belaboring him lustily with a whip, which he flourished with all the satisfactions of an amateur; but as the lash was pointed only with a tuft of untwisted sea-grass, its application merely served to keep open the wounds upon the penitent's back, which had been scarified, as I was informed, with the keen edge of a flint, and was bleeding most profusely.

At first sight, it might appear that Gregg had stumbled upon a simple passion play, of the sort that we know had been performed in Tomé since the late 1700s (see Steele 1978). But the fact that a stone was suspended from a heavy cross to make it even heavier, that one man was wrapped with cords and chains that seemed buried in his muscles, that another man's back had been lacerated with a flint in order to create a bloody appearance—such things leave no doubt but that the four men Gregg observed were Penitentes.

Information about the Penitentes becomes more plentiful after mid-nineteenth century, when New Mexico became a part of the United States. In 1846 Stephen Watts Kearny and his soldiers took possession of New Mexico in the name of the United States; in 1848 Mexico formally ceded possession to the United States in the Treaty of Guadalupe Hidalgo; and by 1850 New Mexico was formally organized as a territory of the United States. Some of the material about the Penitentes from this early post-annexation period originates from within the movement itself. We have, for example, two early constitutions (one dated 1853 and the other 1860) that spell out the rules and regulations governing local Penitente *moradas,* a term that refers both to the buildings used by the Penitentes and to the local organizational unit (see Steele and Rivera 1985, 77–99). The bulk of the post-annexation literature on the Penitentes, however, was generated by two groups of immigrants: the new and mainly French clergy that American church authorities (New Mexico having been severed from the Diocese of Durango in 1850) parachuted into New Mexico, and hostile Anglo-Protestant commentators for whom Penitente activities epitomized Catholic superstition and error. Weigle's (1976b) annotated bibliography, prepared as a supplement to her study of the Penitentes, remains the best guide to the post-annexation literature.

The most well-known member of the Church hierarchy who dealt with the Penitentes in the post-annexation period is almost certainly Jean

Baptiste Lamy, a French-born cleric who had spent more than a decade working in dioceses in Ohio and Kentucky. In 1850 he was appointed vicar apostolic to the newly created Vicariate of New Mexico. When the vicariate became the Diocese of Santa Fe in 1853, Lamy became its first bishop, just as he became its first archbishop when the Archdiocese of Santa Fe was established in 1875. At least for Anglo audiences, Lamy's fame has always rested in part on the fact that he was the model for Bishop Jean Marie Latour in Willa Cather's very popular *Death Comes for the Archbishop*.[2]

Somewhat surprisingly perhaps, given Anglo stereotypes, Lamy seems to have been less bothered by Penitente penitential excesses than was Bishop Zubiría. What did bother Lamy was that the Penitentes were too much like the sort of "secret society" that were a source of nervous concern for anti-modernist Catholic bishops and popes throughout the nineteenth century. By the 1860s, for example, at least four different nineteenth-century popes—Pius VII, Leo XII, Gregory XVI, and Pius IX—had issued edicts prohibiting societies that bound their members to an oath of secrecy, regardless of whether such societies were formed for political or religious purposes (Fanning 1913). In a letter written by Padre Martínez in 1856 (cited in Weigle 1976a, 54), Martínez says that Lamy told him of a papal order to eliminate secret societies like the Penitentes. Although Weigle herself says that "there is no further record of this papal command" (54), it seems likely that Lamy was referring to one or more of the edicts outlawing secret societies that Pius IX had issued in 1846, in 1849, and again in 1854.

Lamy's desire to make sure that the Penitentes did not function like the sort of secret societies that were destabilizing Catholic regimes in Europe is evident in the twelve rules that he issued in 1856 for the proper operation of the Penitentes as a Catholic confraternity (see Weigle 1976a, 201–4). For the most part these rules are concerned with insuring that only men of good character and morals be admitted to local moradas, that members of the Brotherhood respect the authority of their local priest and their bishop, and that local priests have full and complete access to all the meetings, membership lists, and so forth associated with any given morada. None of the twelve rules make any reference to penitential excesses. Only in a supplementary set of rules issued a few months later (Weigle 1976a, 205–6) did Lamy add that while the Brothers could continue to engage in their customary penitential activities, this had to be done in private and without giving scandal.

Generally, as Weigle (1976a, 63) suggests, the attitude of Lamy and his successor, Jean Baptiste Salpointe, toward the Penitentes was ambivalent.

However much they might be suspicious of the Penitentes, they also needed to maintain the allegiance of Hispano Catholics in the midst of a society that seemed to be becoming increasingly secularized and in which religion was on the decline. As a result, and notwithstanding the posture that these clerics might adopt in dealing with the Anglo press, local priests were given a great deal of leeway in dealing with Penitente groups in their area. Although there is no denying that some local priests did take action against the Penitentes, modern commentators seem agreed that there is no evidence of any concerted effort to suppress them at the local level during the latter decades of the nineteenth century (see Weigle 1976a, 66; Sprott 1984, 10).

To Anglo-Protestant commentators, by contrast, the Penitentes represented all that was corrupt and degenerate about Roman Catholicism, and nowhere was this view put forward more forcefully than in Alexander Darley's *Passionists of the Southwest* (1893). Darley was a Protestant missionary who styled himself "Apostle of the Colorado Mexicans," and his account of the Penitentes is infused simultaneously with a hatred for the Roman Church and a patronizing attitude towards Hispano culture. Darley devotes the first two-thirds or so of his book to (1) a general history of flagellation in the Western church, (2) a history of the Third Order of St. Francis, and (3) the presentation of a Penitente constitution provided to Darley by a former Penitente who had converted to Protestantism. The remainder of the book is devoted mainly to Darley's account of the various and sundry ways that the Penitentes had contrived to mortify their flesh in pursuit of what he called "the idolatrous adoration of the blood they switch out of their own backs" (43). Although a simple description of these mortifications would likely have been sufficient to elicit the disgust that Darley wanted to elicit from his (Protestant) target audience, he also chose to pepper his account with the staples of anti-Catholic rhetoric: child abuse (e.g., a young child being forced to lie naked on a bed of cacti during a Penitente ritual, 28); priestly immorality (e.g., priests flagellating themselves in the company of "half-naked women," 30); and Catholic conspiracies to control society (e.g., priests mobilizing the Penitentes on behalf of both Democratic and Republican candidates, 42).

There was one point on which Church leaders like Salpointe and Protestant critics like Darley were in agreement: both groups felt the Penitentes were in decline, mainly because younger Hispanos were no longer joining the organization. In his Preface, Darley said of the Penitentes, "[Their] history has been lived and we now write about it" (1893, 4). Writing only a few years later, Archbishop Salpointe agreed: "Little by little, heed has been given to the voice of ecclesiastical authority, and at the present date, there are only a few interested men who are trying to keep alive yet the old association" (1898, 163). In retrospect it seems clear that in both cases such a conclusion reflected wishful thinking. In fact, well into the early 1900s it was still the case that a sizable majority of all Hispano males were Penitente members, and one or more moradas could still be found in most Hispano villages (Weigle, 1976a, 96). Indeed, the evidence suggests that membership levels in both northern New Mexico and the San Luis Valley of Colorado did not peak until the 1920s (Swadesh 1974, 193–94; Steele and Rivera 1985, 167; V. Simmons 1999, 248–49). Even so, using materials that he had gathered during the 1930s, Lorin W. Brown (1972, 21–22), writing under the pseudonym Lorenzo de Córdova, could still say that all the males in most Hispano villages, with the possible exception of those belonging to one or two high-status families, belonged to the Brotherhood. It was only in the aftermath of World War II that the Penitentes experienced a truly substantial drop in membership, something that Steele (1997a, 45) attributes mainly to the fact that younger Hispano males were moving to the suburbs and so away from communities with established *moradas*.

During fieldwork conducted in a Hispano village in 1950, Edmonson (1957, 43–44) found that the Penitentes were few in number and largely peripheral to Hispano society. The Penitentes, he said, "have not yet disappeared entirely from Hispano culture, but [they] are obviously on the way out." Like Darley and Salpointe before him, Edmonson suggested that the primary cause of this decline lay in the fact that few younger males were joining the organization. Here again, however, the Penitentes have proven more resilient than expected. Notwithstanding a long-term pattern of decline, Penitente membership in particular communities has now and again experienced modest increases. During fieldwork in the hamlet of Cañones, Paul Kutsche and Dennis Gallego (1979, 98) found that seven men under twenty years of age had joined since 1968, while only three of the older members had died. In the Taos area, Sylvia Rodríguez (1994) reports that grassroots opposition to a resort-oriented dam project during the early 1970s produced a religious-cultural revival in San Francisco de Asís parish at Ranchos de Taos, and that one aspect of this revival was an increase in Penitente activity. During the early 1990s, Peterson (1992) suggested that Penitente membership was once again on the increase, in part because the Penitente tradition has been embraced by a number of Hispano artists trying to revive the *santero* tradition. She concedes, however, that the current membership, which she places at around 800 in New Mexico and southern Colorado, is nowhere near what it was earlier in this century.

✢ Lent, Holy Week, and the Theatricalization of Blood

To some extent, the Penitentes were active throughout the year and performed a range of community functions. When a death occurred, for example, a local morada often took charge of the *velorio* (wake), the procession to the *camposanto* (cemetery), and the actual burial. Local moradas might also provide aid to the sick and the needy. Finally, because most males in a village were Penitente members, Penitente leaders often functioned as agents of social control as the need arose.[3] As active as they were throughout the year, however, Lent was a special period for the Penitentes; and it marked the onset of an intensification of their religious activities.[4]

Lent was a time during which Brothers would gather in the privacy of their morada to say prayers, sing hymns, and engage in penitential mortifications. How often they met during Lent varied from community to community. Córdova (1972), who is describing Penitente activity in Córdova and other villages in northeastern New Mexico, suggests that during Lent Brothers gathered in their morada on Wednesday and Friday evenings; De Aragón (1998), who seems to be describing communities further east (on the other side of the Sangre de Cristo mountains) like Las Vegas and Mora, suggests that Brothers met every night during Lent. However often they met during Lent, Holy Week always marked another escalation in Penitente activity.

Sometime on Palm Sunday or Holy Monday, Brothers left their homes entirely and moved into their morada. Special meatless dishes were prepared and brought to the morada by women belonging to the Confraternity of Our Lady of Mt. Carmel. These "Carmelitas" were usually related to men in the Brotherhood (mainly as wives or girlfriends). For the first day or so, Brothers engaged in prayer and penance in the seclusion of the morada and made no public appearances. Tuesday night was usually reserved for the initiation of new members.

Penitente constitutions (presented in Steele and Rivera 1985, 77–154) suggest that the application procedure was fairly standardized from morada to morada. Applicants, usually accompanied by a male relative who was already a member, would come to the morada door with four candles (to be given to the morada as gifts) and ask to be admitted. Blindfolded, they would then be led inside and, once there, told to take off their clothes and put on *calzoncillos* (white cotton pants with drawstrings around the waist and ankles). Initiates were then asked a series of questions. Some of these were questions about the Passion and death of Christ, while others were questions designed to assess the candidate's loyalty to the Brotherhood and willingness to keep secret the affairs of the morada. This was followed by the collective recitation of a prayer, usually *El Veradero Jesús.*[5]

The initiate was then formally made a member of the morada by being "sealed" to the Brotherhood. This was done by a special officer who incised the *sello* (seal) of the Brotherhood on the bare back of each initiate using a piece of glass or sharp stone (like flint or obsidian). Most commentaries suggest that this seal usually consisted of two sets of vertical lines, with one set being incised on either side of the spine (see Steele and Rivera 1985, 117). Here again, however, there was some variation from morada to morada. One informant from the Española area, for example, in describing his own initiation decades previously, recalls being incised both on either side of the spine and on his upper back as he received the seal (quoted in D. Hall 1995, 181). Beshoar's (1949) account of Penitente moradas in southern Colorado suggests that the *sello* there consisted of a cross of some sort. In his words, "In some moradas the cross is cut between the shoulder blades; in others two crosses are cut, one under each shoulder blade, and in still others a cross is formed by making two long, sweeping cuts down the length of the back and one horizontal cut across the center of the back" (4). In any event, however it was done, the person who had just been sealed to the Brotherhood was given a *disciplina,* which he used to whip the cuts made on his back. These new members then asked forgiveness of any Brother they may have offended and correspondingly offered forgiveness to anyone who may have offended them.

Laceration of the back before flagellation has always been a hallmark of Penitente ritual. Recall that in Padre Martínez's letter to Bishop Zubiría, which provides us with our very first reference to the Penitentes, Martínez mentions that the Brothers lacerate their backs with sharp stones. Gregg also mentioned this practice in his account of the Penitentes at Tomé in the 1830s, saying that the purpose of the flagellation he witnessed was only to keep open wounds on the penitent's back that had been made by the keen edge of a flint. Moreover, the various Penitente constitutions that have survived from the second half of the nineteenth century invariably include among the list of officials they delineate a *picador* or *sangrador,* who was charged with cutting other Brothers.

Most accounts suggest that Brothers began their public appearances on Ash Wednesday, though Beshoar (1949, 14), who is describing moradas in southern Colorado, suggests that this happened on Holy Thursday. Much of their public activity consisted of processions to and from the morada to a local church or *calvario* (a cross, or set of three crosses, set onto a hillside) and to moradas, churches, or *calvarios* located in nearby communities. Generally, these Penitente processions were led by a Brother carrying a small cross or banner, a *pitero* (flute player) and a *rezador* (who read prayers aloud from a book). These individuals were followed by two groups, the *Hermanos de Luz* (Brothers of Light) and the *Hermanos de Sangre* (Brothers of Blood), also known as the *Hermanos de Tinieblas* (Brothers of Darkness). The Brothers of Light were the senior members of the morada and the group from which the officers of the morada were chosen; they generally did not engage in displays of penitential mortification. The Brothers of Blood were the newer members, who did engage in such displays. Usually, the Brothers of Blood wore only white cotton pants and a kerchief that covered the lower part of their faces. Finally, it was often the case that Penitente processions were followed by women and non-members who carried holy images of one sort or another.

The penitential activities performed by the Brothers of Blood during Holy Week almost always included flagellation, which was practiced both in the privacy of the morada and in public. Typically a Brother of Blood would either whip himself over the shoulders with a *disciplina*, usually made from plaited yucca fiber, or be whipped by another Brother. Another common penitential activity involved dragging heavy crosses made of rough logs to and from the morada. In addition to these two particular activities, which were common to all Penitente moradas, the Penitentes performed a number of other mortifications—some public, some private—that varied from place to place.

Writing in 1871, the wife of an army officer stationed at Fort Union described the Penitente rituals she witnessed during a visit to Mora on Holy Thursday of that year:

> The first party we met walking barefoot over the stoniest ground, naked with the exception of a pair of cotton drawers on, the weather extremely cold, each beating their bare backs with whips made of the Spanish bayonet & the blood streaming down to their heels. The Spanish bayonet is a plant which grows about 3 or 4 feet high, it is like a blade of shiny grass four or five inches wide & has sharp points on each side one half inch long, something like a saw. They make their whips of several of these plaited together & every time

they strike themselves with it, the points pierce their flesh & bring
the blood. . . . Then we met another party . . . bearing heavy
crosses on their shoulders, walking up a steep mountain barefooted
& chanting all the way, and every little while lying flat on their
faces and eating the dust & then going on their knees & praying.[6]

In an account of the Holy Week activities at Abiquiú and Tierra Amarilla
in 1878, William Gillet Ritch noted that one Penitente "had a heavy wooden
cross lashed to his back [so that] his arms extended horizontally" and that
"his legs were bound with a horse hair lariat or rope, and were much puffed
and swollen" (RITCH 6: RI 1866). Charles Aranda (1974, i) reports that
Brothers would often scatter stones across the floor of the morada and
then kneel on these until their knees bled. Mills and Grove's (1956) overview
of several dozen reports describing Penitente activity suggests that other
mortifications sometimes included: being buried upright with only one's
head above ground; having one's arms tied to a pole across the shoulders
while the hands held two swords, each positioned downwards so that as
one walked, the swords pricked the thighs; having cactus strapped tightly
to various parts of one's body and/or beating oneself with cactus pads; and
allowing oneself to be bound and pulled over rough ground or cactus by
others.

Most Penitente moradas also had a "death cart" (*carreta de la muerte*).
This was a two-wheeled vehicle resembling an oxcart that contained a
wooden statue of Doña Sebastiana. Although Doña Sebastiana images varied somewhat from location to location, most shared a common set of
characteristics: her carved face was usually the face of a skeleton; she usually wore a black robe that was similar in shape (but not in color[7]) to the
robes worn by Franciscan priests in New Mexico; and she usually held a
bow and arrow in her hand (though a significant number of Doña Sebastiana images hold an axe instead). In some ways, as Steele (1994, 59) points
out, the presence of a death cart containing Doña Sebastiana is one of the
defining characteristics of a Penitente morada, since almost all moradas
had one and since these carts are never found outside a morada.

At some point during Holy Week, the death cart carrying Doña Sebastiana would be rolled out of the morada—several moradas still have
ramps at their front doors that were built to facilitate this; (Carlson 1990,
151)—and one or two specially chosen Brothers would pull it to a local *calvario*. In the case reported by Alice Henderson (1937, 26), a lone Brother
pulled the cart using a horsehair rope passed over his shoulders and under

his armpits, and the weight of the cart caused the rope to dig deeply into his skin. Pulling the death cart over rough ground was always a difficult task in itself, but it was typically made more difficult by loading the cart with heavy stones. Stories circulated in almost all Penitente communities suggesting that during some past Holy Week in that particular community, something had caused Doña Sebastiana's arrow to be loosed (by bumping against the death cart, for example) and the arrow had subsequently struck and killed a bystander (Henderson 1937, 26; Weigle 1976a, 170).

✺ The Four Named Rituals

In the midst of the devotions done privately in the morada and the various processions to and from *calvarios* and churches, there were four Penitente rituals staged during Holy Week that stood out as being special and that were given names. These were El Encuentro, Las Tinieblas, La Procesión de Sangre, and a mock crucifixion.

El Encuentro (the Encounter), which took place on Good Friday, memorialized a meeting between Christ and his mother on the road to Calvary. A procession of women, most them Carmelitas, set out from the local church carrying a statue of Mary; while simultaneously, a procession of Brothers started from their morada carrying a statue of Nuestro Padre Jesús. In some cases the Brother who carried Nuestro Padre Jesús was blindfolded, naked to the waist, and had a small cross strapped to his back (see Córdova 1972, 44–45). Eventually the two processions met and merged, and the two statues were raised so as to touch, face to face, for one final embrace.

These is nothing particularly unique about the Penitente El Encuentro ritual. On the contrary, staged encounters between two separate processions, one carrying a statue of Mary and the other a statue of Jesus, have long been common during Holy Week ceremonies in Italy, Spain, and the Spanish Americas. Generally, such staged encounters fall into one of three categories, depending on the precise nature of the event being depicted. Some of the ritual encounters, like the one staged in New Mexico, are meant to depict Mary meeting Jesus sometime *before* the crucifixion. Although there is nothing in the Gospels to suggest that Mary did indeed meet Jesus on his way to Calvary, the belief that such a meeting had occurred became popular in the Middle Ages and was later incorporated into the Stations of the Cross.[8] Sometimes, however, the staged encounter between Mary and Jesus depicts some other pre-crucifixion experience. In many southern Italian communities even today, the staged encounter (in

Italian: the *incontro*) is between an image of Mary and an image of Jesus being flagellated (Di Palo 1992, 78). A second sort of "encounter" commonly staged in Catholic areas takes place on Good Friday afternoon and depicts Mary coming into contact with the *dead* Christ. Finally, in some Catholic communities a third type of "encounter" is staged on Easter Sunday. In this case, the two processions carry, respectively, an image of Mary and an image of the resurrected Christ. When the statue of Mary "catches sight" of the image of her resurrected Son, the two processions run toward each other to effect a meeting of the two images.

Obviously, these three general types of ritualized encounter do not elicit the same emotional response from onlookers. In the first and second cases, onlookers experience the pain and suffering felt by a mother confronting a son who is dead or about to die. In the third case, by contrast, they experience the joy experienced by a grieving mother who finds that the son she thought was dead is now alive. Which outcome comes to be stressed seems to some degree to vary by cultural context. Thus, although all three types of ritual encounter have been staged (and are being staged still) in Italy, the encounter staged most often is the third kind, the "joyous" Easter Sunday encounter (Carroll 1996, 98–100). In Spain and colonial Mexico, by contrast, the encounter staged most often is the one depicting a meeting between Mary and Christ as he makes his way to Calvary (Mitchell 1990, 170–71; Vargas Uguarte 1956, 99–100). The El Encuentro staged by the Penitentes obviously follows the Spanish/Mexican tradition. Although this is hardly surprising, the Italian experience shows us that this ritual could have been shaped into something with a quite different emotional loading if the Penitentes had wanted to do that.

Las Tinieblas (from "tenebrae," a term that in ecclesiastical Latin connotes darkness and affliction) was another Penitente ceremony staged during Holy Week, usually on Holy Thursday evening. This ceremony was open to all members of the community and was held in a church or morada that had been darkened save for a row of candles set on the altar or into a special triangular candlestick. A Brother sang a series of *alabados* (hymns), and as each was completed, one of the candles was snuffed out. Extinguishing the last candle plunged the room into total darkness. After a brief period of silence, general pandemonium broke out as people in the room clapped their hands, stomped their feet, rattled chains, whirled *matracas* (racheted noisemakers), blew whistles, banged on metal washtubs, and even (occasionally) fired guns into the ceiling. Brothers of Blood in attendance would also flagellate themselves. As the tumult died down, someone called for a *sudario,* or prayer for someone who had died. This in turn was followed by another round of pandemonium and another *sudario,* and the process repeated itself several times. Eventually, a single candle was re-lit. If the ceremony was held in a morada, nonmembers left; if in a church, the Brothers left and returned to their morada. Weigle (1976a, 175) says that local moradas elected officers for the upcoming year from among the Brothers of Light following Las Tinieblas.

Las Tinieblas is clearly based to some extent on the traditional Tenebrae service held on each of three different days (usually Thursday, Friday, and Saturday) during Holy Week in a variety of Catholic countries.[9] Indeed, "Las Tinieblas" is what the traditional Tenebrae service was called in Spanish-speaking areas. The fact that the (original) Tenebrae service was celebrated on three different days, and so not tied to any one day in particular, likely explains why the Penitente Las Tinieblas was celebrated on Holy Thursday in some communities, on Good Friday in others, and on both Holy Thursday and Good Friday (see Edmonson 1957, 37) in still others.

In the traditional Tenebrae service a series of psalms and other prayers are recited, and as each section of the service comes to an end, one of the candles set into a pitchfork-shaped candelabra is extinguished. The final extinction is followed—as in the Penitente Las Tinieblas—by a round of noisemaking during which the laity beat their pews (and sometimes each other) with clubs and sticks. Over time, as Thurston (1904) points out, the noisemaking associated with Tenebrae came to be associated with the tumultuous events that the Gospels describe as having occurred in the aftermath of Christ's death (earthquakes, the ripping of the Temple curtain, graves opening up, etc). Penitente members often interpreted the pandemonium associated with their own Las Tinieblas in the same way (A. Henderson 1937, 43; Aragón 1998, 55).

That the traditional Tenebrae service was being celebrated in northern Mexico during the late colonial period (and so would have been available for the Penitentes to imitate) is evident from the fact that the distinctive triangular candle holder used in the service, called a *tenebrario,* is often mentioned in Mexican church inventories of the period. An inventory of the cathedral at Durango prepared by Bishop Tamarón y Romeral in 1762, for example, lists a tenebrario as being in the area of the main altar (AGI, Guadalajara, 558). Similarly, an 1852 inventory of the furnishings in the parish church in Sombrerete, a mining community southeast of Durango, lists a "wooden tenebrario that was used for Tinieblas" (AHAD 312: 699).

On the other hand, unlike what happened in the case of the El En-cuentro ritual (where the Penitente version of that ritual seems to have been modeled directly on the ritual encounters staged in Spain and the Spanish Americas), the traditional Tenebrae service was clearly modified in the process of becoming the Penitente Las Tinieblas. There is only one round of noisemaking during a traditional Tenebrae service, not several, and recurrent pairing of this noisemaking with a prayer for the dead—something that is central to the Penitente ritual—forms no part of the tra-ditional service. Furthermore, that this emphasis on prayers for the dead is a distinctively *Penitente* innovation rather than a more generalized His-panic innovation is evident when we look at the Las Tinieblas ceremony staged in other Hispanic (but non-Penitente) communities. The Tenebrae service celebrated by Hispanic Catholics in Soccoro, Texas, for example, was held (like the traditional Tenebrae service) on the Wednesday, Thurs-day, and Friday of Holy Week and (again like the traditional Tenebrae serv-ice) involved only one round of noisemaking and no prayers for the dead (Stanford 1998). As I will be arguing later in this book (Chapter 7), the *changes* made by the Penitentes to the Tenebrae service are likely more im-portant than the things they left unchanged in coming to understand what Las Tinieblas meant within the logic of Penitente ritual.

Another ceremony staged by the Penitentes during Holy Week, and probably the one that was visually the most impressive, was the *Procesión de Sangre* (Procession of Blood). This procession, which usually took place on the morning or afternoon of Good Friday, started at a local morada and consisted of a large number of Brothers of Blood, who were naked to the waist and who flagellated themselves with scourges as they walked. Usu-ally, but not always, the Procesión de Sangré also included a *pitero* (flute player), *rezador* (prayer leader), and Brothers of Light who walked on ei-ther side of the flagellants.

The last of the public Penitente rituals staged during Holy Week (ex-cept in those communities that celebrated Las Tinieblas on Good Friday night) was a *mock crucifixion*. For this event a large cross was laid on the ground outside a local morada; and a younger Brother, often the man who had carried the statue of Nuestro Padre Jesús during El Encuentro, was lashed to the cross with ropes. The cross was then tilted into a pre-dug hole, and the man (called a *Cristo*) was allowed to hang there in imitation of the crucifixion. Sometimes a support was built onto the cross in order to hold up his weight, but often he was supported only by the ropes that held his arms and legs to the structure of the cross. Support or no, the man's body usually started to turn blue as the ropes cut off his circulation. The Cristo was only allowed to hang on the cross for a brief time, usually no more than thirty minutes, and was removed immediately if he lost consciousness.

There are several eyewitness accounts of these mock crucifixions from the 1860s onward. That such events took place, then, seems indisputable. Nevertheless, popular accounts of the mock crucifixion often included colorful details of dubious authenticity. It was commonly believed, for instance, that the Cristo was sometimes *nailed* to the cross. As early as 1878 Catholic officials considered this rumor sufficiently widespread that they felt the need to refute it in print. Even today I have several times heard this story related as true by people living in New Mexico. Weigle (1976, 171) discounts the claim that nails were sometimes used during the mock crucifixion on the grounds that the claim always appears in second- and third-hand accounts and never appears in the accounts of this ceremony written by eyewitnesses. Other commentators have been less certain. Mills and Grove (1956, 22), for instance, suggest that the intense Penitente emphasis on experiencing the pain of Christ's passion in as literal a manner as possible makes it plausible that some Cristos *were* nailed to the cross. Another common story was that the Brother who played the Cristo in these crucifixions sometimes died. This belief was in turn associated with a cluster of secondary traditions—for example, that the death was kept secret for a year, that relatives were notified only a shoe or piece of clothing put on their doorstep, or that the man's grave was marked by an especially large cross (Weigle 1976, 173).

⁂ The public and very theatrical displays of bloody mortification that once made the Penitentes so distinctive are by now a thing of the past. Aranda (1974, i) suggests that the Penitentes began abandoning their most extreme rituals in the mid-1930s, which would have been around the time that Henderson (1937) was gathering the material for her classic account. Peterson (1992, 20) reports that some Penitente groups continue to stage processions during Holy Week and that they are often called upon by church authorities to lead community services, including rosary sessions and the Stations of the Cross. Certainly Penitente groups continue to walk in procession to and from a local church to their morada carrying statues of Mary or the saints. I witnessed just such a procession at Las Trampas on Good Friday morning in 1999.

What happens today in the privacy of the morada is unclear. Some Brothers are willing to confide to people they know that Penitente members regularly fast and say prayers during Holy Week (Warren 1987, 68), but not much else is known. Charles Briggs's account of the Holy Week ceremonies conducted in public by the Brotherhood in Córdova during the 1970s and 1980s (1988, 292–304) suggests that they celebrated a Las Tinieblas ceremony on both Holy Thursday and Good Friday and the El Encuentro ritual on Good Friday. In both cases, these rituals were accompanied by others that would be familiar to most modern Catholics (e.g., collective recitation of the rosary; recitation of the Stations of the Cross). On the other hand, Peterson (1992, 52), quotes a contemporary member of the El Rito morada as saying, "Some of the younger members have been asking about *Tinieblas;* maybe we'll take it up again." What is significant about such a remark, of course, is that it suggests that the Brotherhood in this particular community have not celebrated Las Tinieblas for quite some time, even though that ceremony used to be a central element in the Holy Week rituals.

It seems likely that the Penitentes have become something quite different than they used to be. Although an account of the Penitente movement today would be an interesting project in itself, if only because the modern movement seems to be attracting so many Hispano (male) artisans anxious to revive the *santero* tradition, my concern in the remainder of this book is with the Penitentes as they were, in the period that stretches from their emergence (see below) to just before World War II.

⚜ Penitente Historiography

The one aspect of Penitente history that has sparked more scholarly debate than any other is the matter of Penitente origins. When and how did the Penitentes come into existence? Since the earliest documentary reference to the Penitentes appears in 1833, and since there is no mention of the Penitentes in the detailed report on the New Mexican missions written in 1776 by Fray Antanasio Domínguez (Adams and Chávez 1956), it was suggested by Angélico Chávez (1954) long ago, and most scholars agree, that the most reasonable answer to *when* is that the group came into existence some time in the period between 1776 and 1833. In fact, given Padre Martínez's letter to Bishop Zubiría in February 1833 (which only came to light in the early 1990s), in which Martínez says that the Brotherhood has been operating at Taos since he took charge of the parish in the early 1820s, we can further narrow the period in which the Penitentes emerged to something like 1776–1823. In regard to the *how* of Penitente origins, however, two quite different hypotheses have been offered.

The first of these is the "indigenous development" hypothesis, which suggests that the Penitentes were an outgrowth of religious organizations and traditions that had been established in New Mexico for some time. Scholars arguing this view almost always see the Franciscan Third Order,[10] a lay religious organization founded in the thirteenth century, as being the organizational precursor of the Penitentes. Most often cited in support of this hypothesis is the fact that church records, including the Domínguez report, indicate that Third Order groups were functioning in New Mexico during the late 1700s and early 1800s; that an undeniable penitential emphasis pervaded the Franciscan traditions associated with the Third Order; that Third Order membership procedures resembled the membership procedures later associated with the Penitentes; and that Third Order chapters—like Penitente moradas—were often concerned with mutual aid and funerals. Chávez (1954) suggests that it was Bishop Lamy who first popularized the view that the Penitentes were an outgrowth of the Franciscan Third Order—partly because he saw no other possibility, and partly because it provided him with a rationale for reforming Penitente practice (i.e., if they were an outgrowth of the Third Order, then reform meant bringing them "back" to the original practices associated with the Third Order).

However it happened, there is little doubt that during the nineteenth century the suggestion that the Penitentes were an outgrowth of the Franciscan Third Order was accepted as a matter of course by both church officials like Lamy and Salpointe (1893, 161–62) and by Protestant critics like Darley (1893). This has also always been—and still is—the hypothesis favored by Penitente members themselves as well as by most modern scholars who have written on the Penitentes (see the literature review in J. M. Espinosa 1993). Indeed, the hypothesis of a Third Order origin for the Penitentes is so much a part of conventional wisdom that many well-known books about the Penitentes—like Ahlborn (1986), Aranda (1974), Chávez (1974), Cordova (1972), Darley (1893), Steele and Rivera (1985), Weigle (1976a)—are given the Library of Congress call number (BX3653) reserved for books dealing with the Franciscan Third Order, regardless of whether or not the book in question endorses the "Third Order" hypothesis.

Some scholars, however, have taken a different tack, arguing that the Penitentes emerged in the early 1800s primarily from organizational models that had only recently been imported into New Mexico. This "late transplant" view was most forcibly argued by the late Angélico Chávez in a series of articles and books that spanned four decades (see especially Chávez 1954; 1974). The fact is, says Chávez, that when the Penitentes first emerged they hardly resembled the Third Order at all (the Penitentes, for instance, included only males, while the Third Order had always included both males and females), but they did resemble *cofradías* known to have existed in Spain and Mexico. In particular, Chávez argues, the Penitentes most of all resembled the famous penitential confraternities that paraded through the streets of Seville during Holy Week in the sixteenth and seventeenth centuries. Like the Penitentes, for example, several of these penitential confraternities were dedicated to Nuestro Padre Jesús Nazareno and/or carried statues of Nuestro Padre Jesús Nazareno in their processions. Then too, Chávez argues, the processions organized by these Sevillan *cofradías* bear a striking visual similarity to the processions organized by the Penitentes. Thus, he says,

> First [came] the Hermanos de Sangre, naked from the waist up, with loose hoods completely covering their heads, and scourging themselves with leather whips studded with metal; next came the Hermanos de Luz, bearing thick candles; then came a third group, the Nazarenos, carrying heavy crosses on their backs and dressed in long red or purple gowns tied at the waist with a thick cord. (1954, 117)

Chávez admits that the "Nazarenos" and the "Hermanos de Sangre" categories seem to have been collapsed in the case of the Penitentes, but says that in all other respects the two groups are similar. Quite obviously, he suggests, knowledge of earlier penitential *cofradías* of the sort that had existed at Seville must have been brought to New Mexico by someone and this person's knowledge used to give shape to the Penitentes. Thomas Steele (1993a), a modern proponent of the "late transplant" theory, allows for the possibility that a book or inspirational tract describing the penitential *cofradías* at Seville and elsewhere, rather than the personal experiences of some Mexican or Spanish immigrant, might have been the inspiration for the Penitentes. In the end, however, Steele, like Chávez, takes it as self-evident that some sort of connection does exist. It is simply the case, Steele argues, that "the New Mexican confraternities exhibit many more resemblances to Iberian and New World models than coincidence alone can possibly explain" (5).

William Wroth (1991) has proposed a weaker variant of the "late transplant" theory. He suggests, first, that Hispano settlers in New Mexico had likely engaged in flagellation and other penitential practices from the earliest days of the colony right through to the late 1700s; but he also argues, with Chávez, that as a result of the interchanges that took place between

New Mexico and Mexico during the eighteenth century, Hispano settlers had likely become familiar with several different Mexican (and Spanish) confraternities that practiced flagellation. Unlike Chávez, however, Wroth suggests that the specific Mexican confraternity that became the model for the Penitentes was *La Hermandad de la Sangre de Cristo*. In support of his theory, Wroth notes that confraternities dedicated to the Sangre de Cristo were operating in northern Mexico in the late 1700s and that early Penitente documents seem to suggest that *La Santa Hermandad de la Sangre de Nuestro Señor Jesucristo* was the original name of the group.

It is not my intention to evaluate the pros and cons of these different accounts of Penitente origins here. My sense is that whatever argument "looks best" depends entirely on which similarities and which dissimilarities (between the Penitentes and the various precursor organizations that have been proposed) one chooses to emphasize and which one chooses to ignore. My concern rather is with how previous commentators have explained the *timing* of Penitente origins, that is, why the Penitentes emerged during the late 1700s and early 1800s rather than earlier or later. It turns out that the answer to this question is always the same, regardless of whether the author in question prefers the "indigenous development" hypothesis or some variant of the "late transplant" hypothesis. The key variable is seen, without exception, to be the *scarcity of clergy* in northern New Mexico during the late 1700s and early 1800s. Because there were so few clergy, the argument goes, Hispano settlers—especially in remote villages—were left to their own devices; and in this situation, individual laymen took the lead in developing their own forms of Catholic religiosity. The result was the Penitentes.

Presumably because it seems so obvious, this argument is usually made in passing and without much comment. The following passages are typical and indicate how amazingly constant this argument has been over the past several decades:

> When the Spanish-born Franciscans were expelled from the country, and the native people were left to perform their own rituals . . . what is more natural than that . . . the laity [in the Third Order] should assume the role and duty of the priesthood, and be loath to relinquish it entirely when the secular priests returned? (A. Henderson 1937, 10)

> The Penitentes seem to have arisen to fill a vacuum in religious direction caused by the lack of enough priests during the eighteenth century, which was later aggravated by the ouster of the Franciscans by

Spain and the Spanish priests by Mexico, and the departure of Mex-ico-trained priests after the American annexation. (Steele 1974, 56)

Sometime after 1776, in the absence of secular clergy for Spanish and genízaro villages, penitential confraternities (cofradías) were estab-lished to administer religious affairs. . . . to meet the needs of the Spanish settlers. (Jones 1996, 149)

The dearth of priests manifested itself in a hundred ways. . . . Cut off as they were from benefit of clergy, they came to rely for community social services and religious expression on their own brotherhoods of charity, de-votion, and penitence. Naturally, there were deviations from canonical practice . . . which Bishop Zubiría sought to correct. (Kessell 1980, 15)

As the eighteenth century advanced, with the decreasing number of Franciscans friars, many of the faithful had taken into their own hands the performance of some of the religious services, especially in the less accessible outlying areas of northern New Mexico. . . . Without the guidance of the Franciscan clergy, and without official authorization from the hierarchy in Mexico, the Penitentes . . . grad-ually emerged. (J. M. Espinosa 1993, 463)

The shortage of priests . . . forced New Mexican vecinos to look for new ways to provide for their spiritual well-being. La Cofradia de Nuestro Padre Jesús Nazareno, a penitential brotherhood emerged to fill this spiritual vacuum. . . . The Penitentes were a pious response to a spiritual need that the Catholic Church was no longer able to satisfy on the frontier. (Mocho 1997, 6)

As [the] inhabitants of an historically isolated territory with little support or direction from a religious clergy, the New Mexico Catholic settlers produced a unique type of Catholicism that was self-reliant and laity centered. . . . From within this history and tradi-tion emerged Los Hermanos Penitentes. (López Pulido 1997, 376)

The initial premise in the passages cited above (and in innumerable oth-ers that could be cited) is undeniable: there *was* an increasing scarcity of clergy (relative to the Hispano population) in New Mexico during the late 1700s and early 1800s.

According to a census taken in 1749, there were 4,170 Hispano settlers and 12,670 Indians in the three villas (Santa Fe, Santa Cruz, and Albu-querque) and twenty pueblos of northern New Mexico and twenty-five res-ident friars to address the religious needs of both groups (Kelly 1941, 19).

The situation was more or less the same in 1760, when Bishop Tamarón found twenty-four friars and one secular priest ministering to a total population of about 16,500. In 1776 Domínguez found that the population had increased somewhat (to a total population of 18,344), while the number of priests had fallen to twenty (Adams and Chávez 1956, 217). Although absolute number of clergy remained relatively constant between 1776 and 1820, rarely fluctuating outside the 20±2 range (see Table 1 in Wright 1998), an expanding Hispano population meant that the *relative* number of priests ministering to Hispano Catholics declined. In the 1820s, the situation worsened still further as the absolute number of priests declined dramatically. A census conducted in 1827, for example, listed only seventeen priests (including both Franciscans and secular priests) in the midst of a total population of just over 43,000 people. In 1829 Manuel de Jesús Rada, who at the time was New Mexico's deputy to Mexico's *Congreso General,* reported that there were only thirteen priests in the territory, including eight secular priests and five Franciscans, and that two of the Franciscans would soon have to leave on account of the law calling for the expulsion of Spanish nationals (MANM 9: 508).

Added to this decline in the relative and (subsequently) the absolute number of priests ministering to the populations of northern New Mexico was a decline in what we might call the "pastoral commitment" of the Franciscans serving in New Mexico from about 1750 onward. Norris's (1994) close examination of the data relating to the background of friars serving in New Mexico after the reconquest of 1692 suggests that after 1750 New Mexican friars were far more likely than previously to be associated with sexual improprieties, drunkenness, and a lack of concern with evangelization. In part, Norris suggests, this was because the New Mexico jurisdiction came increasingly to be used in the late 1700s as a dumping ground for friars who had been defined as a "disciplinary problem" in other jurisdictions.

So if there was indeed an increasing scarcity of clergy relative to the Hispano population from the late 1700s onwards, and if there was, simultaneously, a concomitant decline in the moral character and pastoral commitment of the friars who came to New Mexico, isn't it entirely reasonable to suggest, as countless scholars have, that the laity themselves would craft new forms of Catholic religiosity and that something like the Penitentes might be the result of that process? Of course it is reasonable. Even so, there *are* grounds for challenging this traditional and widely accepted account of Penitente origins.

First, the fact that the ratio of priests to people declined in late colonial

New Mexico does not in itself mean that New Mexico was relatively "short" of clergy when compared to other Catholic areas. For instance, in pre-Famine Ireland there was one priest for every 2,676 Catholics in 1800, and one priest for every 2,996 Catholics in 1840 (Connolly 1982, 33). Using the results of the 1827 census in New Mexico (which reported seventeen priests in a total population of 43,433 people), we get a ratio of one priest for every 2,555 Catholics. Even by the 1820s, in other words, when the priest-to-people ratio in New Mexico was at its lowest point, that ratio was still marginally better than in Ireland during more or less the same period. Moreover, Wright's (1998) analysis suggests that although the number of priests serving in northern New Mexico during the early 1800s may have been small, these priests were usually located in communities that put them within relatively easy reach of most Hispano residents.

Another problem with seeing a "scarcity of clergy" combined with "isolation" as giving rise to the Penitentes is that the earliest Penitente strongholds are not in the locations where we would expect them to be if this argument were true. For example, in the earliest documents that make reference to the Penitentes, namely, those written by Martínez and Zubiría in the early 1830s, only two locations are associated with Penitente activity with any certainty—Santa Cruz de la Cañada and Taos. Not only did both of these communities have resident priests, but neither community can reasonably be considered isolated by the standards then prevailing in New Mexico. Santa Cruz and its environs, for example, was one of the most heavily populated areas of northern New Mexico. In 1800 there were more settlers living in Santa Cruz and vicinity than either in Santa Fe and vicinity or in Albuquerque and vicinity (Jones 1996, 128). By 1827 the total population living in and around Santa Cruz had grown to 12,903—greater than the total (Hispanic) population in all of Texas, Baja California, or Alta California at the time (Jones 1996, 129).

Taos also cannot be classed as an isolated community, though here the matter has less to do with size than with that community's centrality to trade. For most of the eighteenth century, Taos was the site of the most important of the annual trade fairs held in northern New Mexico. Although the fair was for the most part an opportunity to foster trade with nomadic Indians like the Comanches, Utes, and Apaches, it also—as Simmons (1983, 85) points out—attracted Spanish merchants from far to the south and so served as a link tying together the upper Rio Grande valley with the Viceroyalty of New Spain. Simmons (1991, 44) provides a succinct yet colorful account of the social diversity at the Taos fair:

The governor at Santa Fe, accompanied by a soldier escort and pack-loads of personal trade goods, usually journeyed to Taos for the duration of the fair. As the official party approached its destination, it encountered other groups, Indian and Spanish, converging from all directions. The floodtide of people seemed to engulf the level ground surrounding Taos Pueblo.

While the opening of the Santa Fe Trail from Missouri in 1821 produced a dramatic decline in the popularity of the Taos fair, it simultaneously promoted an influx of foreigners, and many of them settled in Taos and the surrounding area. Chávez (1981, 27) suggests that the *majority* of foreigners who settled in New Mexico during this period settled in the Taos area. Finally, an 1832 report (reproduced in H. B. Carroll and Haggard 1942, 96) lists Taos and Santa Cruz as being among only six communities in New Mexico with public schooling for the primary grades (the other four communities being Santa Fe, San Miguel del Vado, Albuquerque, and Belén).

In summary, then, when the Penitentes first appear in the documentary record, they appear in association with two locations—Santa Cruz and Taos—that were among the *least* isolated and most cosmopolitan of the communities then existing in New Mexico and that both had resident priests.

Santa Cruz and Taos aside, the only other community that can with certainty be associated with Penitente activity before 1840 is Tomé, where Josiah Gregg witnessed a Penitente procession in the early 1830s. Here again, though, we are not dealing with a rural backwater abandoned by the Church. On the contrary, a chapel dedicated to Our Lady of the Conception had been built at Tomé in 1750 with the approval of the bishop of Durango, and the Domínguez report indicates that the image of Our Lady kept in this chapel was well adorned with precious jewels and reliquaries. Moreover, there had been a priest resident at Tomé since 1821 (Steele 1978, 243). In 1828 both the priest and people of Tomé worked together to get the old chapel relocated to a safer site away from the river. The project secured the approval of Governor Armijo, but it failed because the people in a neighboring community failed to cooperate (see Chávez and Adams 1956, 153n). Yet it was in this community—with its old and established local church and a conscientious resident priest who worked with his flock to promote Catholic piety—that the Penitentes make one of their earliest documented appearances.

The "scarcity of clergy" argument also runs into difficulty when we consider the later history of this group. After all, as Robert Sprott (1984) points out, if the Penitentes were a response to a lack of local clergy, then we might reasonably expect that Penitente membership would have started to decline in the latter half of the nineteenth century when the shortage of clergy was eased considerably—and yet that did not happen. On the contrary, as already noted, Penitente membership continued to build during the late nineteenth and early twentieth centuries and peaked only during the 1920s.

In short, whether we look at the very earliest accounts of the Penitentes or at their later history, there seems to be no basis for drawing a link between Penitente activity and the absence of local clergy.

But perhaps the most serious objection to the Penitentes as a response to the "scarcity of clergy" argument is that it rests implicitly on a model of Hispano religiosity that has never been examined critically and that is likely false.

❧ Sacramental Presuppositions

Implicit in all claims that an increasing scarcity of priests prompted the emergence of the Penitentes is the suggestion that Penitente ritual was a popular attempt to create functional alternatives to the sacramental rituals that had previously been administered by priests. In a well-known work that is still widely cited in the scholarly discussions of the Penitentes, Thomas Steele argues that "left without sufficient priests, [Hispano Catholics] understandably felt a deep need to find a satisfying substitute for confession, the mass and the Eucharist" (1974, 62). He goes on to suggest that Penitente ritual was that satisfying substitute. Thus, for Steele, Penitente ritual generally is the "folk equivalent of the Catholic Mass" (61) and the *bulto* of Jesús Nazareno carried in procession "served in many a priest-less village as a substitute for the reserved Eucharist" (63). Steele has repeated this argument, with only minor changes, in several subsequent publications (in particular, Steele and Rivera 1985, 4–7; Steele 1992; 1993a).

Robert Sprott (1984, 18–26) improves upon Steele's argument by suggesting that while Penitente ritual may have come into existence to replace sacramental rituals like the Mass and the Eucharist, these (Penitente) rituals proved to be even more emotionally satisfying than the official rituals they replaced. Sprott argues that Penitente rituals "functioned kerygmatically" (20), by which he means that these rituals were a public proclamation in the here and now of the offer of salvation made possible by the death and resurrection of Christ. Although the Mass and the Eucharist do the same thing (i.e., function kerygmatically in this sense), Sprott suggests that Penitente rituals were in the end more appealing than the Mass because these rituals were tied to the local village context in New Mexico in a way that the Mass was not.

Louisa Stark (1971) makes an argument similar to those put forward by Steele and Sprott, but sees confession, not the Mass and the Eucharist, to have been the critical ritual. She suggests that as priests became scarce, they were not available to hear confession and give absolution, and that in this context Penitente ritual emerged as a folk equivalent to confession as a way of expiating sin and so avoiding the punishments of hell.

✢ Grounds for Skepticism

Unfortunately, there are several reasons to be skeptical of *all* arguments that see Penitente ritual as an attempt to create "folk equivalents" to the sacramental rituals of the official church. First, such arguments feed too easily into longstanding Anglo-Saxon stereotypes of Hispanics. After all, what is being suggested, in the end, is that in the absence of the restraint provided by a local priest, Hispano Catholics moved easily into bizarre penitential practices characterized by messy emotional excess. The Hispanos who emerge from the logic of these arguments, in other words, are an emotionally volatile people greatly in need of external constraint. They are, in other words, precisely the sort of "hot-blooded Latins" that so many Anglos expect them to be.

A second basis for skepticism is that the sort of argument developed by commentators like Steele and Sprott seems to conform all too conveniently to the biases of the official church. At least since the Council of Trent, for example, the Church has argued that regular attendance at Mass and, more generally, participation in the sacramental life of the Church are central to the definition of a "good Catholic" and that it is the function of local parish priests to provide the guidance that ensures that those under their care become good Catholics according to these standards. Within the logic of this Tridentine vision, it "makes sense" that Hispanos would be good Catholics, devoted to the Mass and to the sacraments as long as they had reasonable access to priests, but would start to stray into error as priests became scarce and they tried on their own to recreate their beloved Catholic rituals. In short, constructing Hispano Catholics as being especially attached to official rituals like the Mass and the sacraments, and seeing a scarcity of priests as leading to the emergence of well-meaning but ultimately inappropriate rituals serves to reinforce and thus legitimate the Tridentine emphasis on the laity's need for priestly guidance.

But perhaps the most important reason for being skeptical of all arguments that suggest that Hispano Catholics fashioned Penitente ritual as a substitute for the sacramental rituals that would otherwise have been administered by priests is that there is really no evidence that Hispano Catholics before 1800 were an especially religious people, whether we measure "religiosity" using the standards of the Tridentine church or using the standards that emerge from the study of popular Catholicism in other areas. Such a bold statement, of course, needs to be justified; and that is the goal of the next chapter.

TWO

The Golden Age That Wasn't

HISPANO PIETY BEFORE 1800

In a now-classic sociological study published originally in 1940, George Sánchez (1996) called the Hispano population of New Mexico a "forgotten people." Sánchez himself was concerned with the dramatic decline in Hispano well-being since the American Annexation and with the unresponsiveness of U.S. governmental organizations (educational institutions in particular) to their worsening situation. Hispanos had been "forgotten," he argued, by the very government that had promised them enlightened rule and a better life. But the term "forgotten people" seems equally applicable to the historiographical plight of New Mexican Hispanos.

Until relatively recently, histories of New Mexico were concerned most of all with "pivotal events" such as Oñate's entry into New Mexico in 1598 and his subsequent colonization of the area, the Pueblo Revolt of 1680, the reconquest under Vargas in the 1690s, the struggles between Franciscan missionaries and Spanish colonial officials, and so on. One consequence of this historiographical fascination with pivotal events was that the day-to-day life of the great mass of Hispano settlers was generally ignored. In the past two decades or so, to be sure, a few historians have fought to reverse this historiographical tide. Oakah Jones (1996, 109–65) has pulled together a great deal of information relating to Hispano lifestyles and settlement patterns during the colonial period. Marc Simmons (1991) has written dozens of short essays on topics ranging from "how colonial ladies painted their faces," to playing cards, to Hispano use of *acequias* (irrigation ditches). Ramón Gutiérrez (1991)—in a book that proves that sex and violence sell as well with academics as with the general public—has provided much information on the institution of marriage among Hispanos during the colonial period and on the sexual exploitation of Pueblo women by Hispano males. But even these accounts by Jones, Simmons, and Gutiérrez, which

have otherwise done so much to shed light on Hispano culture, have re-
markably little to say about Hispano *religiosity*. There is no mystery as to
the proximate cause of this lacuna: the surviving documentary record simply does not say very much about the religious beliefs and practices of Hispano settlers in colonial New Mexico.

Partly, this failure of the documentary record to make much reference
to Hispano religiosity is a function of the social and political processes that
produced that record. As any number of commentators have noted, many
of the surviving documents relating to New Mexico's colonial history were
generated during the course of the recurrent conflicts between civil authorities and the Franciscans over access to the kingdom's most valuable
resource: the labor of the Pueblo Indians. As a result, those documents are
rife with claims and counterclaims regarding what was or was not happening in the pueblos and how well (or poorly) the missionaries or civil
officials were treating the Indians. Information relating to the religious activities of the Hispano settlers was not information that would have been
particularly useful to either side in this conflict and so went unmentioned.

Something else that militated against paying much attention to Hispano religiosity was the stated rationale for the Franciscan presence in New
Mexico. The Franciscans were in New Mexico to convert the Pueblo Indians. This was their primary goal and the reason that their activities were fi-
nanced by the royal treasury. Administering to the Hispanos living in the
settlements scattered along the Rio Grande Valley or living in one of the
villas was thus very much an "add on"—something the Franciscans were
expected to do but not something germane to their primary goal, and so
not something of much importance in judging how well or how poorly
they were meeting that primary goal. The net result, as even Angélico
Chávez, himself a Franciscan, had to concede, was that for most of the
colonial period the Franciscans regarded Hispano Catholics in New Mexico in a more or less casual manner (1974, 208).

I might add here that the Franciscan inattention to Hispano religiosity likely explains something that is usually glossed over in most commentaries: throughout the entire colonial period not a single native-born
Hispano entered the Franciscan order. This is true even though by 1610 a
majority of those entering the Franciscan Order in the Province of the
Holy Gospel generally (of which New Mexico was a part) were *criollos*, that
is, males of Spanish descent who had been born in the Spanish Americas
(Morales 1973). Moreover, this failure of Hispano males to enter the Franciscan order is not an artifact of there having been no priestly vocations in

New Mexico. On the contrary, starting with the ordination of Don Santiago Roybal sometime in the 1720s (see F. A. Chavez 1948a), a few Hispano males did enter the priesthood; but in all cases they joined the diocesan clergy. It would appear, in other words, that the Franciscans' lack of interest in the spiritual well-being of the Hispano community was matched by a corresponding lack of interest on the part of the Hispano community toward the Franciscans.[1]

The fact that Hispano religiosity was not central to the Franciscan purpose in New Mexico also likely explains why there are no assessments of Hispano religiosity in sources where we might otherwise expect to find them. Three different bishops of Durango, for example, visited New Mexico during the eighteenth century; and two of them—Benito Crespo, who came in 1730, and Pedro Tamarón y Romeral, who came in 1760—left detailed reports of what they encountered.[2] Anyone familiar with the pastoral visits made by bishops in Spain and Italy might reasonably expect that Crespo and Tamarón would have paid attention to the things established as important by the Council of Trent—whether the people understood the core doctrines of the Church; how many Catholics fulfilled their Easter duty; how often people went to Mass, and so on. In fact, both bishops did address exactly these questions, but only in regard to the Pueblo Indians. Crespo, for example, calls attention to the fact that the rule requiring annual confession and communion was not being fulfilled in any of the pueblos (Adams 1954, 102). The reason, he felt, was that none of the Franciscans understood the languages of the Indians. Confessions therefore had to be made through an Indian interpreter, and most pueblo residents were reluctant to do that. He adds that all the pueblos remained tied to their idolatry and paganism (103). The important point, however, is that Crespo made no similar attempt to assess the frequency of communion and confession among the Spanish settlers.

Three decades later, in 1760, Bishop Tamarón also called attention to the fact that the Franciscans had made little or no effort to learn the languages spoken in the pueblos. As a result, Tamarón argued, Pueblo Indians had learned to recite their catechism in Spanish by rote and so had little or no understanding of what they were repeating (Adams 1954, 78–79). The fact that the Franciscans did not speak the language of the Indians explained, for Tamarón as for Crespo, why the Indians rarely confessed (49, 78–79). But like his predecessor, Tamarón made no attempt to assess the frequency of confession or communion among Hispano settlers nor to assess how well they knew and understood core Catholic doctrines.

This seeming indifference on the part of Crespo and Tamarón to Hispano religiosity was in large measure a function of the fact that they too, like so many of the civil leaders in New Mexico, were locked in a battle with the Franciscans over jurisdictional matters. Since the mid-1600s the bishops of Durango had insisted that New Mexico was subject to their jurisdiction; and the Franciscans, with equal insistence, had resisted this claim. Crespo himself had intensified this dispute by becoming the first bishop of Durango to make a pastoral visit to northern New Mexico, since visitations of this sort presume that the bishop involved has jurisdiction over the area visited. In his letter to the viceroy describing his 1730 visitation, Crespo set the matter of jurisdiction front and center by declaring in his opening sentence that the Franciscan *custos* of the New Mexico missions had expressed "opposition to my exercising jurisdiction in said province" (Adams 1954, 100). Tamarón appears to have been received more favorably by the Franciscans than was Crespo (for speculation on why, see Adams 1954, 27–28), but in the end he too was working to solidify his jurisdictional hold over the area. In his report to the king on his visit, he notes explicitly that "the Order of St. Francis has opposed with inflexibility and vigor the Bishop of Durango's being bishop of and exercising jurisdiction in New Mexico, but the King has permitted it" (Adams 1954, 78).

Because both Crespo and Tamarón were concerned with solidifying their jurisdiction at the expense of the Franciscans, it was inevitable that, like earlier commentators, they too would focus on Indian religiosity, since in so doing they could demonstrate that the Franciscans had failed in their primary mission. Once again, in other words, the state of Hispano religiosity—being unrelated to the central Franciscan purpose in New Mexico—was ignored in the documentary record.

❧ Imagining the Past Nevertheless

Unfortunately, the fact that Hispano religiosity was not systematically assessed during the colonial period has not prevented modern commentators from making sweeping generalizations about the nature of this religiosity. Typically, this is done by taking the sort of Hispano Catholicism that existed in New Mexico during the late nineteenth and early twentieth centuries and projecting it onto the colonial past. It is common, for example, in both scholarly and popular accounts of New Mexico, for an author to make a statement about Hispano religiosity during the colonial period and then refer the reader to Cleofas Jaramillo's *Shadows of the Past* (1941) or Lorin W. Brown's *Hispano Folklife of New Mexico* (1978) for evidence in support of that statement. Yet Jaramillo's work is an account of her childhood experiences in Arroyo Hondo at the turn of the twentieth century, and Brown's work consists mainly of material collected during the 1930s. Neither work, in other words, has anything to do with the colonial period.

Sometimes, but only sometimes, this historiographical tendency to project the recent past onto the distant past results in characterizations of Hispano religiosity that can easily be falsified, even given the deficiencies of the documentary record. For example, in describing Hispanic life during the seventeenth and eighteenth centuries, George Sánchez says very matter-of-factly: "Social life in the villages revolved around church festivals. Each settlement had its church or chapel which was dedicated to a patron saint. The more important settlements had a resident priest, who in addition to his duties in his home parish, paid periodic visits to the villages in his circuit" (1996, 7). At first sight, Sánchez's characterization here might seem unproblematic, if only because it seems so similar to characterizations that can be found in ethnographic or historical studies describing Catholic communities in other parts of the Latin world. Nevertheless, the specific claim that he makes in his second sentence, namely, that "each settlement had its church or chapel which was dedicated to a patron saint," is incorrect. The evidence for this comes from the one document that provides more information on religious matters in eighteenth-century New Mexico than any other: the already-mentioned report written by Fray Atanasio Domínguez in 1776 (reproduced in Adams and Chávez 1956).

Thomas Steele and Rowena Rivera's characterization of Fray Domínguez and the report he eventually wrote is refreshingly blunt, and I cannot improve upon it: "In [1776] the Order of Friars Minor sent a visitor to New Mexico with not only a license to snoop but the greatest natural gift for snooping in the history of the colony. Fray Francisco Atanasio Domínguez returned home to draft a doggedly thorough and cattily opinionated report about everything religious that New Mexico had to offer" (Steele and Rivera 1985, 3). For each of the three villas (Santa Fe, Albuquerque, Santa Cruz de la Cañada) and twenty-three pueblos that he described, Domínguez first provided a fairly detailed account of the physical structure and contents of the local church and *convento* (the residence of the local friar) and then an account of the local friar and his administration of the local mission or church.

Toward the end of each entry, Domínguez was also always careful to say something about any Spanish settlements that happened to be nearby. Often this meant nothing more than giving an indication of the number of families living in a settlement. Sometimes he makes a patronizing or snide comment about the Spanish spoken by the settlers or about their appearance. When these settlements had a church, however, he tells us that. He tells us, for example, that there was a small chapel maintained by a local family in the settler community of Rio Arriba near San Juan Pueblo at which a Mass was said annually (90) and that there was a church in the community of Las Trampas near Picurís Pueblo (98–100). For the vast majority of Hispano settlements, however, Domínguez makes no mention of a church or chapel, and this almost certainly means that none existed. In fact, as Kessell (1980, 15) points out, churches did not begin to proliferate in Hispano villages until shortly after Domínguez's visit.

The lesson to be learned here is that we must proceed cautiously when reconstructing the nature of Hispano religiosity during the colonial period. In particular, we must be careful not to assume that patterns common in later periods were common as well in earlier periods. This means that statements about Hispano religiosity during the colonial period must be supported as much as possible by evidence drawn from the same period. What happens when we try to reconstruct the nature of Hispano religiosity by doing just that?

⋅⋇⋅ Ritual Observances

In a deposition taken from a Spanish soldier during Governor Otermín's attempted reconquest of New Mexico in 1681, the soldier made reference to two attempts at rebellion that had preceded the Revolt of 1680 (Hackett 1970, 2:299). The first of these, he said, had occurred in 1650; and the second, a few years later. In both cases, the rebellions had been detected in time and the ringleaders executed or sold into slavery. He added as well that in both cases the plotters had planned "to attack in all districts on the night of Holy Thursday, because the Spaniards would then be assembled." Whether or not this remark should be taken at face value is problematic. Sometimes the Indian populations in the Spanish Americas who rose in revolt did wait until Spaniards were gathered together, but often they did just the reverse: attacked when the Spaniards were dispersed (which is what they did during the Pueblo revolt of 1680). The witness's remark, in other words, may derive more from Spanish fears about an Indian uprising than from what Pueblo populations did or did not intend to do. Even so, the remark itself would not have made sense either to the speaker or to his audience unless it were the case that Hispano settlers throughout New Mexico did routinely gather together on Holy Thursday evening.

In a similar vein, Bishop Tamarón tells us that during his 1760 visitation he was told of a rumor that had circulated widely the previous year (1759) to the effect that the Indians were going to revolt on Corpus Christi. "The governor took precautions and made inquiries," he says, "but he was unable to clarify the matter" (Adams and Chávez 1956, 73). Here again, whether the planned rebellion was real or simply a projection of Spanish fears[3] is not particularly important. What is important is that the rumor would only have made sense to the settlers (who relayed it to Tamarón) if they generally gathered together to celebrate Corpus Christi.

References like the two (from 1690 and 1760) just mentioned provide clear evidence that Hispano settlers during the 1600s and early 1700s did gather together and engage in collective rituals on particular feast days like Holy Thursday and Corpus Christi. Moreover, some information on the different ritual activities associated with these feast days and on the relative importance of these different activities can be derived from the Domínguez report.

Domínguez identifies nine separate confraternities, including two chapters of the Franciscan Third Order, operating in New Mexico's three villas. Five of these confraternities were located in Santa Fe, two in Santa Cruz de la Cañada, and two in Albuquerque. Generally, each confraternity sponsored (1) Masses said on a weekly or monthly basis, and (2) more elaborate activities on a particular feast day, usually involving a sung Mass and a procession through the local community. Several of the confraternities had been unable to meet their expenses, however; and during the period of his visit, Domínguez says, many of their sponsored activities were cut back. Looking carefully, we can detect a pattern to the cutbacks. The Confraternity of the Rosary at Santa Fe, for example, traditionally sponsored a Mass and a procession on each of six different feast days throughout the year, a Mass and procession once a month on a Sunday, and weekly Masses on Mondays and Saturdays (Adams and Chávez 1956, 27). Because its income was insufficient to meet these expenses, the weekly Masses on Mondays and Saturday were suspended, but the confraternity continued to sponsor the monthly Sunday Mass and the annual feasts in honor of Our Lady (which included five of the six feasts they had traditionally sponsored; Adams and Chávez 1956, 241). Similarly, the Confraternity of the Blessed Sacrament at Santa Fe had traditionally sponsored a Mass during Corpus

Christi, a Mass on the feast of the Ascension, a procession at Easter, and a Mass every Thursday (19). Here again, toward the end of Domínguez's visit, lack of funds forced a cutback and so the weekly Masses were suspended (241).

The pattern, in other words, is that confraternity cutbacks were usually achieved by eliminating weekly Masses rather than by eliminating the annual celebrations that involved both a Mass and a procession through the community. What this suggests is that these annual celebrations were especially important to Hispano settlers, and certainly more important than simple attendance at Mass on a regular basis.

The festivities associated with particular feast days aside, there is also solid documentary evidence that Hispano settlers participated in the sacramental activities—notably those associated with baptism, marriage, and burial—that marked passage through the life cycle. Although no records relating to baptisms, marriages, and burials in New Mexico for the period 1598–1680 have survived (Esquibel 1998, 28)—likely because of the Pueblo Revolt—such records are available for most New Mexican communities for most of the eighteenth century (see Brugge 1968, 3–17; A. Chávez 1957). Also available for the Hispano community during the eighteenth century are 1,592 *diligencias matrimoniales,* that is, matrimonial investigations carried out in order to determine if there were any impediments to marriage between prospective spouses (Gutiérrez 1991, 245).

The general impression from this material is that most Hispanos were indeed baptized and married in the Church and came to be buried in consecrated ground—something, I might add, that is not always true in all supposedly Catholic areas.[4] Doesn't this, especially when taken in conjunction with the fact that Hispano Catholics also participated in various religious festivals throughout the year, provide clear evidence that Hispano Catholics were a deeply devout people? In fact, it does not.

✵ The Methodological Implications of Pueblo Catholicism

The Indians in most Pueblo communities, like their Hispano neighbors, were also baptized and married by Catholic priests, attended Mass, participated in Catholic festivals at particular points during the year, and, when they died, were buried in consecrated ground. In this case, however, we have abundant evidence that participation in all these rituals was not indicative of a deeply rooted Catholic religiosity. As already mentioned, for example, both Bishop Crespo and Bishop Tamarón called attention to the ways in which the Pueblo Indians fell far short of Tridentine standards.

The most candid and forthright characterization of Catholic religiosity in the pueblos, however, comes, as always, from Domínguez. At the end of his report, he says:

> As Christians, a saint's name is given them in holy baptism as is the custom in our Holy Mother the Church, but . . . most of them do not know their saints' names and those who know them do not use them. . . . They are not in the habit of praying or crossing themselves when they rise or go to bed, and consequently have no devotion for certain saints as is customary among us. And if they sometimes invoke God and His saints, it is in a confused manner to comply in their confusion with what the fathers teach and explain. For example, they pay the father for a Mass, and he asks them what their intention is . . . and they reply: "You know, that saint what is more good, more big, him you make Mass. I do not know, maybe him Virgin, maybe St. Anthony," etc. . . . They do not confess annually. . . . They are exceedingly fond of pretty reliquaries, medals, crosses, and rosaries, but this does not arise from Christian devoutness (except in a few cases) but from love of ornament. (Adams and Chávez 1956, 254–56)

Domínguez himself suggested that the Indians only participated in the externals of Catholic ritual because of compulsion by the local friars. Although compulsion was certainly an element, modern anthropological commentators have suggested that something a bit more complicated was going on.

Dozier (1958; 1961; 1964) argues that Pueblo communities actively embraced Catholic ritual as a way of constructing a "facade" behind which they could practice the traditional religion that the friars so often sought to eradicate. Because the goal was to protect their traditional religion, the two religions were, to use Dozier's term, "compartmentalized"; that is, they were kept strictly separate in the thinking of the Pueblo peoples so that Catholic elements did not become assimilated to the traditional system and vice versa. The result was "the presence in Pueblo culture of two mutually distinct and separate socioceremonial systems, each of which contains patterns not found in the other" (Dozier 1961, 175). Although Catholicism was clearly less important than traditional religion, in the sense that it was less intimately involved with what was considered sacred, this is not to say that it was unimportant or that Pueblo participation in Catholic ritual was hypocritical. On the contrary, Catholic ritual ultimately served the same functions as traditional ritual. When performed properly but separately, both sets of rituals "accomplish the same ends—health and well-being for all humanity" (Dozier 1961, 177). Even today, long after any compulsion that might have been associated with the missionary friars has vanished, Roman Catholic practice, notably including marriage and baptism in the Church, continues to coexist with traditional religion in most Pueblo communities, although the strict compartmentalization noted by Dozier seems to have eroded over the past century or so (see Eggan 1979, 230; Parmentier 1979).

In summary, then, Pueblo Indians did participate in the "life-cycle" rituals of the Church and did participate in a number of church festivals throughout the year, and this may not entirely have been the result of simple coercion. But they were still not "devout" in the usual sense of that term: they had no serious understanding of Catholic doctrine, no strong devotion to Mary or to the saints (and certainly none to Christ); and they placed no great value on non-life-cycle Catholic rituals like confession and communion.

Although there is little in my characterization of Pueblo Catholicism that will come as a surprise to readers familiar with Pueblo history and ethnography, the methodological implications of this characterization for the study of *Hispano* Catholicism has generally been ignored by previous commentators. To put it simply: If participation in the life-cycle rituals of the Church (baptism, marriage, funeral services) and in special ritual celebrations scattered throughout the year (on Holy Thursday, Corpus Christi, or whatever) was not associated with a Catholic religiosity that was coherent, deeply-rooted, and interiorized in the case of the Pueblo Indians (which seems to have been the case), then why take these things as reflecting this sort of religiosity in the case of the Hispano settlers? The answer, of course, is that we shouldn't.

In the case of the Hispano settlers, I am not suggesting that participation in Catholic rituals was a way of diverting attention from another sort of religion as it was (if Dozier is correct) in the case of the Pueblo Indians.[5] Marriage and baptismal ceremonies, however, can serve important social and economic functions that have little if anything to do with religiosity. As George Foster (1953) pointed out long ago, it was common in Latin America, even more so than in Spain, for sacramental rites like marriage, baptism, first communion, and confirmation to serve as the occasion for establishing and/or reaffirming social ties between individuals and families within the local community. These ties established a range of mutual obligations that had social and economic value for all parties involved. In many areas of Latin America, marriages and baptisms continue to be occasions on which such ties are established (Norget 1999, 98). Indeed, the fact that baptisms and marriages perform important social functions having little to do with religiosity would explain why in many areas of Latin America participation in these particular church-sponsored ceremonies are high even though rates of attendance at Sunday Mass are low (see Bibby, Hewitt, and Roof 1998).

It seems likely that marriages and baptisms in colonial New Mexico performed the same social and economic functions that these ceremonies performed elsewhere in the Spanish Americas. Certainly, careful analysis of surviving baptismal records from colonial New Mexico reveals that *compadrazgo* (godparent) relationships did function to establish systematic interrelationships between the same families over time (Esquibel 1998, 31). Participation in these rituals, then, cannot be advanced as indicators of Hispano religiosity.

In the end, if we want to advance the view that Hispano Catholics during the colonial period were a deeply devout people (and this, remember, is the view implicit in virtually all existing commentaries on Penitente origins), we need to bring forward evidence that goes beyond the simple fact that they participated in the life-cycle rituals like marriage, baptism, and burial within the Church, and beyond the fact that they participated in religious rituals and processions on selected feast days. The problem is that when we go looking for such evidence, we are far more likely to turn up evidence suggesting the reverse, namely, that Hispano Catholics were *not* a particularly devout people.

❧ Jacals in the Wilderness

Fray Alonso de Benavides was given charge of the Franciscan *custodia* of New Mexico in 1623 and arrived in Santa Fe early in 1626. He subsequently wrote a report on the *custodia* that was published in Spain in 1630 and produced a revised version of the same report in 1634 (1916; 1945). Benavides's two reports constitute the first systematic effort to assess the Franciscan effort in New Mexico and remain one of the only sources we have for assessing the state of the Catholic religion in New Mexico during the seventeenth century. Generally, Benavides's discussion is taken up with accounts of the various Indian groups being missionized by the Franciscans. Only in his account of Santa Fe does he say anything that bears on the religiosity of the Spanish settlers, and in this regard he tells us two things.

First, he says that the two hundred and fifty or so soldiers there are "well indoctrinated," that is, well versed in their knowledge of the doctrines of the Church. Possibly this was correct, but in evaluating such a claim it must be remembered that Benavides routinely made the same claim about the Pueblo Indians, and we know—from later reports by commentators like Crespo and Tamarón—that the Indians were generally repeating what they had learned by rote with little if any understanding of the words they were repeating.

Benavides's next remark, however, is a simple observation that is, I think, more revealing of Hispano religiosity: the settlers at Santa Fe lacked a church. In his original report, Benavides says that religious services had been held in *"un malo jacal"* (a poor hut); but in his second report, he admits that even this had collapsed sometime before his arrival. Benavides himself tried to put a good face on all of this. Thus, he suggested, the settlers had wanted to build churches for the Indians first; and in any case, when he himself did start construction of a proper church, the wives and children of the settlers / soldiers helped him build it. Benavides's argument here, however, is not especially convincing.

It is true that the Franciscans had been busily building churches in the Pueblo communities before Benavides's arrival. Between 1609 and 1620, for instance, they built eleven such churches (Ivey 1998). What is not obvious is why building a church at Santa Fe during this period would have hindered the building of these mission churches. Furthermore, given the ease with which a church was built at Santa Fe after Benavides's arrival, there seems no particular reason why it could not just as easily have been built few years earlier if the local Spanish residents had wanted it.

In any event, even Franciscan commentators would eventually come to admit that the absence of a church at Santa Fe before Benavides's arrival was problematic. In an account of the Province of Santo Evangelio (of which the Custodia of New Mexico was a part) written in the 1760s, for example, Fray Francisco Antonio de la Rosa Figueroa says that before Benavides's arrival, "divine services [at Santa Fe] were held in a galerrón, which here means horreum, which must have been some xacalón used as a granary" and that it was "in view of *such an indignity*" that Benavides ordered the construction of a proper church (Hodge, Hammond, and Rey 1945, 205; emphasis added). At the very least, such an account must be taken as an implicit criticism of Hispano religiosity, since it suggests that the settlers at Santa Fe routinely confronted this "indignity" offered to the celebration of the Mass and yet did nothing (before Benavides's arrival) to correct the situation.

Here and there, other remarks by Franciscan commentators also criticize Hispano religiosity. Writing in 1778, for example, on the basis of reports collected from friars living in New Mexico, Fray Juan Agustín de Morfi (1977, 12) suggested that Hispano Catholics in New Mexico "know less about religion than the Indians themselves." In a report written for the Bishop of Durango in 1821, Padre don José Francisco Leyva y Rosas, pastor of the parish church at Albuquerque, made much the same point. Speaking of the fifty-seven or so families living in two isolated communities near Albuquerque, he says that they "never hear Mass during the greater part of the year . . . to the detriment of their children, who grow up without the nourishment of the Word of God, never hearing it from their pastor" (cited in Steele 1995, 173).

But perhaps the most sweeping condemnation of Hispano (and Indian) religiosity in New Mexico is found in a report that Juan Bautista Ladrón de Guevara made to the Bishop of Durango in 1820, just after Guevara had completed an official visit to New Mexico: "Of 35,500 and more souls, one thousand Spanish and mixed know the Christian doctrine. . . . The Indians of all missions except Senecu barely know any more of God than do the Gentiles. . . . From so much irreligion comes the indecent state of the churches, lack of ornaments, the fatal desolation of the House of God" (quoted in Boyd 1974, 163). Remember that Guevara's harsh judgment here on Hispano religiosity was being delivered during precisely that period of time when (at least in the opinion of all previous commentators) the supposedly deep-seated attachment of the Hispano population to Catholic rituals, coupled with a increasing scarcity of clergy, was driving Hispano Catholics to create new devotional forms like the Penitentes!

❧ So far, I have been citing scattered judgments of Hispano religiosity made by priests who were implicitly measuring that religiosity by paying attention to those things (like knowledge of church doctrine, regular attendance at Mass, interiorized religiosity, and so on) that were considered important within the logic of Tridentine Catholicism. That Hispano religiosity during the colonial period might come up short using such standards is not especially problematic. After all, it was routine for the Counter-Reformation missionaries sent into the European countryside in the two centuries after the Council of Trent to suggest that local populations there, too, fell far short of Tridentine standards. Indeed, one of the dominant metaphors appearing in missionary accounts of the Counter-Reformation period suggested that the European countryside in areas like southern Italy and Spain constituted an "Indies right here," whose inhabitants were as ignorant of core Catholic beliefs and rituals as the inhabitants of the overseas Indies.[6] The only difference, it would appear, was that New Mexico's isolation insured that this sort of Tridentine ignorance lasted longer there than elsewhere.

But there are ways of "being Catholic" that have little to do with Tridentine Catholicism—and here too we encounter some problematic patterns in northern New Mexico. Simply put: colonial New Mexico before 1800 was virtually unique among Catholic societies in Western Europe or Latin America in that several traditions that are the hallmarks of deeply rooted (if non-Tridentine) forms of popular Catholicism in these areas are nowhere to be found in New Mexico. Take the matter of apparitions.

❧ "Santiago is with us . . . briefly"

In December 1598, the Indian inhabitants of Acoma fell upon a visiting detachment of Spanish soldiers and killed eleven soldiers and two of their servants. Among the dead was Juan de Zaldívar, Oñate's nephew and the detachment's commander. A month later Oñate sent an expedition to Acoma under the command of Vicente de Zaldívar, younger brother of the slain commander, to request the surrender of those responsible for the attack, and failing that, to subdue the community by force. The Acomans refused to surrender, and the ensuing battle lasted three days. The Spanish emerged victorious, with no deaths and few casualties, largely because they had been able to raise two cannons to the top of the great rock on which Acoma sat. Among the Acomans, by contrast, six to eight hundred warriors were killed and about five hundred people, mainly women and children, were taken captive.[7]

In a letter written in late February 1599, Alonso Sanchez, who fought at Acoma and who had been on the six-member Council of War that advised Vicente de Zaldívar, said that some of the captured Indians asserted "that in the heat of battle they had seen someone on a white horse, dressed in white, a red emblem on his breast, and a spear in his hand" (Hammond and Rey 1953, 427). Sanchez does not name the individual, but he does say that "without [this] special aid from our God it would have been impossible to gain such a victory." The mysterious figure, in other words, was an apparition; and to anyone familiar with the iconographical traditions prevailing in Spain, there would have been little doubt about his identity: Sanchez is clearly describing Santiago (St. James the Moorslayer) himself, Spain's national patron. (The fact that Sanchez's description seems based so clearly on traditional representations of Santiago is of course evidence that the apparition report originated with the Spanish soldiers at Acoma, not with the Indians, as he suggests.) Although none of the depositions taken from other witnesses at Acoma (see Hammond and Rey 1953, 464–79), either Spanish or Indian, say anything about an apparition, there seems little doubt that the Spanish soldiers thought they saw something of supernatural origin. Thus, in an account of the battle written in 1610, Gaspar Pérez de Villagrá—who had also fought at Acoma and who, like Sanchez, had been a member of the Council of War advising Vicente de Zaldívar—has the captured Indians saying they saw *two* mysterious figures. The first was a noble Spaniard astride a white horse who wielded a broad sword as he flung himself into the forefront of the fighting; the second was a "maid more beautiful than the sun or heavens" (Villagrá 1992, 298). Villagrá goes on to identify the noble Spaniard as Santiago and the beautiful maid as the Virgin Mary. Finally, in the report on New Mexico that he sent to Rome in 1634, Fray Alonso de Benavides (1945, 166) suggested that it had been St. Paul, not Santiago, who appeared with the Virgin at Acoma, mainly because, he said, the apparition had occurred on the feast of St. Paul's Conversion. Still, however much Benavides might quibble over the "who" of the apparition experience, neither he nor any other church leader of the time expressed any doubts over the fact that an apparition had taken place.

The apparitions at Acoma, I must add, were not the only visionary experiences endorsed in Benavides's report(s). In his first report on New Mexico (written in 1626, published in 1630), Benavides says the Jumano Indians (who lived in what is now eastern New Mexico and Texas) were constantly requesting missionaries to come amongst them because (they said) they had been so instructed to do this by a "woman dressed in blue" who spoke to them in their own language. One of the missionaries happened to have in his possession a picture of Luisa de Carrión, a nun and mystic living in Spain, which depicted her wearing a blue habit in honor of the Immaculate Conception. The Jumanos were shown this picture and said that their visitor was dressed the same way but was younger and more beautiful. Although Benavides says no more about the identity of the mysterious woman dressed in blue in his original (1630) report, he came to believe that she was María de Ágreda (1602–65).

A Spanish mystic whose popularity was on the rise in the late 1620s, María de Ágreda claimed the ability to bilocate (to be in two places at once). In 1631, after having returned to Spain, Benavides visited María (who was twenty-nine at the time) at her convent in Ágreda, where she told him that she had been making miraculous visits to New Mexico (and elsewhere) since 1620. Although she supplied considerable detail regarding New Mexico, much of it was wrong and—as Frederick Hodge (Hodge, Hammond, and Rey 1945, 7) suggests—the rest could easily have been derived from Benavides's own report, published the year before. Even so, for the revised report that he published in 1634, Benavides rewrote the section dealing with the conversion of the Jumanos and now suggested that he had "no doubts whatsoever" (95) but that the woman in blue had been María de Ágreda. He added (96) that Luisa de Carrión also claimed to have made miraculous visits to New Mexico and that he believes she visits tribes living to the west of New Mexico (like the Zuñi, Hopi, and Navaho) just as María de Ágreda visits tribes (like the Jumanos) living to the east.

In summary, it would appear that Benavides was quite open to the possibility of apparitions of Mary, the saints, or other holy persons occurring in New Mexico and quite willing to give such events legitimacy. Indeed, the ease with which Benavides seems willing to populate New Mexico with bilocating nuns almost reads as if he were extending an invitation to the inhabitants of New Mexico to have visionary experiences. Nor was he alone in this; on the contrary, Benavides's account of the apparitions of María de Ágreda in New Mexico would be quoted approvingly by any number of other commentators over the next century and a half (see reports cited in Hackett 1937, 2:465–990). Nevertheless, it was an invitation that Hispano settlers declined. That very first apparition (or apparitions) at Acoma in 1599—which occurred, remember, among Spanish soldiers who had been raised outside New Mexico—was also the last.[8] Unlike Catholics in Spain or elsewhere in the Spanish Americas, subsequent generations of Hispano settlers simply did not have visionary experiences.

This absence of apparitions among Hispano settlers is all the more puzzling, given that New Mexico was characterized by a number of structural conditions that should have facilitated the experience of apparitions. In the case of Spain, for example, William Christian (1981, 90–91) has suggested that the likelihood of an apparition was inversely correlated with ecclesiastical control; that is, apparitions were more common in communities or time periods where control by Church authorities was weakest. Not only was New Mexico a substantial distance from the centers of ecclesiastical power in Durango and elsewhere, but the Hispano settlers there, by virtue of their predilection for dispersed settlement, were far less under the watchful eye of the local Franciscan missionaries than Indians living in the pueblos. Writing in the late 1700s, for instance, Fray Juan Agustín de Morfi suggested that "since [the settlers] do not live under the scrutiny of the authorities, it is not easy for the latter to keep track of the conduct of these subjects [and this] permits their larger crimes to go unpunished because they are not detected" (1977, 12). Yet unlike what happened in Spain, this relative freedom from ecclesiastical control did not foster apparitional experiences.

Something else that should have proven conducive to the experience of apparitions in New Mexico was the prevailing subsistence pattern, especially as it related to herding. Under the communal agricultural system that prevailed in northern New Mexico, grazing stock (mainly sheep and goats) was moved to pasturage some distance away from agricultural fields in the spring and kept away until harvest was completed. Since only a few shepherds were needed to supervise even a large number of animals, this task was usually given to a few young males (Van Ness 1991, 190–91). In European contexts, this sort of system, which insured that shepherds would spend long periods of time watching their flocks in isolated hillside pastures, routinely produced apparitions. Indeed, "the Virgin appears to a shepherd" motif is one of the most commonly encountered motifs found in European apparition stories.[9] And yet the same isolation that facilitated hallucinations/apparitions among countless shepherds in European contexts simply did not have the same effect on shepherds in New Mexico.

Apparition experiences are also usually facilitated by the familiarity of local populations with earlier apparition traditions. Not only does such familiarity make the possibility of an apparition in the present seem more credible to local audiences, but earlier apparition stories can provide would-be visionaries with details that can be incorporated into their own visionary experiences. Bernadette Soubirous's apparitions at Lourdes in 1856, for example, induced a spate of similar experiences by others in the area (Thurston 1933); and details associated with the apparitions at Fatima in 1917 were routinely incorporated into many of the apparitions that occurred in Europe and North America over the next several decades (Carroll 1986, 136–40). Certainly imitation was one of the processes that produced that first (and last) New Mexican apparition at Acoma. By 1599, after all, Santiago had appeared in at least nine other locations scattered throughout the Spanish Americas, usually to Spanish soldiers during or just before a battle (Valle 1946). The Spanish soldiers at Acoma, in other words, were simply appropriating for their own use an apparitional motif that had long proven popular with Spanish soldiers elsewhere in the Americas.

There was also a long tradition of Mary appearing at various locations in Spain and the Spanish Americas,[10] and Hispano settlers in New Mexico could easily have been familiar with any of these apparition traditions. The one apparition tradition, however, that we *know* they were familiar with was the tradition associated with Nuestra Señora de Guadalupe.

Devotional accounts suggest that Nuestra Señora de Guadalupe appeared to an Indian named Juan Diego at Tepeyac, near Mexico City, in 1531. Although a shrine dedicated to Mary did exist at Tepeyac in the early part of the sixteenth century, modern scholars have now established that the apparition story did not emerge and become attached to that shrine until sometime in the first half of the seventeenth century (Lafaye 1976; Poole 1997). Although initially this story and the associated cult was popular mainly in the Mexico City area (where it seems to have appealed most of all to the local *criollo* population), the cult's popularity soon spread to other areas. By the mid-eighteenth century, the cult of Our Lady of Guadalupe was a popular devotion throughout Mexico as a whole (Poole 1997; Taylor 1996, 282–83). That the cult had achieved a high visibility in New Mexico by this time is evident from the Domínguez report.

Titles of the various images of Mary encountered by Domínguez during his 1776 visitation of New Mexico churches (and the relative frequency of each title) include:

Nuestra Señora de Dolores (15 images)
Concepción (15 images)
Nuestra Señora de Guadalupe (14 images)
Nuestra Señora de la Luz (3 images)
Nuestra Señora de la Soledad (3 images)
Nuestra Señora del Rosario (3 images)
La Asunción (3 images)
Nuestra Señora de Valvanera (2 images)
Nuestra Señora de Los Angeles (2 images)
La Conquistadora
Nuestra Señora del Pilar
Nuestra Señora de los Reyes
Nuestra Señora del Carmen
Nuestra Señora de Belén [Bethlehem]
Nuestra Señora de Loreto
Nuestra Señora de los Remedios

As is clear, Nuestra Señora de Guadalupe was one of the three most common Marian titles encountered in New Mexican churches. In at least one case, involving the large painting of Nuestra Señora de Guadalupe at Nambe, Domínguez tells us explicitly that the various apparitions of this Madonna were depicted in the corners of the painting (53). Yet despite their familiarity with the Guadalupe story and (most likely) with other apparition traditions as well; despite New Mexico's distance from the centers of ecclesiastical control; and despite the isolation that was a defining feature of Hispano settlement patterns, Hispano settlers simply did not have visionary experiences.

I will concede that the apparent absence of apparitions in colonial New Mexico might be explained away as a methodological artifact (i.e., whatever apparitions may have occurred left no trace in the documentary record precisely because of New Mexico's isolation) or simply as a function of the fact that the absolute number of Hispano settlers was relatively small compared to Hispanic populations elsewhere. By itself, then, the absence of visionary experiences cannot be taken as saying very much about Hispano Catholicism during the colonial period. The problem is that apparitions are not the only thing missing.

◆ Also Missing: Image Cults

Over the centuries, countless images depicting Mary, Christ, or one of the saints have come to be seen as dispensing miraculous favors and so become the basis of a cult. Mary Lee and Sidney Nolan (1989), for instance, have identified 3,635 different miraculous images distributed across various Catholic shrines in Western Europe. Since the Nolans only surveyed images located at pilgrimage sites that are still active, this number almost certainly underestimates the total number of miraculous images that have existed in Western Europe.

Although a miraculous image comes into existence mainly because ordinary Catholics come to believe that appeals directed to the image can result in miraculous favors, these images could never become the basis of a continuing cult unless they were legitimized and encouraged by both ecclesiastical and civil authorities—and such legitimation and encouragement was generally forthcoming. Indeed, although there seems to be a widespread belief that the Church took a hard line against image cults following the Council of Trent, in fact, just the reverse is true: if anything, the Church was *more* predisposed to promote image cults during the Counter-Reformation than before.[11] In Spain, in particular, Church authorities were increasingly more likely, from the sixteenth century onward, to approve a cult organized around a miraculous image than around an apparition (Christian 1981, 75–93); and this official willingness to legitimize miraculous images carried over into the Spanish Americas.

Between 1530 and 1812 imperial bureaucrats in Spain sent off several dozen questionnaires to officials through the Spanish Americas. These questionnaires (reprinted in Solano and Ponce 1988) interrogated local officials on a wide range of topics, including the flora and fauna found in their region, local geography, demography, mining activities, and local government. Quite often too, especially when the questionnaires were sent to local bishops, they asked about the condition and contents of churches in their jurisdiction and, in particular, about any miraculous images that those churches might contain. A questionnaire sent out in 1635, for instance, asked bishops "if their cathedral had any important relic, and if so, to indicate the saint involved" and also "what devotional images are found in the churches of the diocese and what miracles may have occurred [in connection with those images]" (Solano and Ponce 1988, 114). A questionnaire sent out in 1648 asked "what important relics are to be found in the churches and *conventos* of the diocese, on what day are they shown and with what degree of solemnity" and also "if any of these churches and conventos have a miraculous image [*imagen milagrosa*] and what miracles are verified [*comprobados*]" (117). Notice that although the officials framing these questions inquired after both relics and images, only images (and not relics) were explicitly associated with miracles. Similar questions (associating miracles with images but not relics) were also included in questionnaires sent out in the eighteenth century (see Solano and Ponce 1988, 144). In short, it would appear that both the bureaucrats who crafted these questionnaires and the bishops who answered them took it as obvious that the sort of supernatural power that might result in miracles was associated most of all with miraculous images.

Generally, image cults sprang up throughout the Spanish Americas just as they had sprung up in Spain itself. A Jesuit commentary published in the mid-eighteenth century (Florencia and Oviedo 1755), for example, lists forty miraculous images in Mexico City alone. The same commentary identifies 105 such images for Mexico and Guatemala (which included Nicaragua) as a whole. Rubén Vargas Uguarte (1956, 1:201–94) provides detailed information on thirty-eight miraculous images that became the focus of especially large cults in colonial Mexico. The emergence of these cults by century looks like this:

sixteenth century	11 cults
seventeenth century	15 cults
eighteenth century	10 cults
nineteenth century (to 1821)	2 cults

Remembering that we are dealing with cults that survived until the nineteenth century (the older cults remained in place even as newer ones appeared), these data suggest that the cumulative number of miraculous images in Mexico was constantly on the increase throughout the colonial period. D. A. Brading (1994, 18) suggests that the proliferation of cults organized around miraculous images was especially intense in the period 1640 to 1760, when sanctuaries housing such images came to be erected with regularity in virtually every Mexican province.

Yet despite the long tradition of cults organized around miraculous images in the Catholic tradition generally, and in Spain and Mexico in particular, and despite the legitimacy given these cults by Spanish authorities (both religious and civil), popular cults organized around miraculous images simply did not emerge in New Mexico. Images, of course, had been present in the mission churches of New Mexico since the beginning of the colony. Furthermore, the Domínguez report indicates that many of the images he inspected were adorned with jewels or *relicarios* (small silver lockets containing a relic or holy image). Martha Egan (1993, 34) may be correct in asserting that some of these items were votive offerings (i.e., that some of these images were being "thanked" for supernatural favors received), but other interpretations are possible. In some parts of the Catholic world, for example, giving expensive gifts to a local cult was a way of enhancing a family's prestige within the community (Miele 1998; Carroll 1996, 178–86). The more important point, however, is that the available evidence from both Mexico (Larkin 1999) and New Mexico (Ward 1999, 171) suggests that jewels and silver *relicarios* of the sort mentioned by Domínguez were donated by relatively wealthy local elites. What is missing in New Mexico, in other words, is any evidence that image cults had a large *popular* following among either the Hispano or the Indian populations.[12] What is also missing, in New Mexico, are popular traditions associating any of the images found in New Mexican churches with dramatic miracles of the sort associated with miraculous images in Mexico and elsewhere. In his 1776 report, for example, Domínguez never once uses the term "miraculous" in describing any of the images he encountered and never relates a story associating any of those images with a miracle.

What is at stake here can be seen more clearly by considering what is undeniably the most well-known image in New Mexico: the statue of Mary as *La Conquistadora* that now resides in a side chapel of the Cathedral at Santa Fe.[13]

⤲ A Cult Promoted by Elites

At the time of the Domínguez visit in 1776, the statue of La Conquistadora at Santa Fe was adorned with more jewels and *relicarios* than any other that he encountered. Domínguez, in fact, lists seventy-six separate items. Popular tradition has long held that this statue was the image that Vargas carried with him during his campaign to reconquer New Mexico in 1692–93. Fray Angélico Chávez (1948b) has pointed out, however, that documents from the period suggest that the image carried by Vargas as he went from community to community was, in fact, a standard bearing the likeness of Nuestra Señora de los Remedios.

In Chávez's own reconstruction, La Conquistadora was one of the many images of Mary brought out of New Mexico by the settlers expelled during the Pueblo Revolt. It subsequently became the focus of a confraternity established in the Spanish community of San Lorenzo in what is now southwestern Texas. The image was brought back to New Mexico during de Vargas's second campaign in 1693 and once again became the focus of a confraternity. Vargas does seem to have had a special attachment to this confraternity, Chávez notes, because he allowed himself to be elected *mayordomo*. This confraternity, however, died out in the 1720s and seems to have been forgotten. In 1770, during a period of intense predation by the Apaches, Comanches, and Navahos, La Conquistadora was chosen as patroness of New Mexico as a whole; and a new confraternity was established in order to organize the feast in her honor.

Although Chávez (1948b, 104) characterizes the 1770 selection of La Conquistadora as patroness of New Mexico as deriving from a "popular movement," such a conclusion seems unwarranted. As Chávez notes, we have only two accounts of the events surrounding the selection of La Conquistadora as patroness of New Mexico: the one set down in 1776 by Domínguez (1956, 240–41) and the other set down in 1777 by Juan Candelaria (b. 1692), a resident of Albuquerque (see Candelaria 1929). Although the two accounts differ in a few details, they both make clear (1) that a petition signed by six men, all of whom seem to have been relatively well-to-do, was presented to Governor Pedro Fermín de Mendinueta, asking that a feast be established in honor of Our Lady of the Rosary (the official title of the La Conquistadora statue);

and (2) that the expenses for the first feast held in her honor (in 1770) were borne by the governor himself. Candelaria adds that in 1770 the governor—apart from covering the expenses of the feast—also paid for a "complete outfit of vestments and robes for the image of the very best found in Mexico" (1929, 296). In short, the La Conquistadora cult came to be implanted in New Mexico mainly because it was promoted by social elites (de Vargas in the first instance, and the governor and other local elites in the second).

This is not to deny that, once established, the festival in La Conquistadora's honor became a popular event. On the contrary, Domínguez says that this festival lasted for three days and involved "performances of Moors and Christians, tilts, a comedy and bullfights" (241). Even so, neither Domínguez nor Candelaria use the term "miraculous" in discussing La Conquistadora, and neither mentions any special miracles associated with this image. Nor is there any mention of miracles in the documents (reprinted in Chávez 1948b) associated with the confraternity(ies) that maintained the La Conquistadora image in the decades following the Pueblo Revolt. In the end, then, unlike what was true of the miraculous images of Mexico and elsewhere, it would appear that La Conquistadora's cult rested more on her association with local elites than on any popular perception that she was associated with supernatural power.

❧ The Absence of Localized Madonnas

The fact that popular cults organized around miraculous images did not exist in New Mexico probably explains something else that makes New Mexico different from other areas of the Catholic world: the absence of "localized" Madonnas, that is, the absence of Madonnas whose titles tie them to the local community in some distinctive way. For example, in the list below are titles associated with the miraculous images identified by Ruben Ugarte (1956, 1: 1-294) as being at the center of especially important cults in Mexico. Although each of these images had usually started life with a fairly standard title (Our Lady of the Rosary, the Immaculate Conception, etc.) most of them came to acquire a more distinctive title when they started dispensing miracles. As in Spain and Italy, this was usually done by incorporating the name of the community in which the image was located into the title (e.g., *Nuestra Señora de San Juan de Lagos, La Virgen de Izamal, Nuestra Señora de Talpa*). In other cases, a title was created using some detail from the origin legend surrounding the image. Thus, *Nuestra Señora de la Bala* was called that because a bullet (*bala*) fired by a jealous husband missed his wife, the intended victim, and lodged in the pedestal of an image of the Madonna to which the wife was clinging; *Nuestra Señora de las Aguas* was a statue of Mary as the Dolorosa that was seen (in a vision) holding back the floodwaters (*las aguas*) that threatened a community and whose clothes were found to be wet when the image was inspected; the *Virgen del Roble* was found in an oak (*roble*); and so on.

List of titles associated with the miraculous images that Vargas Ugarte (1956) identifies as being the focus of especially important cults in Mexico: (The number in parentheses indicates the number of separate and distinct miraculous images with this title; e.g., there are two "Guadalupe" images: one is the famous image at Tepeyac, near Mexico City, and the other is an image in Villagarcía that has the same title but a quite different origin legend.)

Nuestra Señora de Guadalupe (2)
Nuestra Señora de los Remedios
Nuestra Señora de la Asunción
Nuestra Señora de la Soledad (3)
Nuestra Señora de la Bala
Nuestra Señora de las Aguas
Nuestra Señora de la Macana
Nuestra Señora de la Piedad
Nuestra Señora de los Angeles (4)
Nuestra Señora de la Raíz
Nuestra Señora de la Salud (2)
Nuestra Señora de la Ocotlán
Nuestra Señora de Guanajuato
Nuestra Señora del Pueblito
Nuestra Señora de San Juan de Lagos
Nuestra Señora de Zapopan
Nuestra Señora de los Zacatecas
Nuestra Señora de la Bufa
Nuestra Señora de Refugio
La Purísima de Celaya
Virgen de Izamal
Nuestra Señora de Hool
Nuestra Señora de la Laguna
Nuestra Señora de los Terceros de León
Virgencita de Tlaltenango
Nuestra Señora de la Luz (2)
Nuestra Señora de la Defensa (2)

Nuestra Señora de Juquilla
Nuestra Señora de los Dolores de Acatzingo
Virgen de Roble
Nuestra Señora del Rayo (2)
Nuestra Señora de la Escalera
Nuestra Señora del Zape
Nuestra Señora de Talpa
Santísima Virgen de la Presentación
Nuestra Señora del Sagrario
Nuestra Señora de Santa Anita
Santísima Virgen de la Aurora

The presence of "localized" Madonnas in this list contrasts sharply with the absence of such Madonnas in the earlier list, which gives the titles associated with the images encountered by Domínguez in his tour of New Mexican churches. In the New Mexican list, the titles are overwhelmingly associated either with generic cults that were being promoted by Church authorities throughout the Catholic world (*Purísima Concepción, Asunción, Nuestra Señora del Carmen, Nuestra Señora del Rosario*) or with cults that had been established at particular locations outside New Mexico. *Nuestra Señora de Guadalupe,* of course, was associated with the celebrated sanctuary near Mexico City. The cult of *Nuestra Señora de la Luz,* which had originated in Sicily, was established at the Jesuit church in León in 1732 and from there had spread throughout New Spain. Other Madonnas in New Mexico came ultimately from Spain: *Nuestra Señora de Valvanera* was originally an image associated with one of the most important sanctuaries in northern Spain, though her cult subsequently spread to Mexico (Fontana 1983); *Nuestra Señora del Pilar* was and is a famous image whose sanctuary is located at Zaragoza; *Nuestra Señora de la Reyes* was a image found in the Royal Chapel at the cathedral in Seville. The important point is that not one of the titles associated with any of the images that Domínguez found in New Mexican churches, with the possible exception of La Conquistadora, ties the image involved to a New Mexican locale[14] or hints at a story of miraculous origins set in New Mexico.

Miraculous images—like apparitions—were simply absent in New Mexico. Images in New Mexico did not become surrounded by mysterious lights, cure the blind or the lame, save people from impending doom, bring dead children back to life, and so on, in the way that images did these things elsewhere. Here again, as in the case of apparitions, what makes the absence of miraculous images all the more striking is the presence of conditions that in other parts of the Catholic world *facilitated* the proliferation of miraculous images. Consider, for example, what happened elsewhere in the Catholic world when images were attacked.

❧ The Persecution and Mutilation of Holy Images

One of the most common legends surrounding miraculous images in Spain and Italy suggests that the image had originally been hidden during a period of persecution and was then rediscovered at a later date. In a typical case, somebody (often a shepherd) is guided to a secluded spot by miraculous means (e.g., a mysterious light or an apparition of Mary) and uncovers an image that has been buried, hidden in a tree, or something similar. The discovered image, which is usually an image of Mary, subsequently comes to dispense miraculous favors. In Italy, it is conventional in stories of this sort to suggest that the discovered image had hidden during the Iconoclast Controversy of the eighth and ninth centuries, when different Byzantine emperors and various leaders of the Eastern Church mounted an attack on image cults.[15]

In Spain, it is more common to suggest that the discovered image had been hidden by Christians fleeing Muslim persecution. The origin legend associated with the miraculous image of *Our Lady of Guadalupe* in Estremadura, Spain, for example, suggests that it was hidden originally by Christians from Seville fleeing Muslim persecution in the eighth century and was subsequently recovered, centuries later, when the Virgin Mary directed a shepherd to the hiding place (Lafaye 1976, 217–24). The origin legend surrounding *Nuestra Señora de la Hiniesta* is similar. In this case, a group of devout Sevillans fleeing Muslim forces in 714 are said to have hidden the image in a wooded grove in Catalonia, where it was subsequently discovered by a group of noble hunters in 1380, who in turn returned it to Seville (García Guttiérez and Martinez Carbajo 1994, 166). *Nuestra Señora de Valvanera* (one of whose images was encountered by Domínguez in New Mexico) was supposedly hidden in a hollow oak at Valvanera, in northern Spain, during the Muslim invasion and rediscovered centuries later by a group of Christian hermits (Fontana 1983).

Another type of legend that is quite common in Europe suggests that an image becomes associated with a miraculous sign and/or comes to dispense miraculous favors after it has been desecrated in some way. Writing in the early thirteenth century, Gonzalo de Berceo (1997, 123–28) tells a story that he says happened in Castile in his own time. Two thieves, one a cleric and the other a layman, broke into a church in order to rob it. As they proceeded to gather various furnishings, however, the cleric made the mistake of stealing a wimple draped around the head of a statue of Mary. In response, the image made the wimple stick to his hand, causing both thieves to become disoriented and ultimately to be captured. Another variant of the "desecrated image" story, one that became especially popular in Spain during the late seventeenth and early eighteenth centuries (see Alpert 1997) suggests that as a group of crypto-Jews start to whip a crucifix, the figure of Christ starts to bleed and asks them in an audible voice why they are whipping their God. In Italy, the most common "desecrated image" story (see Carroll, 1996, 46–48) involves the "impious gamesplayer." In these stories some people are playing a game (the precise nature of which varies from story to story) near an image of Mary; one of the players loses his temper and strikes the image with an ax (or a sword, a rock, etc.) and the image bleeds. The impious gamesplayer is later killed, and the image itself acquires a reputation for dispensing miraculous favors.

Common to all these "hidden image rediscovered" and "desecrated image" stories is the idea that holy images that are attacked will not only survive the attack but will become even more powerful. In the end, then, the message underlying these stories is that the supernatural power associated with image cults is real and that attempts to eradicate such cults are futile. Such a message would obviously be appealing to ordinary Catholics who had a deep and abiding faith in the supernatural power vested in holy images and would be appealing as well to Church authorities anxious to promote image cults. It was only to be expected, then, that these European stories would be imported into the Spanish Americas by both settlers and Church officials who continued to believe in image cults. Moreover, the many Indian revolts against Spanish rule, which almost always involved the smashing and desecration of images found in Catholic churches, provided the perfect context in which to develop distinctively American variants of these older European stories.

As an example, consider the traditions associated with the miraculous image of Nuestra Señora del Hachazo (*hachazo* = blow of an ax) at Zape, a community northwest of the city of Durango. In 1616 Jesuit missionaries at Zape planned a formal dedication of a statue of the Virgin as the Immaculate Conception on November 21st, the feast of Mary's Presentation. Five days before the planned dedication, however, the local Tepehuanes Indians rose in revolt. During the course of the revolt, both at Zape and elsewhere, church buildings were vandalized, images (including the image at

Zape) were smashed, and a number of Spaniards, including several missionaries, were killed along with their servants and slaves.

A few years later, according to the most common story associated with this cult, a pious soldier who had survived the 1616 revolt (he felt) by appealing to the image of the Virgin at Zape sent the image to Mexico City to be repaired. The restored statue was eventually installed in the mission church at Zape on August 14 (the feast of the Assumption), 1623, and became the focus of a popular cult. There was a mark on the face of the image, and popular tradition held that this was from an ax-blow that the image had sustained during the revolt. Tradition also suggested that after three attempts to repair the mark, with the mark reappearing each time, it was decided that the Virgin herself wanted the mark to remain visible as a reminder of the calamity that had fallen on the country in 1616.[16]

A slightly different tradition concerning the Zape cult is preserved in a Jesuit account published in the mid-eighteenth century (see Florencia and Oviedo 1755, 321–25). In this version, the Indian rebels hacked the statue into several pieces, which they then threw into a well. The pious soldier who made the vow commissioned a completely new statue, and it was this statue that subsequently became miraculous. On the other hand, the same source (324–25) also reports that pieces of the original statue were still in existence and that many people had been miraculously cured of various infirmities by drinking water in which small bits from these pieces had been dissolved.

The image cult at Zape persisted well into the eighteenth century. Bishop Pedro Tamarón visited Zape in 1763 during the course of a pastoral visit; and in the report describing that visitation, he provided a relatively extensive account of the cult, giving both an account of its origin (Tamarón preferred the first of the traditions mentioned above) and of the current condition of the image (AGI, 556: f38–f44). The image, he says, was one and a third *varas* in height; and the gash, which ran from the middle of the left cheek down to just before the neck, was about four fingers in length. He also says that it seemed as if the image's coloring had only just been touched up and refreshed (which of course is likely just what had happened in anticipation of the good bishop's visit). Zape was sufficiently important to Tamarón that it was one of the only locations that he visited more than once during the five visitations that he made during his tenure as Bishop of Durango (Gallegos 1969, 236)

The origin legend surrounding the miraculous image at Zape can be seen as merging the "persecution" element from the discovery-of-hidden-image stories common in Spain and Italy with the "image struck by impious person" element from the impious gamesplayer stories. Although in this case the wound did not bleed, it was nevertheless associated with something miraculous, namely, that it did not heal despite repeated attempts at repair. Most importantly, of course, the message implicit in the legends surrounding this Mexican image is the same that is implicit in the older European stories: Catholic images are a source of supernatural power; and these images will prevail, even grow stronger, despite attempts by unbelievers to suppress them.

Although the Zape story was particularly well known in the diocese of Durango (and so could easily have been known to both the settlers and the Franciscans in New Mexico), there were many other miraculous images in Mexico associated with similar stories. The Franciscans, in particular, seem to have been predisposed to popularize image cults organized around miraculous images that had been attacked during Indian revolts. Writing from Mexico City in 1777, for example, Fray Juan Agustin de Morfi (1935, 79) noted that the church associated with the Franciscan *convento* of San Francisco had a miraculous image of Mary called "del Mezquital" because it had been from the community of San Francisco de Mezquital (which is just to the south of Durango) where it had been profaned (like the Zape image) during the Tepehuanes revolt. It is against this Mexican tradition of cults organized around images profaned during a revolt by Indians that we need to look carefully at what did and did not happen in the aftermath of the Pueblo Revolt in New Mexico.

In 1680 the inhabitants of most of the Pueblo communities in northern New Mexico rose in revolt against Spanish rule. Several hundred Spaniards, including twenty-one Franciscan missionaries, were killed; the rest were forced to retreat to El Paso del Norte in the southernmost portion of the province. As with Indian rebellions elsewhere in the Spanish Americas, the rebels ransacked local Christian churches and destroyed the images found there. Judging from the reports of the devastation given by Spanish eyewitnesses (collected in Hackett 1970), these images were most commonly burned or smashed. Sometimes, however, the Indians showed the intensity of their disdain in other ways. A report of the revolt drawn up in October 1680 by the Cabildo of Santa Fe at La Salineta (during the course of the Spanish retreat) suggested that the rebels:

> set fire to the holy temples and images, mocking them with their dances and making trophies of the priestly vestments and other things belonging to divine worship. Their hatred and barbarous

ferocity went to such extremes that in the pueblo of Sandia images of saints were found among excrement, two chalices were found concealed in a basket of manure, and there was a carved crucifix with the paint and varnish taken off by lashes. There was also excrement at the place of the holy communion table at the main altar, and a sculpted image of Saint Francis with the arms hacked off. (Hackett 1970, 1:178).

Yet unlike what happened at Zape and at other locations in Mexico, not a single one of the images profaned during the Pueblo Revolt became the center of an image cult in New Mexico when the colony was reestablished in the 1690s. Just how easily images profaned during the Pueblo Revolt *might* have become the focus of a cult can be seen by considering the one such profaned image that did become the focus of a cult, though not a cult located in New Mexico.

◈ Nuestra Señora De La Macana

In his *Teatro Mexicano,* published in Mexico City in 1698, Augustin de Vetancurt, himself a Franciscan, presents a brief synopsis of the Pueblo Revolt of 1680 and then says:

Six years earlier [in 1674] a nine year old girl . . . who was crippled and in great pain entrusted herself to an image of Nuestra Señora del Sagrario de Toledo that she had with her—and instantly found herself cured. And amazed at the miracle that had been wrought, the girl said that the Virgin had said to her: "My child, arise and say that this Custody [New Mexico] will soon be destroyed because people have so little reverence for my priests, and this miracle will be testimony that this [prophecy] is the truth. They must make amends for their wrong-doing if they do not want to experience this punishment. (Vetancurt 1971, 103–4)

Vetancurt goes on to say that when all this came to be known, a Mass was celebrated with the girl present, and grievances that had been filed against the friars were burned.

Taken at face value, Vetancurt's account seems to provide evidence of two things that seem generally to be missing in New Mexico: miraculous images and apparitions. Unfortunately, there are several reasons why his story *cannot* be taken at face value. First, the simple fact that the story "foresees" the Pueblo Revolt is evidence that the story, at least in its current form, developed sometime after 1680. Second, the legend seems a little too similar to stories about other miraculous images that were circulating in the Spanish Americas at the time. Sometime in the 1660s or so, for example, the Virgin is supposed to have appeared to another young girl, also crippled, near the village of Maras, northwest of Cusco in Peru; subsequently, the image of this Virgin became well known for miraculous cures (Sallnow 1987, 82). Third, Vetancurt's account seems too clearly to serve Franciscan aims, in that it has the Mother of God herself siding with the Franciscans in their never-ending disputes with the civil authorities. Certainly, later Franciscan commentators were alert to the propaganda value of the Vetancurt story. In a report written in 1761, for example, Fray Pedro Serrano repeated the Vetancurt story and then blamed the entire Pueblo Revolt on the fact that following this incident the civil authorities in New Mexico had relapsed into their persecution of the Franciscans and so caused the punishment promised by the Virgin to be carried out (see Hackett 1937, 495). Finally, and most importantly, Vetancurt himself (however inadvertently) provides some evidence that this story originally had a much simpler form and was unconnected to anything that happened in northern New Mexico.

In the *Menologio Franciscano* that was included in his *Teatro Mexicano,* Vetancurt tells us (88) that he received the story from Fray Joseph Traxillo (José Trujillo). Traxillo had become a friar in 1634, and after serving in various places—including the Philippines—he was eventually assigned to the Hopi Pueblo of Xongopavi (in what is now northeastern Arizona). Vetancurt continues by saying:

> It was from here [Xongopavi] in the year 1672 that he wrote to a P. of this Province about how the Virgin had healed a crippled girl of twelve years and had warned everyone that within a few years this land would be destroyed on account of the lack of reverence in which the priests were held, and about how he hoped that when this happened he would be able to use the occasion in order to give his life for his Redeemer. And, to his glory, give his life is just what he did on August 10, 1680, along with the others that I have already described.

Note that this version of the story lacks the "lawsuits against the priests" element that seems to tie the other version so clearly to New Mexico. Indeed, if this were the *only* version we had, we might reasonably conclude that the events described took place at Xongopavi and that most of all the story reflected the bitterness of an old priest at the lack of respect shown him by his Hopi charges[17] and his consequent eagerness for martyrdom. It would be a story, in other words, that had nothing to do with the Hispano settlers in northern New Mexico.

On balance, then, it seems entirely possible that the story repeated by Vetancurt at the end of his account of the Pueblo Revolt is really a post-1680 creation that mingles together (1) memories of Fray Traxillo's story from Xongopavi, which originally referred to events there; (2) memories of the quarrels that undeniably did take place between the Franciscans and the civil authorities in New Mexico; and (3) the stark fact of the Pueblo Revolt itself. I grant that such a reconstruction is entirely conjectural, but at least it would account for something that otherwise seems quite puzzling: the fact there is no verification of this apparition story from sources located in New Mexico and no mention of the story in any of the depositions taken from settlers who had fled New Mexico during the Pueblo Revolt. Angélico Chávez (1959, 96–97) says simply that New Mexicans "forgot" about the incident. A much simpler explanation is that they never knew the story in the first place because it was not something that happened in New Mexico.

No more is heard about the image mentioned by Vetancurt until the mid-1700s, by which time it had become the focus of a cult in Mexico City and had acquired an expanded origin legend. The most complete account of this new legend appears in a devotional booklet first published by Fray Felipe Montalvo in 1755 and subsequently reprinted several times in the late 1700s.[18] Montalvo's account repeats the origin legend found in Vetancurt's work but then goes on to say that during the Pueblo Revolt an Indian chieftain entered a house where the image had been hidden by Christians fearful for its safety and struck the head of the image with *"una aguda macana"* (literally: "a sharpened club"). This chieftain was later hanged by the devil himself. Eventually, we are told, the image found its way to the Franciscan convent at Tlalnepantla (which was just northwest of Mexico City). Although attempts were later made to repair this gash, the mark continued to remain visible so as to demonstrate that this image was to be set apart for special veneration as *Nuestra Señora de la Macana*. In 1755 the image was transferred to the Convento Grande of the Franciscans in Mexico City.

At least some of the additions to the origin legend that appear in Montalvo's work—in particular the mark-that-won't-heal element—seem clearly to be borrowed from similar legends surrounding other profaned images in Mexico, like Nuestra Señora del Zape. The influence of European traditions, for example, can be seen in the fact that in Montalvo's expanded legend the image is said to have been hidden by local Christians fearful for its safety (just like so many images in Spain and Italy were hidden during times of persecution) and in the fact that the impious person who strikes the image, just like the impious gamesplayer in the European stories, eventually dies. The similarity to the impious gamesplayer story is even more evident in a slightly different version of La Macana's origin legend set down in Mexico City in 1754.[19] In this version of the legend, the chieftain gives the image a blow to the head with his club, and blood issues forth (just as it does in the impious gamesplayer story), with the mark of the wound still being visible today ("*y dió con ella un golpe a la Santa Imagen de Nuestra Señora en la cabeza de donde le salió sangre, y asta oy conserva la señal*").

What seems to have happened, then, is that Franciscans residing in Mexico, who had a history of establishing cults organized around profaned images, took in an image that had been profaned during the Pueblo Revolt and that was supposedly the image mentioned by Vetancurt. The origin legend surrounding this image was then expanded by borrowing elements from stories about persecuted images that had long been circulating in continental Europe and the Spanish Americas. The final result, in this case as in so many others, was an origin legend that legitimized the belief that a holy image could be infused with supernatural power *and* that this power would persist even in the face of determined attacks by unbelievers.

But remember: what is most significant about the story of Nuestra Señora de la Macana is that it shows just how easily any one of the images profaned during the Pueblo Revolt could have become the focus of a popular cult in New Mexico if the desire to do this had been present. The fact is that such a desire was absent. In the end, Nuestra Señora de la Macana was the focus of a *Mexican* cult; neither she nor any other image profaned during the Pueblo Revolt became the object of a cult located in *New* Mexico.

❧ In other parts of the Latin Catholic world, the experience of an apparition or the presence of a miraculous image were ways of sacralizing the landscape, that is, of associating particular locations with supernatural beings whose power could be accessed for the benefit of human beings. Sites that were sacralized in these ways quite often became the object of pilgrimage, and many of the pilgrims who came to these sites brought with them ex-votos, that is, objects that testified to their having received favors from the supernatural being associated with that site. In New Mexico, however, the absence of apparitions and miraculous images meant that the landscape there was *not* sacralized in the way it was elsewhere. This, I think, helps to explain some other patterns that have not previously been acknowledged and that I now want to discuss, namely, the fact that pilgrimage sites were generally nonexistent in New Mexico for most of the colonial period and that Hispano Catholics never embraced certain ex-voto traditions that were common elsewhere.

·⁓ Pilgrimage

Today the most famous pilgrimage site in northern New Mexico is the sanctuary dedicated to Nuestro Señor de Esquípulas at Chimayó. Although this sanctuary draws pilgrims throughout the year, the most intense period of pilgrimage activity occurs during Holy Week, on Good Friday especially (see plate xx), when hundreds of pilgrims can be seen walking along the highways and roads of New Mexico towards Chimayó and thousands more arrive by car or bus. Yet as important as it now is, the Chimayó sanctuary is not really very old. On the contrary, the present sanctuary started life as a simple public chapel built over the period 1813–16 at the initiative of Bernardo Abeyta,[20] a resident of Chimayó. Furthermore, both Abeyta's original petition asking permission to erect this chapter (reproduced in de Borhegyi 1953, 93), as well as the various documents that passed back and forth between Church authorities in New Mexico and in Durango,[21] suggest that the chapel's purpose was only to provide a place where Hispano families living in and around Chimayó could display their devotion to Our Lord of Esquípulas. There is no indication in any of these documents that the chapel was expected to attract pilgrims from further afield. Indeed, there is no evidence that the church at Chimayó began attracting any significant number of pilgrims from outside the Chimayó area before the mid-1800s. What makes this significant is that Chimayó was the very first pilgrimage site in northern New Mexico.

At first sight, the absence in New Mexico of sacred sites that drew pilgrims from distant communities might seem attributable to the fact that during the colonial period Hispano settlers were legally required to obtain permission from their local *alcalde* mayor to travel within the province (and from the governor to travel outside the province). In fact, this legislation seems to have been aimed mainly at vagabonds and other undesirables in both the Hispano and Indian populations. By the late 1700s, Hispano settlers who were well established and well known generally did not need to obtain travel permits (Simmons 1968, 184). Furthermore, whatever the law may have said about travel outside local communities, the many trade fairs that existed in New Mexico—the most well-known of which was the annual fair at Taos in October (see Simmons 1991, 40–46)—insured that travel outside local communities was in fact a common occurrence during certain times of the year. Indeed, the fact that trade fairs, but not pilgrimage sites, were common in colonial New Mexico is in itself an unusual pattern, given that in other areas pilgrimage and attendance at regional trade fairs were mutually reinforcing activities. Thus, it was common in both Spain (Christian 1981, 117–18), Peru (Sallnow 1987, 92–94), and northern Mexico (Teja 2001) for towns that were the object of pilgrimage to be simultaneously the site of an important regional trade fair.

Regional pilgrimage sites aside, what is also missing in New Mexico is any evidence of "local" pilgrimage, that is, pilgrimage by the members of a particular community to nearby sacred sites. It was common in Spain, for example, for the countryside around towns and villages to be dotted with chapels or outdoor shrines erected at locations that had been sacralized by an apparition, the discovery of a hidden image, the fact that a hermit or other holy person had lived there, and so on. Community-sponsored pilgrimages (romerías) to these sacred sites, often involving an overnight stay, were central to the local experience of Catholicism in Spain during the early modern period (Christian 1981, 70–91; Kamen 1993, 194–98; Poska 1998, 20–25). In Ireland, local pilgrimages of this sort (though not involving an overnight stay) were usually made to springs and stone cairns dedicated to particular saints (Carroll 1999, 19–44).

What all of this means, of course, is that—even setting aside any difficulties that might have been associated with travel too far outside the local community—Hispano Catholics, like Catholics in Spain and Ireland, could easily have developed traditions of local pilgrimage that drew them to sites located near to where they lived. That this did not happen is further evidence that Hispano Catholics simply did not have the sorts of experiences that sacralized local and regional landscapes in other areas of the Catholic world.

❧ Painted Ex-votos

A painted ex-voto is a small painted tablet that is brought to a sanctuary by someone who has received a favor from the supernatural being associated with that sanctuary. These tablets are typically not painted by the person who received the favor but are commissioned from artisans who specialize in producing such paintings. Occasionally the person who received the favor is depicted in the painting in the act of prayer. More usually, however, a painted ex-voto depicts the danger from which a person was delivered. Thus, painted ex-votos routinely depict people being run over by the wheels of a cart, escaping from a house that has collapsed or caught on fire, evading soldiers or thieves bent on killing them, being saved in the nick of time as their mule or coach almost runs off a cliff, being pulled from a well into which they have fallen, being tortured by the authorities, and so on. Invariably, the supernatural being to whom the appeal for help was made is depicted somewhere in one of the upper registers of the painting.[22]

In Italy the use of such painted ex-votos by ordinary Catholics became common in the sixteenth century (Carroll 1992, 84), and it quickly spread to other Catholic countries. Henry Kamen (1993, 197) suggests that painted ex-votos came into widespread use at Spanish sanctuaries during the seventeenth century. Today painted ex-votos are especially common at sanctuaries in Andalucía and Catalonia (Rodríguez Becerra and Vásquez Soto 1980, 50).

In Mexico the use of painted ex-votos received a boost in the late eighteenth century when technological advances allowed a thin coat of tin to be applied to a leaf of iron, since in this way folk artists in central Mexico were given access to a relatively inexpensive but durable surface that was well suited to the use of oil paints. The result was an upsurge in the production of "tin *retablos*," that is, paintings made on square or rectangular sheets of tin.[23] Some of these tin *retablos* depicted particular saints, Madonnas, and images of Christ, and were intended for devotional use within homes and churches. Others, however, were commissioned as painted ex-votos and depicted the same range of "dangerous situations" encountered among painted ex-votos in Spain and Italy.[24] Even now, for example, the use of ex-votos painted on tin *retablos* is common among Mexican migrants to the United States who want to thank Mary or one of the saints for favors received or dangers avoided during the course of the immigration experience (Durand and Massey 1995). But what is most interesting (for us) about the tin *retablo* tradition in Mexico is that it emerged in the early 1800s, that is, more or less contemporaneously with the *santero* tradition in northern New Mexico.

There is an enormous body of scholarly literature dealing with the *santero* tradition in New Mexico, most of which has been written by art historians.[25] That literature suggests that between 1790 and 1830 a relatively small number of *santeros* (estimates range from six to ten) arrived or emerged in New Mexico and established workshops for the manufacture of *santos* (holy images), including both *bultos* (three-dimensional images carved of wood) and *retablos* (two-dimensional images painted on sections of wooden plank). Generally, these New Mexican *santos,* both *bultos* and *retablos,* were characterized by an emphasis on frontal (or at best, three-quarter) views and were nonnarrative (i.e., except in the case of images tied to Christ's passion, the holy person depicted in a *santo* is not engaged in a recognizable activity). There was also little concern with perspective, so that foreshortening was usually missing from *bultos;* and *retablos* were painted in a "flat" style that did not aim to convey three dimensions. In *retablos,* outlines were emphasized and filled in with simple colors.[26] Within the defining limits of this common tradition, however, there were minor stylistic differences that differentiated one *santero* from another, and much of the existing scholarly literature on the *santero* tradition is concerned with using these differences to decide which *santero* (or which *santero's* workshop) made what particular *santo* or *retablo.*

In some ways, the two traditions of religious folk art that developed in Mexico and New Mexico, respectively, were linked. Mexican and New Mexican artists, for example, often depicted the same saints and the same Madonnas and often drew upon the same iconographical traditions in doing so. This is why Giffords (1992, xv-xvi) was able to use existing scholarship on the New Mexican *santos* to identify some of the more obscure saints depicted on Mexican tin *retablos.* In at least one way, however, these two folk art traditions were quite different. While folk artists in Mexico made tin *retablos* that were destined for devotional use in private homes and for use as painted ex-votos, *santeros* in New Mexico made the one type of image but not the other. New Mexico *santeros,* in other words, made *retablos* for devotional use but did not make painted ex-votos. Why not? I think the answer to that question has already been given: unlike what was true in Mexico (and in Spain, in Italy, and in so many other parts of the Catholic world), the landscape in New Mexico had not been sacralized by apparitions or miraculous images and so had not come to be associated with supernatural beings whose power could be accessed for the benefit of human beings. To put it more simply, a tradition of painted ex-voto use did not develop in New Mexico because there was no one there to thank.

❧ Conclusion: Deaf Saints and Absent Madonnas

According to an investigation carried out in 1706 by Fray Juan Álvarez, who had been appointed to act for the Inquisition in Santa Fe, a sorceress called La Chispa advised her clients to turn to magic because prayer would not work. "The saints of this territory are deaf," she said, and the "mother of God had not come to this land" (cited in Greenleaf 1985, 32). The patterns reviewed in this chapter suggest that La Chispa's summary comment here was right on the mark. Statues of Mary and the saints may have existed in New Mexico's churches, but the conceptualization of Mary and the saints as supernatural beings whose power could be accessed by direct contact was missing from the mind-set of Hispano Catholics during the colonial period. This, I suggest, explains why Hispano Catholics did not experience apparitions of Mary and why they did not invest images of Mary or the saints with miraculous powers—even though these are things that their co-religionists in Mexico, Spain, and Italy did with regularity.

⚜ There is one final aspect of Hispano piety in the period before 1800 that must be assessed, if only because it concerns something that has always been front and center in the thinking of all commentators concerned with Penitente origins. That something is public flagellation, and it is a topic that merits its own chapter.

THREE

Awash in a (Very Small) Sea of Crimson Blood

FLAGELLATION IN PRE-PENITENTE
NEW MEXICO

On the Thursday of Holy Week in the year 1598, Don Juan de Oñate and his party stopped somewhere just to the south of present-day El Paso as they made their way northward into what would become New Mexico. Twelve years later, in 1610, Gaspar Pérez Villagrá—who had been a captain under Oñate's command—wrote an epic poem about the Oñate *entrada*, and part of that poem tells us what happened on that Holy Thursday (Villagrá 1992, 102–3). First, Villagrá says, Oñate ordered a chapel to be built of logs and draped with canopies, in which was enclosed a consecrated host.[1] That night the entire camp engaged in prayer and penitential behaviors. The women and children came to the chapel barefoot and prayed. The Franciscan friars sang hymns and prayed while wearing hair shirts. But it is Villagrá's account of what Oñate and the other soldiers did on that Holy Thursday eve that would come to be of greatest interest to modern scholars:

> The soldiers, all together, with both hands
> Laying their backs all open on one side
> And on the other with the cruel whips,
> Were begging aid of Him and in great haste. . . .
> The General, in a secret place
> That he wished only I should know
> Kneeling upon the ground did shed
> Two fountains from his eyes and then,
> Lashing his shoulders, he poured out
> A sea of crimson blood while imploring
> His Divine Majesty that he have mercy on
> All that great camp that in his charge

Was placed and entrusted.
Also, his two nephews at their posts
Did lacerate themselves with whips,
Until the dawn came. . . .[2]

The soldiers, in other words, engaged in bloody self-flagellation. In a note added to the modern translation of Villagrá's work, the editors suggest that the "scene depicted by Villagrá cannot help but recall the later penitentes of New Mexican history" (1992, 102n)—and given the centrality of flagellation to Penitente ritual, they are certainly correct. As a result, it has become something of a convention in all existing accounts of the Penitentes to cite Villagrá's account of the self-flagellation practiced by Oñate and his men as evidence that the Penitentes who emerged in the early nineteenth century were the outgrowth of continuing flagellant traditions that had been present in New Mexico since the colony's foundation.

The case for a pre-Penitente tradition of flagellation in New Mexico does not, of course, rest on this one instance alone. On the contrary, Penitente scholars who mention the Holy Thursday self-flagellations practiced by Oñate and his men are always quick to associate that incident with two other instances of pre-Penitente flagellation in New Mexico. The first is an incident that Alonso de Benavides mentions in both of the reports that he wrote in the 1630s (1916, 21; 1945, 66). Benavides says that in the pueblo of Xumanas, to the southeast of Albuquerque, he was confronted by an angry wizard, who shouted that Spaniards were crazy because they went about flogging themselves and shedding blood in the streets and because they were now trying to teach his people to do likewise. Likely, Benavides suggests, the wizard had seen a flagellant procession (*algún procesión de disciplina*) staged during Holy Week in some Christian pueblo. The other incident appears in the Domínguez report. In his account of the services conducted by Sebastián Fernández, the Spanish-born friar resident at Abiquiú, Domínguez says that every Friday during Lent, Fernández first conducts a Via Crucis (Stations of the Cross) service in his church and then, "after dark, [leads in the practice of] discipline attended by those who come voluntarily, because the father merely proposes it to them, and, following his good example, there is a crowd of Indians and citizens" (1956, 124).

I should make it clear that these three incidents—the flagellations by Oñate and his men on Holy Thursday, Benavides's reference to flagellant processions during his conversation with the Pueblo wizard, and Domínguez's reference to the flagellation at Abiquiú—are not simply the incidents cited most often to support the claim for a preexisting tradition of flagellant piety in New Mexico, they are the *only* incidents cited in this regard. In other words, outside of the evidence provided by these three incidents, there is absolutely no other documentary evidence attesting to the practice of flagellation in New Mexico for the entirety of the colonial period. Yet as crucial as these three incidents have been in discussions of Penitente origins, each incident is problematic.

Angélico Chávez (1974, 63–68) has already brought out some of the problems with Villagrá's account. First, there is no mention of penitential exercises, and in particular no mention of flagellation, in the official log of the expedition. On the contrary, that log says simply that on Holy Thursday "we adored the Most Holy Sacrament." Second, Villagrá wrote his epic poem several years after the events he described and at a time when Oñate's reputation had been tarnished in a number of ways. Given Villagrá's admiration for Oñate, Chávez suggests, he would have had every incentive to embellish the log-keeper's laconic account by making those Holy Thursday services simultaneously a bit more flamboyant and more indicative of a deeply felt religious piety on the part of Oñate and his lieutenants.

But even taking Villagrá's account at face value, while it may provide evidence that some of the adult males in the expedition practiced self-flagellation, it makes no reference to anything resembling the public processions of flagellants that would come to be associated with the Penitentes or that (as we shall see) were commonly sponsored by penitential *cofradías* in both Spain and Mexico in the early seventeenth century. Villagrá says only that Oñate flagellated himself in a secret place that only Villagrá knew about, that Oñate's two nephews (Juan and Vicente de Zaldívar) whipped themselves at their posts, and that the remaining soldiers did likewise while gathered together as a group.

There are problems too with the other two incidents. As Wroth (1991, 41) points out, Benavides's remarks can be read as referring only to flagellant processions in Indian villages and so do not necessarily provide evidence that Spaniards in New Mexico also participated in such processions. In the case of the Domínguez report, what Domínguez is describing at Abiquiú is flagellation at night in the privacy of a church. Here again, in other words, there is nothing to suggest that Hispano Catholics participated in public processions involving flagellation.

But what is most problematic about these three often-cited incidents is that if they are read against the known history of flagellant confraternities and flagellant processions in other areas of the Catholic world, these same three incidents can be taken as providing evidence that public flagellation in New Mexico had *died out* long before the emergence of the Penitentes.

❧ A Brief History of Public Flagellation

During the European Middle Ages the practice of flagellation, both in private and in public, was shaped by two separate though complementary beliefs. First, flagellation was seen (first within the monastic orders, then among the laity generally) as a particularly efficacious way of expiating sin and sinfulness. Given this conceptualization, it was only a short step to the view that communal flagellation in public would be an especially effective way of appeasing vengeful supernatural powers who sent catastrophes as a punishment for society's sinfulness. This is why public processions of flagellants in the Middle Ages so often followed upon natural disasters. The Black Death, which appeared in the middle 1300s, for example, and which devastated nearly a third of the population in most areas of Europe, provoked waves of public flagellation. But the disasters that provoked public flagellation could be social as well as natural. Thus, for example, the flagellant movement that broke out at Perugia in 1260 and soon spread across northern Italy, and that represents the first appearance of large-scale public flagellation in a European context, was likely more the result of the political instability that was gripping Italy at the time than anything else (J. Henderson 1978).

The second view shaping the practice of flagellation was that it was a way of participating in (and so honoring) the passion of Christ. Flagellation, in other words, was an expression of Christocentric piety that was valuable in itself, irrespective of its value in expiating sin or ameliorating natural or social disasters. It was this second view of flagellation that came increasingly to be promoted by the Observant branches of the mendicant orders, and it was this view that most of all gave rise to the flagellant confraternities established during the late medieval and early modern period. As Giovanna Casagrande (2000, 52–53) has pointed out, the fact that communal flagellation was seen to be a very public way of imitating, and so identifying with, the suffering Christ likely explains why women were generally excluded from the flagellant confraternities established during this period (just as they we excluded from the priesthood).

In Italy, there was a fairly dramatic proliferation of flagellant confraternities during the late fifteenth century. Quite often such confraternities were established by subdividing existing confraternities into a *Stretta* group, which practiced flagellation, and a *Larga* group, which did not (Terpstra

1990; Fontaine 1999). In Spain, a similar proliferation of flagellant confraternities occurred a bit later, in the early 1500s, and was mainly the result of efforts by the Franciscans. In most Spanish cities of the period, for example, the first Holy Week confraternities to incorporate flagellation into their public rituals were almost always confraternities dedicated to the *Vera Cruz* (True Cross); and these were usually based in a local Franciscan church or convent (Flynn 1999; Mitchell 1990, 42; Moreno Navarro 1982, 116; Webster 1998, 21). William Christian provides a succinct overview of the pace at which flagellant brotherhoods spread from city to city in Spain over the course of the sixteenth century: "Formal flagellant brotherhoods of the True Cross . . . were formed at Cáceres in 1521, Cabra in 1522, Villalpando in 1524, and formed or reformed in Toledo before 1536, Seville in 1538, Baeza in 1540, Jaén in 1541, and Jerez in 1542. Similar brotherhoods of the Blood of Christ were formed in Valencia in 1535 and were a regular part of penitential processions in Barcelona after 1544" (1981, 185).

Further evidence of the increasing popularity of flagellant brotherhoods in the sixteenth century is found in the proliferation of such brotherhoods *within* particular cities during this period. At Seville, for instance, the flagellant confraternities established during the sixteenth century (either by reorganizing existing confraternities or by establishing new ones) included: the Cofradía de la Santísima Trinidad y de las Cinco Llagas (1535); the Cofradía de Nuestro Padre Jesús de la Pasión (1531); the Cofradía de la Vera Cruz (1538); the Cofradía de Nuestra Señora de la Soledad (c. 1550); the Cofradía de Nuestro Señor Jesucristo Crucificado y Nuestra Señor de la Hiniesta (1560); the Cofradía de los Azotes que sufrió nuestro amabilísimo Redentor (1563); the Cofradía de Nuestro Padre Jesús Nazareno (1564); the Cofradía del Gran Poder (1570); and the Cofradía del Dulce Nombre Jesús y Primera Sangre de Nuestro Señor Jesucristo (1574) (see Llompart 1969, 43; Montoto 1976, 138).

By the early seventeenth century, the public processions staged by flagellant confraternities in Spain had become among the most elaborate such processions in the Catholic world. Writing from Valladolid in 1605, for instance, a Portuguese observer said that "the Holy Week processions here are more numerous and more organized than in Lisbon, with the result that the least of those seen here is more remarkable than the best of ours" (cited in Llompart 1969, 38). The same observer went on to describe two processions. The first, he said, consisted of 800 flagellants marching in double file; 550 brothers carrying torches or candles of one sort or another; and two *pasos* (platforms carried in procession) that each carried a statue or statues depicting a scene from the Passion. The second consisted of 2,000 flag-ellants; more than a thousand brothers carrying candles; and seven *pasos*. This same observer also reported that some of the flagellants scourged themselves so savagely that their garments were encrusted with "more than a pound of coagulated blood [*sangre coagulada de más de a libra*]," something that he personally found both scandalous and excessive (Llom-part 1969, 38).

Flagellant brotherhoods also came to be established in Mexico—and here again, Franciscans took the lead. Flagellant brotherhoods dedicated to the Vera Cruz, for example, were established in Mexico City in 1527 and in both Guadalajara and Zacatecas in 1551 (Wroth 1991, 21–26). If contem-porary reports are to be believed, the sheer size of the processions organ-ized by these New World brotherhoods, especially when they included In-dians as members, were quite impressive. One Franciscan commentator, writing in 1609, suggested that one of the *cofradías* associated with the Chapel of St. Joseph in the Franciscan Convento Grande at Mexico City staged a procession on Holy Thursday that included 20,000 Indians, of whom more than 3,000 were flagellants, and that a procession staged by another *cofradía* on Good Friday included more than 7,000 flagellants (Torquemada 1986, 229). The same commentator goes on to name several other cities in Mexico where similar processions (usually smaller in size, but sometimes larger) were staged.

The popularity of flagellant confraternities received a further boost fol-lowing the Council of Trent (1545–63), given that local bishops committed to implementing Tridentine reform, of whom Carlo Borromeo of Milan was the prototypical example, routinely saw flagellation as a useful way of implementing the emphasis on discipline and control that was a central element in those reforms. (The link between flagellation and Tridentine re-form will be discussed at length in the next chapter.)

Up until the mid-sixteenth century, flagellant brotherhoods in Europe were primarily an urban phenomena, mainly because cities were the areas most accessible to the mendicant orders who were promoting flagellant brotherhoods as a form of Christocentric piety. In the century and a half following the Council of Trent, however, there was an explosion of mis-sionary activity in the European countryside; and many of these rural mis-sions—especially those conducted by the Franciscans and the Jesuits—were characterized by a strongly penitential emphasis that often involved flag-ellation. These penitential missions were especially common in Spain and southern Italy (Rienzo 1980, 442; Orlandi 1994, 434–36) and usually incorporated flagellation into the mission experience in two ways. First, at particular times during the mission (usually after a sermon), missionaries would flagellate themselves in order to get onlookers, at least male onlookers, to do likewise. Speaking of the penitential missions conducted by the Jesuits in the late seventeenth century, for instance, Paola Vismara Chiappa (1982, 822), says:

> On this point, the [archival] records are extremely repetitive: during the course of the mission, the preacher was constantly offering himself up as an example of the sort of flagellant that was common in this era. Thus, we see him described with his clothing open at the back, the instrument of flagellation in his hand, and with his blood gushing out here and there. These actions induced strong emotions in those looking on, which the preacher sought to transform into a desire to imitate his own actions.

Second, and more importantly, flagellation was a central element in the grand penitential procession held toward the end of the mission.[3] Partly, Counter-Reformation missionaries included public flagellation in the mission experience because they, like their urban-based predecessors in the fifteenth and early sixteenth centuries, saw it to be form of Christocentric piety. But these missionaries also had another, and more pragmatic, reason for promoting flagellation.

When missionaries wrote about their mission experiences, as they often did, they were quite explicit in saying that overtly theatrical techniques were often necessary in order to secure the emotional involvement of rural populations in the mission experience. As a result, during the course of their sermons missionaries often held up skulls, cut their own hair, passed their arms through flames, and so on (see Rienzo 1980). The most efficacious techniques, however, were always those that involved what Luigi Lombardi Satriani (1981) has called the "theatricalization of blood." In other words, ritual activities that were public and that involved much shedding of blood—including, but not limited to, flagellation—were seen to be (and were) a form of visual entertainment that best secured the involvement of onlookers in the mission as a whole. Some idea of just how bloody mission activities could become can be found in an account of Jesuit missionary activity written in 1651 by Scipione Paolucci, himself a Jesuit. Speaking of the penitential processions staged toward the end of a mission, Paolucci says that it was common to see a great multitude of men throw caution to the winds and beat themselves repeatedly, sometimes on their backs and sometimes on the front of their legs, so as to draw blood; many others struck themselves on the head with canes so as to drive the thorns [they wore] even more deeply into their skulls and so cause even more shedding of blood; others struck their legs and arms with bunches of sharp twigs, whose points easily broke off and stuck in the living flesh. Several raked their skin with wire brushes of the sort used for carding [fibres]. Some rolled gruesome pointed spurs over their breasts. Still others attacked various parts of their body with iron pinchers. . . . Others bloodied their tongues by rubbing them with the thorny part of a certain plant. Finally, there were others, who had twenty or so lancets, of the sort used during [medical] blood-letting, stuck in their thighs and other parts of their body. These men walked with their arms bound to a cross and with each movement they experienced the most intense tearing of their flesh in several locations. (Cited in Di Palo 1992, 24–25)

As a theatrical technique, public blood-shedding activities like these had the special advantage that the very fact of such activities being public predisposed practitioners to greater excess, which meant more blood, and which thus served to intensify the overall dramatic effect. As one Spanish cleric said in the mid-seventeenth century in speaking of the special benefits of public flagellation, "Those who might otherwise beat themselves lightly and timidly in private often find themselves so animated in the presence of company as to perform vigorous and harsh flagellation" (cited in Flynn 1999, 238).

None of this is to say that the flagellant confraternities of the early modern period or the Counter-Reformation missionaries who staged penitential processions in the countryside abandoned the medieval view that flagellation was a method of expiating sin and appeasing vengeful supernatural force. On the contrary, when the occasion arose, public flagellation could still be pressed into service as a way of ameliorating natural catastrophe. This is evident, for instance, in Cervantes's well-known account of the comic encounter between Don Quixote and a procession of flagellants, where Cervantes says very explicitly that this procession had been organized by a local brotherhood in response to a drought (1981 [1605], 396–400). Similarly, Kamen (1993, 435–36) reports that Jesuit missionaries in Catalonia regarded natural disasters like plague or drought as conditions that facilitated the organization of flagellant processions. As late as 1714, a confraternity in Nice organized a procession of several hundred penitents who whipped themselves with iron-tipped scourges in response to a lack of rain and a wave of exceptionally cold weather (Bordes 1978, 386).

In short, by the mid-seventeenth century public flagellation meant several different things simultaneously both to Church authorities and to the laity: it was an expression of Christocentric piety, a way of expiating sin and so a way of ending natural and social disasters, and a form of entertainment.

In Spain the popularity of public flagellation started to decline in the late seventeenth century (Christian 1981, 199–200). By the early 1700s, in cities like Seville, many confraternities that had previously staged flagellant processions during Holy Week had come to abandon the practice; and in those confraternities that still staged such processions, the number of flagellants was much reduced from what it had been a century earlier (Bermejo y Carballo 1882, 44). It was during that this same period that the practice of public flagellation came increasingly to be criticized by a vocal minority within the missionary orders themselves, on the grounds that such bloody activity did little to induce interiorized religiosity (Rusconi 1992, 253).

The most serious assaults on the practice of public flagellation, however, came in the latter half of the eighteenth century, when a variety of Catholic leaders, both secular and ecclesiastical, sought to implement the Enlightenment emphasis on rationality by eliminating from Catholic ritual anything that smacked of "superstition" or "irrationality." In practice, this meant eliminating (or at least regulating) Catholic rituals that (1) were not related in an obvious and direct way to the sort of Christocentric Catholicism envisioned at Trent, and/or (2) involved public displays that seemed to be infused with emotionalism.

The most well-known reform of the period, at least as regards Spain, is the royal *cedula* issued by Carlos III in February 1777. This decree regulated public processions in several different ways. First, it prohibited specific forms of penitential behavior, notably including those that involved flagellation and walking with arms bound to a large crossbar. Second, it prohibited the practice of walking in procession with faces covered. Finally, it prohibited processions at night. The 1777 decree, however, was only one part of a whole series of reforms promulgated during this period whose intent was to rationalize Catholic practice. In 1768, for instance, Carlos III issued a series of regulations that put seminaries firmly under the control of local bishops and that set standards for both the content and organization of the clerical training that took place within these seminaries (F. M. Hernández 1979). In the early 1770s, the Bourbon administration systematically collected information on all existing *cofradías* in Spain as part of a concerted effort to make these organizations more subject to the authority of the state (Arias de Saavedra and López Muñoz 1998).

Attempts were also made in this period to regulate and reform a number of popular religious rituals, notably those that involved the very visible display of behaviors marked by emotional excess. At Seville, for example, ecclesiastical authorities regulated the masked dances held during Carnival in 1768; prohibited fireworks in 1771; reformed the processions and brotherhoods associated with Holy Week in 1777; prohibited the use of giant puppets, giant heads, and the *tarasca* (serpent-monster) in Corpus Christi processions in 1780; and issued regulations relating to the practice of bathing in the river[4] in 1784 (Sánchez Herrero 1999, 47). In Italy, the Synod of Pistoia (1786) passed a number of resolutions whose purpose was likewise to eliminate various superstitious and emotionally extravagant behaviors that had crept into Catholic practice (Carroll 1996, 18–24). In particular, it was during the second half of the eighteenth century that Italian authorities, both civil and religious, acted to suppress the practice of public flagellation, nocturnal processions, and religious ceremonies (of any sort) that incorporated a visible penitential emphasis (Zardin 1987, 122–23; Bernardi 2000, 240–42).

Authorities in the Spanish Americas quickly came to adopt the same rationalist policies that were becoming commonplace in Spain and, more generally, throughout Catholic Europe. In Mexico during the late 1700s, a series of reform-minded bishops campaigned against the use of overly elaborate musical scores in church that distracted from the Word of God, against religious dances and live representations of the Passion, and against draping statues of Mary and the saints with expensive jewelry and clothing (Larkin 1999). Nor were these bishops alone in this campaign. In 1790 the viceroy banned giant puppets and the serpent-monster from the Corpus Christi procession in Mexico City (Gómez 1986, 19) just as they had been banned from that same procession in Seville a decade earlier. Similarly, writing in 1788, José Antonio Alcocer (1958, 192), who himself had conducted a great many Franciscan missions in northern Mexico, reported that his missionary college (El Colegio de Nuestra Señora de Guadalupe de Zacatecas) had stopped conducting penitential missions of the sort outlawed in the royal *cedula* of 1777 even before that date, and in any event had *never* permitted bloody flagellations (*las disciplinas de sangre*) in their public processions.

None of this is to say that these rationalist reforms were always and everywhere fully effective. Public flagellation, in particular, was never completely extinguished. In both Spain and Italy flagellant processions continued to be staged in some communities (and in a few communities are staged even to this day; see Christian 1981, 204–5; Carroll 1996, 77–79). The same was true in Mexico. The 1805 Constitution of the Hermandad de Nuestro Amo Jesús El Nazareno in Cuencamé, for instance, says:

> On the Fridays of the Holy Spirit,[5] the brothers should go out into the streets and walk the Via Sacra carrying a cross and wearing a crown of thorns and a noose, and on the penultimate and last Fridays, [they should do this] while disciplining themselves . . . and at each station [they should give themselves] fifteen lashes [*azotes*]. On one Friday [they should do this] in memory of the sorrows of Our Lady the Virgin Mary and on the other Friday in memory of the Passion and death of Our Lord Jesus Christ. (AHAD 212: 663)

Similar processions were staged in other communities in northern Mexico. Nevertheless, taking all the evidence into account, Wroth (1991, 30–39) is almost certainly correct in arguing that during the late 1700s and early 1800s public displays of flagellation, though by no means extinguished, were very much on the decline in northern Mexico.

On the other hand, while Enlightenment leaders were opposed to public displays of flagellation, they were more flexible in the case of penitential activity carried out with moderation in the privacy of a church. One of the decrees issued by ecclesiastical authorities at Seville in 1777, for example, after receipt of the Royal decree prohibiting public flagellation, suggested that "those who truly felt penitent should henceforth, in consultation with their confessors, choose forms of penance that were more rational and private and less open to public view" (cited in Sánchez Herrero 1999, 49). The language here is virtually identical to the language used by Bishop Zubiría in responding to the 1833 letter from Padre Martínez in which the Penitentes are mentioned for the first time. Thus, after giving his approval to Martínez's decision to suspend the public activities of the brotherhood, Zubiría says that the members should be told that "the best way to please God is to listen to the voice of their pastors and to obey those pastors without resistance, [and so] to content themselves for now with doing Penance in the privacy of their church, always in moderation" (cited in Wroth 1991, Appendix I).

Morada at Ojo Caliente (no date). Alice Bullock Collection, Center for Southwest Research, General Library, University of New Mexico. NEG. NO. 000-478-4393.

Morada at San Francisco, in the San Luis Valley, Colorado.

Morada at Truchas, New Mexico.

(ABOVE) Penitentes near Wagon Mound, New Mexico, circa 1896. Courtesy of the Colorado Historical Society. NEG. NO. F-389. Photo by E. M. Cosner.

Opposite page

(TOP) *Disciplinas* used by Penitentes during ritual flagellation, circa 1896. Courtesy of the Colorado Historical Society. NEG. NO. F-3434. Photo by E. M. Cosner.

(BOTTOM) A Picador lacerating the back of a Brother, from Darley's *The Passionists of the Southwest* (1893). Courtesy of the Bancroft Library, University of California, Berkeley.

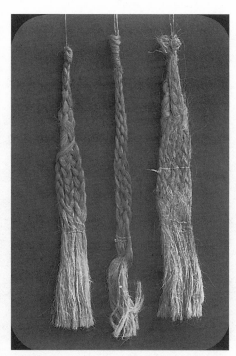

Doña Sebastiana image from the church of San José de Gracia de Las Trampas at Las Trampas. Photo by Jesse L. Nusbaum, courtesy of the Museum of New Mexico. NEG. NO. 13671.

Opposite page

(TOP) Penitente procession at San Mateo, New Mexico, in 1888. Photo by Charles F. Lummis. Courtesy of the Southwest Museum, Los Angeles. PHOTO N.20141A.

(BOTTOM) A Penitente crucifixion on Good Friday, 1888, in San Mateo, New Mexico. Photo by Charles F. Lummis. Courtesy of the Southwest Museum, Los Angeles. PHOTO N.36551.

Copyright 1888
by C F Lummis

Crucifixion of the
Penitentes

Pilgrims entering the sanctuary at Chimayó on Good Friday (1999).

Bulto of Jesús Nazareno by José de Gracia Gonzales, New Mexico, 1860s (FA.1989.40.1). International Folk Art Foundation in the Museum of New Mexico, Santa Fe. Photo by Blair Clark.

(LEFT) Daguerreotype of Padre Antonio José Martínez (ca. 1847–48). Casa San Ysidro Collection, The Albuquerque Museum Purchase, 1997 G.O. Bond. 1998.27.29. (RIGHT) Title page of the manual for parish priests published by Padre Martínez in 1839. Center for Southwest Research, General Library, University of New Mexico.

A traditional "Jesús Nazareno" image, under a "Tres Caídas" (Three Falls) designation, being carried into a church in Taxco, Mexico, circa 1905. Photo by C. B. Waite, Center for Southwest Research, General Library, University of New Mexico. NEG. NO. 996-003-0068.

✤ Re-viewing Flagellation in New Mexico

If we now view the three overly cited incidents of flagellation in New Mexico against the general history of public flagellation in Catholic societies, what do we see? First, two of these three incidents (the flagellation practiced by members of the Oñate expedition in 1598 and the penitential processions staged in Indian pueblos during Holy Week mentioned by Benavides in his reports) appear in precisely the "right" time period (i.e., in the late 1500s/early 1600s, when public penitential processions were in vogue throughout the Catholic world) and among precisely the "right" groups (among Hispanic colonists who had lived in areas where flagellant confraternities were well established and in Indian pueblos that were under the direct control of the Franciscans, a religious order that was promoting public flagellation as a matter of policy throughout the Catholic world). Moreover, the one brief mention in the Domínguez report of the flagellations performed in the church at Abiquiú does not change the fact that there is not a single reference to public penitential processions in New Mexico at any point during the eighteenth century, which is precisely the period when such processions were in decline elsewhere. Furthermore, that one instance of flagellation at Abiquiú—as Domínguez himself is at pains to tell us—was conducted at night in the privacy of a church, was closely supervised by Fray Fernández, and does not seem to have involved much shedding of blood. The flagellation at Abiquiú, in other words, was much closer to the sort of restrained and private penitential practice that was being *encouraged* during the late 1700s than to the extravagant processions of bloody flagellants that were being *prohibited* during this period.

Imagine that we had to reconstruct the general history of flagellation in Catholic areas during the two centuries following the Council of Trent using only the three New Mexican references to flagellation as our guide. What would we conclude? We would undoubtedly conclude that the popularity of public flagellant processions reached a peak in the late 1500s and early 1600s and that such processions died out in the eighteenth century in favor of restrained flagellation done in the privacy of a church. And, of course, that more or less *is* the history of flagellation after Trent.

Three cases, of course, cannot really be used to establish a pattern; but in some ways, that is precisely the point I am trying to make: these three cases, despite the fact that they are routinely cited as "evidence" that the Penitente emphasis on flagellation was the outgrowth of a longstanding tradition of Hispano flagellation, prove nothing of the sort. Public flagellation in New Mexico may have existed up until some point in the seventeenth century, but these three cases can easily be read as suggesting that it died out long before the emergence of the Penitentes in the early nineteenth century.

In the end, then, what I am suggesting is that the public flagellation that was still being practiced during the early 1800s in a few Mexico communities like Cuencamé and the public flagellation of the Penitentes in the 1820s were fundamentally different phenomena. The flagellant processions at Cuencamé and elsewhere were the last remnants of a documented tradition that persisted in Mexico right up to the rationalist reforms of the late 1700s. In New Mexico, by contrast, public flagellation, as I have suggested, had likely died out more than a century and a half earlier. This would mean that what the Penitentes were doing in the early 1800s was for all practical purposes something quite new, rather than the continuation of something old.

⁘ Conclusion

The vision of Hispanic piety that has emerged from the analysis presented in this chapter and the last is obviously quite different from the vision that underlies most existing scholarship on colonial New Mexico. The more traditional vision constructs Hispano Catholics during the colonial period as a deeply pious people clinging to impeccably Catholic and distinctively Hispanic traditions that stretch back to dim medieval mists. By contrast, the vision that has emerged from the examination of the available evidence in this chapter and the last suggests that Hispano Catholics were not particularly devout, and that this is true whether we focus on the Tridentine standards favored by the official church (which emphasize knowledge of core doctrines, interiorized religiosity, regular attendance at Mass) or on the hallmarks of popular Catholicism prevailing in other Latin Catholic areas—apparitions, image cults, localized madonnas, painted ex-votos.

The new vision of Hispano religiosity that has been articulated here is not the result of any new discoveries. On the contrary, the "data" relating to the Penitentes has remained more or less constant for quite some time now. Rather, what I have proposed is a gestalt shift in the way that that data is perceived. Such a shift is made possible, on the one hand, by the setting aside of what are essentially confessional concerns (in particular, a desire to shape the past in order to construct Hispanos as "good Catholics" according to standards prevailing among contemporary Catholics) and, on the other, by incorporating into the study of the Penitentes a systematic awareness of the conclusions reached by scholars studying popular Catholicism in other cultural areas.

For those scholars whose approach to Hispano history is shaped by confessional concerns (i.e., who are themselves Catholics in good standing with the contemporary church and who want to demonstrate that Hispanos in previous centuries were good Catholics) the conclusions being offered here will no doubt seem disrespectful. My response, simply, is that there can be no disrespect in seeking to recapture the lived reality, whatever it might have been, of an undeniably strong people who had to adapt to difficult conditions—even if that lived reality did not include elements (like a deeply rooted Catholic piety) considered to be important by contemporary Hispanos.

Of course, what is most significant about the vision of Hispano piety that has emerged in this chapter and the last, given the concerns of this book, is that it forces us to reconsider all previous accounts of Penitente origins. After all, if the Penitentes were not the outgrowth of a strong and preexisting tradition of Catholic piety, which is the contention implicit in all previous accounts of Penitente origins, where *did* they come from? What explains their great popularity? What is the source of the emotional intensity so obviously associated with Penitente ritual? Ultimately, all these questions must be answered if we are to truly understand the Penitentes. As a start, however, I assume that if the Penitentes were something new, then they likely had their origin in something new that was happening at that time in Hispano society—and it is now time to consider what that might have been.

FOUR

Suffering Fathers and the Crisis of Patriarchal Authority in Late Colonial New Mexico

The figure of *Nuestro Padre Jesús Nazareno* has always been central to Penitente ritual. Most commonly, Nuestro Padre Jesús Nazareno is a freestanding image depicting Christ wearing a full-body tunic with wide sleeves and with a crown of thorns on his head. If the image is a *bulto,* the tunic is often made of real cloth and fitted over the carved statue underneath. The face, neck, hands, and feet of this Christ are usually marked by a relatively large number of bloody lacerations; and removal of the tunic (in the case of a *bulto*) typically reveals even more bloody lacerations on other parts of his body.[1]

There are several things about this figure that might strike Anglo audiences, even Anglo Catholic audiences, as odd. First, Christ is being called "Padre" (after all, official doctrine, in both the Catholic and the Protestant tradition, holds that Christ is the *Son* of God). Second, it quickly becomes apparent when discussing such images that "Jesús Nazareno" does not mean (or mean simply) "Jesus of Nazareth." Finally, the amount of blood depicted on these Penitente images is usually far in excess of what is found on the Christocentric images (even those associated with the Passion) that are more familiar to Anglo audiences. Nevertheless, all of the iconographical elements that define Penitentes' Nuestro Padre Jesús Nazareno have clear precedents in Christocentric cults found in other areas of the Catholic world.

For example, however much at variance it may seem with official Catholic doctrine, it has long been common practice in Spain, especially in Andalucía (Mitchell 1990, 114), to use the term "Padre" when referring to certain images of Christ. At one time or another, for example, the Sevillan *cofradías* that stage processions during Holy Week have carried aloft images of Nuestro Padre Jesús del Gran Poder, Nuestro Padre Jesús Nazareno,

Nuestro Padre Jesús de las Tres Caídas, Nuestro Padre Jesús de la Pasión, Nuestro Padre Jesús de la Salud y Buen Viaje, Nuestro Padre Jesús del Silencio, Nuestro Padre Jesús Descendido de la Cruz, Nuestro Padre Jesús con la Cruz al Hombro, Nuestro Padre Jesús de las Penas, and Nuestro Padre Jesús ante Anás (see Bermejo y Carballo 1882; Moreno Navarro 1983; Gonsález Gómez and Roda Peña 1992).

"Jesús Nazareno," like "Nuestro Padre," is a common Christocentric title and, in particular, a title that has long been incorporated into confraternity dedications in both Spain and the Spanish Americas. One of the most well-known of the Passion Week *cofradías* at Seville, for example, was founded in 1564 and dedicated originally to the Santa Cruz de Jerusalén; however, by the early 1600s it had come to be dedicated jointly to the Santa Cruz de Jerusalén and to Nuestro Padre Jesús Nazareno (Montoto 1976, 135). A *cofradía* dedicated to Jesús Nazareno was established at Jaén in 1592 (Ulierte Ruiz 1991), and by the mid-1600s Jesús Nazareno *cofradías* could be found in any number of Spanish cities.

At least by the late 1700s (i.e., in the period just before the emergence of the Penitentes), such dedications were common in Mexico as well. In Mexico City, for example, one of the *cofradías* associated with the guild of the tailors was dedicated to Jesús Nazareno (Carrera Stampa 1954, 123), and a miraculous image of Jesús Nazareno was located in the church associated with a hospital of the same name (Florencia and Oviedo 1755, 115). Jesús Nazareno was also a common *cofradía* dedication both in the rural areas around Mexico City (Lavrin 1988, 71) and in the diocese of Michoacán (Brading 1994, 136). In the city of Durango (even closer to New Mexico), a brotherhood (*hermandad*) dedicated to Padre Jesús Nazareno coalesced around an image of the same name that had been set up in the church of San Nicolás de Tolentino in 1673 (Gallegos 1969, 181). Elsewhere in the Diocese of Durango, a *cofradía* dedicated to Jesús Nazareno, founded under the auspices of the Franciscan Third Order, existed in Sombrerete in 1790 (AHAD 128: 0084); and in 1813 several parishioners from Chalchihuites submitted a plan for the establishment of another *cofradía* dedicated to Jésus Nazareno (AHAD 226: 0783).

The title "Jesús Nazareno" denotes an image depicting Christ on his way to Calvary. Traditional "Jesús Nazareno" images in Spain, Italy, and the Spanish Americas usually wear a full-body tunic with wide sleeves that is cinched at the waist. Such images typically have long hair, which often falls across the image's face, and wear a crown of thorns (see gallery following p. 86). In Spain and Mexico, Jesús Nazareno images often have three metallic plumes sprouting from the top of their heads[2] and wear nooses around their necks; whereas Jesús Nazareno images in Italy often have the noose around the neck but lack the metallic plumes. Most commonly a Jesús Nazareno image depicts Christ with the cross over his shoulder as he drags it along the route toward Calvary, but other variations are possible. One of the most well-known Jesús Nazareno images at Seville, for example, shows Christ receiving his cross; that is, he holds the cross over his shoulder, but the long vertical beam is in front of him, not behind (see Webster 1998, 91). It is also common, in both Spain and Mexico, for a Jesús Nazareno image to depict Christ during one of the three falls occasioned by the weight of the cross. In this case the image is likely to be called "Padre Jesús de las Tres Caídas" (Father Jesus of the Three Falls[3]) or something similar. In the early 1700s, for instance, one of the most important processions staged in Mexico City on Good Friday was the one staged by the Cofradía de las Tres Caídas de Jesús Nazareno (García Ayluardo 1994, 80).

In the end, then, while the "Padre Jesús Nazareno" central to Penitente ritual may have lacked some of the iconographical elements mentioned above (the noose around the neck, the metallic plumes from the head) and was only occasionally depicted with some of the others (the long hair, carrying a large cross), his title, his full-body tunic, and his crown of thorns leave no doubt but that he was to some extent modeled on these Mexican/Spanish/Italian predecessors.

On the other hand, although there is no denying that the Penitentes borrowed from earlier "Jesús Nazareno" traditions when constructing their Padre Jesús Nazareno, it is also the case that they added some things. Most importantly, they added elements that had the effect of intensifying the (apparent) suffering of their Padre Jesús. Mostly this meant covering his body with more bloody lacerations than was typical of Spanish/Mexican Jesús Nazarenos. In this regard William Wroth (1982, 57; 1991, 71) suggests that the Penitentes were drawing on iconographical traditions associated with the Ecce Homo, the image of Christ as he appeared just after having been flagellated by Pilate.[4] Certainly, traditional images of the Ecce Homo do depict Christ with a large number of bloody lacerations (caused by his flagellation), though they usually do not depict him with a full-body tunic.

Usually the Penitentes also gave their Padre Jesús nail marks in his hands and feet and sometimes (at least in the case of *bultos*) a spear wound in his side (see, for instance, plates 76 and 79 in Wroth 1991; plate 188 in L. Frank 1992). Indeed, depicting nail marks in the hands and feet of free-standing images of their Padre Jesús is so much a part of Penitente iconography that the occasional failure on the part of a *santero* making Penitente *santos* to do this is cause for comment (see for example Birner 2000, 40). What is most interesting here is that such nail marks (or spear marks) are not part of the traditional iconography associated with either Ecce Homo images or Jesús Nazareno images in Spain, Mexico, or Italy—which in itself makes perfect sense, given that both of these images are supposedly depictions of Christ *before* his crucifixion (and so before he was nailed to the cross and speared). Larry Frank (1992, 211) suggests that in giving their Padre Jesús Nazareno the nail marks of the crucifixion, the Penitentes were drawing on the iconography associated with the *Man of Sorrows*. This was an image depicting Christ as a freestanding figure clothed only in a loin cloth and wearing a crown of thorns; marks on his body usually included lacerations caused by the flagellation, abrasions on his knees and elbows caused by falling under the weight of the cross, puncture wounds in his hands and feet, and a spear wound in his side. The general idea, in other words, is that the Man of Sorrows embodies *simultaneously* all the things that caused Christ pain during his Passion. Although European in origin, the Man of Sorrows cult did exist in Mexico (Giffords 1992, 31) and so would indeed have been available for the Penitentes to imitate as they set about intensifying the apparent suffering of their Padre Jesús Nazareno.

In summary, then, there is nothing especially unique or novel about the title that the Penitentes gave to the image of Christ that was at the focus of their ritual activities, nor anything unique or novel about most of the elements that came to define his iconography. On the contrary, both that title and those iconographical elements were preexistent in both the Spanish and Mexican Catholic traditions and thus would easily have been available to Hispano settlers during the period (the late 1700s/early 1800s) when Penitente ritual was being developed. Still, while there seems little mystery about *how* the Penitentes constructed their Nuestro Padre Jesús Nazareno, none of this tells us anything about *why* they constructed him in the way they did.

After all, there were many different images of Christ, with many different titles in the Hispanic world (let alone the Catholic world). Given all the iconographical bits and pieces floating in this Christocentric sea, why did the Penitentes select some elements and not others when constructing the Christ who was to be at the center of their cult? Why, in fact, did they choose a representation of Christ at all, rather than some representation of Mary or a saint? Why did they merge different traditional iconographies (those associated with Jesús Nazareno, the Ecce Homo, the Man of Sorrows) in order to intensify his suffering? And why did they call him "Nuestro Padre"? As common as this title was in Spain and Mexico, there were also a great number of Christocentric images in those same societies who were not called "Padre." Questions such as these cannot be answered by a purely art-historical approach, and yet these are the questions that have to be answered if we are to truly understand the Penitentes.

❧ Why "Nuestro Padre"?

For commentators like Richard Ahlborn (1986) and Thomas Steele (1998a), use of the title "Nuestro Padre" by the Penitentes derives simply from a metaphorical emphasis on the family that pervades all aspects of Penitente practice and that itself reflects the strong cultural emphasis on the family that has long been a core value in Hispano villages. At first sight, I grant, such an argument seems plausible. After all, the Penitentes dedicated themselves to a "father," sang hymns to a "mother" (Mary), and referred to each other as "brothers"—all of which does sound a lot like a family. Then too, Penitente moradas, which are almost always one-story structures consisting of three rooms arranged end to end, seem clearly to have been modeled more on the domestic household structures in which Hispano families lived than on the churches in Indian Pueblos or Hispano villages. Indeed, the fact that the design of most Penitente moradas was so obviously tied to traditions of domestic architecture in New Mexico led George Kubler (1940, viii) to exclude any discussion of these moradas in his book on the religious architecture of New Mexico.

Nevertheless, there are at least two reasons why we should be cautious about a too-easy acceptance of the Ahlborn/Steele view that Penitente moradas were pervaded by familial imagery. First, however unintentionally, it is a view that accords all too well with those conceptual dichotomies that underlie the Black Legend,[5] that cluster of anti-Spanish and anti-Catholic biases that has for centuries structured Anglo accounts of Spain and its colonial empire. After all, within the logic of the Black Legend, Anglo-Saxon cultures are associated with rationality and restraint, innovation and modernity; whereas Latin cultures are associated with emotionalism and excess, passivity and tradition. Seeing the Penitentes as pervaded by a familial emphasis (given that most Anglos would likely see the family as a "traditional" form of social organization) both reflects and reinforces this old bias. But a more important reason for being cautious about the view advanced by scholars like Steele and Ahlborn is that it is less consistent with the available evidence than first appears.

First, unlike what happens in "real" families, women are excluded from full membership in local Penitente moradas. True, the Carmelitas did engage in number of tasks that have an undeniably domestic flavor. They prepared and brought food to the morada during Holy Week, and they often cleaned the morada throughout the year. Carmelitas also marched in Penitente processions behind the Penitentes themselves. Even so, Carmelitas were never sealed to the Brotherhood, did not take part in the private activities that were most central to Penitente ritual, and were not permitted to be physically present in the morada when those activities were taking place.

Sometimes modern Penitente members seem to sense that the exclusion of women from core Penitente ritual is inconsistent with the inclusiveness that should be present if local moradas were indeed modeled on the family. For example, in a recent book (Varjabedian and Wallis 1994) that presents a sympathetic and fairly uncritical account of the Penitente movement, a modern Brother is quoted as saying that if we had access to documents describing Penitente activity in the 1790s, "we would discover that women were once equal participants in the moradas" (19). True, he goes on to say, we might find evidence of a division of labor between males and females, and evidence that men had more authority (read: we would find evidence that the earliest moradas resembled a stereotypical Hispano family!), but we would still find, he suggests, that women were originally as much a part of the membership as men. Never mind that there are no documents that support the view that this modern Brother is advancing here; never mind that the earliest documents we do have suggest something quite different; and never mind that allowing women into a flagellant *cofradia* would have been inconsistent with the traditions in place in Spain, Mexico, and Italy. The Penitentes-modeled-on-the-family view *requires* a Penitente past in which men and women participated on a roughly equal footing, and if that sort of past is not available, its existence can simply be asserted!

Another problem with the suggestion that Penitente moradas are pervaded with familial imagery has to do with Mary. Although the Carmelitas sang a range of hymns in honor of Mary, most of the hymns that are sung by the Penitentes themselves and that mention Mary are hymns concerned with Christ's Passion and Mary's sorrowful reaction to that Passion (Aragón 1998, 99). This would suggest that Mary-the-sorrowful-mother functions in these hymns just as she functions in the El Encuentro ritual: as a device that intensifies our experience of Christ's Passion. This raises the possibility that it is not an emphasis on the family that brings Mary into Penitente ritual, but rather an emphasis on the Suffering Christ.

Also significant here, I think, is the fact that the Penitentes were a brotherhood dedicated solely to Padre Jesús Nazareno. Although Angélico Chávez made much of the many similarities between the *cofradías* at Seville and the Penitentes, what he failed to mention (as far as I can tell) is that Sevillan *cofradías* were usually dedicated simultaneously both to Christ and to Mary. Sometimes these joint dedications were the result of the merging and remerging of different confraternities during the sixteenth and seventeenth centuries; sometimes a joint dedication had been in place since the confraternity's foundation; and sometimes one or the other dedication was simply added as the confraternity developed over time. To take an example already mentioned: the Cofradía de la Santa Cruz de Jerusalén, founded at Seville in 1564, and which by the early 1600s had added "Jesús Nazareno" to its dedication, added "Nuestra Señora de la Concepción" to its dedication in 1636 (Montoto 1976, 135). By the late 1700s, certainly, joint dedications to Christ and Mary were the norm. Félix González de León (1852), for example, describes thirty-six Passion Week confraternities that were still functioning at Seville in the eighteenth century; and of these, thirty-four carried a joint dedication of this sort (e.g., Santo Cristo de las cinco llagas y María Santísima de Esperanza; Santo Cristo de la Columna y Azotes y Madre de Dios de la Victoria; Prendimiento de Cristo y María Santísima de Regla; Nuestro Padre Jesús de la Salud y María Santísima de las Angustias; and so on). The Penitentes, in other words, although they borrowed much from preexisting iconographical traditions in both Spain and Mexico, chose not to borrow a common dedicatory formula for Passion Week *cofradías* that would have associated their organization simultaneously with Father Jesús *and* with Mother Mary.

A final difficulty with the "family" model being proposed by Ahlborn and Steele is that it requires us to see Mary as the strongest female presence in Penitente ritual (given that Mary is an obvious mother figure)—but a reasonable case can be made that the strongest female presence in Penitente ritual is Doña Sebastiana, not Mary. As already mentioned, Doña Sebastiana images were in many ways a defining feature of Penitente moradas, in that all moradas had one and that these images were never found outside moradas. Unlike Mary, who is brought into Penitente ritual only because of her involvement with Christ's Passion, Doña Sebastiana is very much an independent personality; her presence in death-cart rituals is not part of a narrative that necessarily includes Christ. This is problematic (for the Ahlborn/Steele theory) because Doña Sebastiana—with her skeletal appearance and her association with Death—hardly seems the sort of warm and positive "maternal" figure we would expect if the organization of local moradas were indeed based on stereotypical images of the Hispano family.

All of these considerations seem sufficient grounds for taking a fresh look at Penitente iconography and at least considering the possibility that, the comments made by scholars like Steele and Ahlborn notwithstanding, something other than a cultural emphasis on the family made the "Padre Jesús" title appealing to the Penitentes—and I think that a useful starting point here lies with a minor iconographical puzzle that has been ignored by previous commentators.

❧ Why a Red Tunic?

As has already been mentioned, *bultos* of Padre Jesús Nazareno usually wear a full-body tunic made of real cloth. Although the practice of dressing statues in cloth vestments happens only occasionally in the Anglo Catholic tradition (in the case of the Infant of Prague, for example), it was a well-established and popular practice in Spain by the early modern period (Webster 1998, 57–62) and quickly spread to Mexico. Evidence that it was a practice well established in *New* Mexico as well is provided by the Domínguez report (Adams and Chávez 1956), since the good friar describes a great many of the images he encountered during his 1776 visitation as "dressed." In particular, Domínguez describes seven different statues depicting Jesús Nazareno; and in all seven cases, he says explicitly that the image was dressed in a cloth tunic. On the other hand, while there is nothing unusual in the fact that the Penitentes dressed *bultos* of their Padre Jesús Nazareno in a cloth tunic, the color of that tunic merits careful consideration.

Although Jesús Nazareno images in both Spain and Mexico sometimes wear a red tunic, it is far more common to find them wearing one that is purple or white. The Jesús Nazarenos carried in procession at Seville, for example, have traditionally worn tunics made of purple velvet (see the pictures and text in Moreno Navarro 1983; Gonsález Gómez and Roda Peña 1992). In Mexico during the late 1600s, the Brothers belonging to the Hermandad de Nuestro Padre Jesús Nazareno at the church of San Nicolás de Tolentino (later the church of San Agustín) in Durango wore purple tunics as they walked in procession (Gallegos 1969, 181). Similarly, the 1805 constitution of the Hermandad de Nuestro Amo Jesús El Nazareno in Cuencamé (a community just to the northeast of Durango) specifies that Brothers are to wear a purple tunic and a crown of thorns when they carry their crosses in procession during Lent (AHAD 212: 664). In New Mexico, by contrast, although the Penitentes' Padre Jesús Nazareno sometimes wears a white surplice over a red tunic, he is far more usually, as already mentioned, depicted wearing a red tunic alone. Why the greater emphasis on red in the Penitente tradition as opposed to the more usual (for the Spanish world) purple?

The matter is not resolved by appealing to local tradition. Domínguez (Adams and Chávez 1956) identifies the color of the tunics worn by three of the seven Jesús Nazareno images that he encountered during his inspection: the image of Jesús Nazareno at San Jeronimo de Taos wore a purple tunic (104), the image at Laguna wore a white tunic (184), and the large Jesús Nazareno found in the chapel of the Third Order at Santa Cruz de la Cañada wore a purple tunic over a white tunic (75). As limited as it is, in other words, the evidence from the Domínguez report suggests that in the pre-Penitente era, New Mexican Jesús Nazarenos wore tunics that were the same color (purple or white) as the tunics worn by Jesús Nazarenos most everywhere else in the Catholic world. So the question remains: Why did the Penitentes choose to dress their Padre Jesús in a bright red tunic? A possible answer, I think, is suggested by Roberto Cipriani's (1981) analysis of the "red Christs" (i Cristi rossi) who appear in the Holy Week celebrations of some communities in Puglia (the heel of the Italian boot).

Most of the Jesús Nazarenos associated with Holy Week processions in Italy (whether we are talking about images or about actors who take the role of Jesús Nazareno in these processions) wear white tunics or white tunics with red mantles (see Lancelloti 1951; Cipriani 1981, 260–61). In a significant minority of Pugliese communities, however, Jesús Nazarenos wear red tunics. In trying to account for this use of red tunics, Cipriani brings forward much evidence from the Classical and Christian traditions suggesting that the colors red and black are often linked as symbolic opposites, with red (because of its association with blood) connoting "Life" and black connoting "Death." Given this symbolism, Cipriani argues, associating a processional Jesús Nazareno with red is nothing more than a quasi-theatrical device that functions to heighten the contrast between the *living* Christ, who is carrying his cross on the way to Calvary, and the Christ who is soon to be *dead*. Furthermore, Cipriani argues, using red in this way is facilitated by certain ambiguities in the Gospel accounts of Christ's passion.

Three of the four Gospels say that Christ was brought before Pilate after having been scourged and dressed as a mock king with a crown of thorns, a reed scepter, and a mantle. These accounts, however, are not consistent among themselves as to the color or nature of the garment that was placed on Christ. Matthew 27:27–29 says that soldiers put a "scarlet robe" on the scourged Christ; John 19:2 says that it was a "purple robe"; and Mark 15:17 says that they "clothed him in purple." Given that two of the three accounts mention a robe, most depictions of the Ecce Homo have Christ draped in something like a cloak that falls across his shoulders but leaves his chest bare. On the other hand, because these two accounts vary as to the color of this cloak, artists have been free to choose whichever of the two colors (purple or red) they prefer; and they have usually chosen red (see, for instance, the Ecce Homo in Gifford's book on Mexican *retablos* [1992, 19]). By contrast, Mark's account, which says that they "clothed him in purple," permits the garment put on Christ to be more substantial than a simple cloak, and this presumably legitimates the full-body tunic so often worn by Jesús Nazarenos. The fact that the garment in this case is specifically described as purple would also explain why the tunics worn by the Jesús Nazarenos at Seville and in most other Spanish and Hispanic contexts are purple.[6] Cipriani's point, however, is that given these inconsistencies, a little mixing and matching from the different Gospel accounts could easily give scriptural legitimation to the "red tunic" worn by Jesús Nazarenos in various southern Italian communities.

In summary, then, Cipriani's argument is that giving Jesús Nazareno a bright red tunic in a Holy Week procession is a theatrical device adopted by some communities to give greater visual emphasis to an element that is central to all representations of the Passion, namely, the living Christ's impending death, and that using a red tunic in this way has a certain legitimacy because it is at least roughly consistent with the biblical text. It seems to me entirely plausible that a process similar to the one that Cipriani is describing could account for why the Penitentes dressed their Padre Jesús Nazareno in a red tunic.

Certainly, within the context of Penitente art, black *is* associated with death. Penitente crosses, for instance, both those that appear in *bultos* of the crucifixion and those carried in procession, are routinely painted black; and Doña Sebastiana, who is explicitly associated with death, wears a black robe. If we grant the premise that red connotes life, then the visual contrast between a red-robed "Jésus Nazareno" and the blackness of Penitente crucifixes and Doña Sebastiana images would function in Penitente ritual to establish that same heightened contrast between the suffering-but-still-living Christ and the soon-to-be-dead Christ in Passion Week rituals in Puglia.

✠ Putting together all the various considerations that we have so far been discussing, we can perceive, I think, an identifiable logic lying beneath the iconography of the supernatural figure who was the focus of Penitente ritual. Thus, it would appear that the Penitentes started with an image of the suffering Christ, whose title ("Jesús Nazareno") and iconography were well known in the Hispanic world, and then modified that image in order to intensify his already-apparent suffering. This was done partly by borrowing from the iconography associated with other common images of Christ (like the Ecce Homo and the Man of Sorrows) and partly by adding in elements that were relatively rare in the Hispanic tradition (like giving their image a red tunic). What this suggests (to me) is that an especially intense emphasis on suffering—an emphasis that was even stronger than would normally be associated with typical Jesús Nazareno images—was central to what this newly created image meant to the Penitentes. But this new image was also very explicitly identified as a "father." More than anything else, in other words, the Penitentes chose to make *an intensely suffering father* central to their rituals; and it is this emphasis on an intensely suffering father (rather than, say, a general emphasis on the family) that lies at the core of Penitente symbolism.

If we are considering the possibility that the Penitentes were a response to something new that was happening in Hispano society (and we are), this symbolic emphasis on a "suffering father" suggests that the emergence of the Penitentes was tied in some way to something new that was happening to the patriarchal order that had prevailed in New Mexico. In fact, such a conclusion dovetails very nicely with conclusions that have been reached by a new generation of historians specializing in the study of late colonial New Mexico.

✠ A Period of Change and Stress

Until relatively recently it was common for historians specializing in the study of the Spanish Americas to suggest that colonial New Mexico had been a stagnant agricultural backwater. Partly this view derived from the controlling influence of the Black Legend, which suggested that Spaniards were cruel, superstitious, lazy, corrupt, avaricious, and predisposed to accept tyranny and authoritarian rule, and that as a result of these character traits, Spanish colonial rule had everywhere and always been oppressive

and a barrier to progress. Although the Black Legend first came to domi-
nate English-language historiography in the aftermath of England's conflicts with Spain in the late sixteenth century, its influence persisted well into
this century (for examples, see Powell 1971). Given the pervasive influence
of the Black Legend, it is hardly surprising that New Mexico, being one of
the most isolated areas of Spain's colonial empire, would in particular
come to be associated with a lack of progress.

What is somewhat surprising is that even those (Anglo) historians like
Hubert Howe Bancroft (1832–1918) and Herbert Bolton (1870–1953), who
are now seen as having done so much to undermine the first part of the
Black Legend (having to do with distinctively "Spanish" character traits),
were quite accepting of the second part (which associated Spanish rule
with lack of progress). For example, in explaining why he devoted only one
volume in his *History of the Pacific States* series to New Mexico and Arizona
jointly, Bancroft (1888, vi) suggested that "all Spanish-American provinces
are in certain respects so similar in their annals one to another" that a detailed history of one is sufficient to provide insight into them all. He felt
that California (to which he devoted seven volumes) was the ideal case for
his "one" detailed history, partly because it was less isolated than most
other areas under Spanish rule and partly because the Russian presence
made things a bit more interesting. New Mexico, he argued, was not worth
writing about at length because that "country's isolation and non-inter-
course with the outer world" (vii) insured that the result would be tedious
reading. Reading about New Mexico in the eighteenth century, he felt,
would be especially tedious since "from 1700 [onward] New Mexico settled
down into that monotonously uneventful career of inert and non-pro-
gressive existence, which sooner or later is to be noted in the history of
every Hispano-American province" (225).

Similarly, while Herbert Bolton is now routinely criticized for extolling
the achievements of individual Spanish leaders in North America while
simultaneously ignoring the devastating effects of European colonization
on indigenous populations (see, for example, Kessell 1990), he too saw
Spanish colonial rule as stultifying, especially in New Mexico. In his widely
read *The Spanish Borderlands* (1921), for example, after discussing the Pueblo
Revolt and the subsequent reconquest of New Mexico by Vargas, Bolton
summarizes the remainder of the colonial period in this simple paragraph:

For another century and a quarter, New Mexico continued under
Spain; then it became a part of independent Mexico. It was a typical

Spanish outpost, isolated and sluggish, quite unlike the lively mining and political centers of New Spain farther south. At Santa Fé a long succession of military governors ruled over the province and engaged in unsavory quarrels with the missionary superiors. (181)

This view of late colonial New Mexico as a "stagnant backwater" persisted well into the 1970s. Alicia Tjarks (1978, 85), for example, suggested that New Mexico in the late 1700s was "a closed, practically self-sufficient economy [which] had been based for centuries on the exploitation of farmland and small domestic industries, forced by need to replace with local manufactures the lack of imported goods and clothes."

Within the logic of this traditional perspective, it was the removal of trade barriers imposed by Spanish government (something that came about as the result of Mexican independence in 1821) and the subsequent opening of the Santa Fe trail to overland trade with Missouri in the 1820s that stimulated the otherwise stagnant New Mexican economy and saved it from the fate of other areas that had been under Spanish rule. What this argument suggested, in other words, was that social change and economic prosperity in New Mexico had been contingent on an economic reorientation *away from* the corrupt and stagnant Spanish/Mexican centers to the south, and *toward* the dynamic and expanding economy of the American Republic. As Ross Frank (1992, 17) points out, such an argument has always been appealing to Anglo historians because it allows the American annexation in 1846 to be seen as an inevitable continuation of a shift toward progress and economic vitality that had begun with the opening of the Santa Fe trail in 1821 and so as something that was generally beneficial to New Mexico.

Over the past several decades the traditional image of late colonial New Mexico as a stagnant and isolated society has been challenged by a number of historians, including Thomas D. Hall (1989), Ramon Gutiérrez (1991), and Ross Frank (1992; 1996). These historians have demonstrated that during the closing decades of colonial rule, New Mexico was not only enjoying unprecedented economic prosperity but was also undergoing a number of fairly dramatic social transformations. The processes they have most often identified as setting in motion these economic and social changes include: (1) an intensification of the raids made on Hispano settlements by nomadic Indians, (2) the differing demographic experiences of the Hispano and Pueblo Indian populations, and (3) the social and economic consequences of the Bourbon reforms.

Nomadic raids. In the early decades of the eighteenth century, Hispano settlers routinely obtained slaves from neighboring Indian tribes either by direct raiding or by barter; and nomadic groups (mainly Utes, Navahos, Apaches, and Comanches) just as routinely raided settled communities (both Hispano and Pueblo) in New Mexico for captives and agricultural produce. The result was a cycle of raids and retaliatory raids that devastated communities on all sides.

During the 1740s and 1750s raids by nomadic groups on settled communities in New Mexico intensified; and, following a lull in the 1760s, such attacks skyrocketed during the 1770s and 1780s. Burial records, for example, indicate that 211 New Mexicans were killed during the 1770s by nomadic Indians (mainly Comanches); these same records indicate that this was greater than the sum total of all the New Mexicans killed by nomadic Indians over the preceding seventy years (see the data in Brugge 1968, 31). Reports written by Governor Mendinueta from 1767 to 1777 (cited in R. Frank 1992, 43) mention 195 separate raids on 30 different villages, which collectively resulted in 382 deaths, 130 Hispanos or Pueblo Indians wounded, and another 94 captured.

What is difficult for modern audiences to understand is that these raids often served an economic function for the Indian groups involved that did not necessarily carry along with it an unwillingness to cooperate with other Hispano communities. As Spanish officials of the time so often complained, it was common for raiders to attack a particular settlement; seize livestock, agricultural products, and human captives; and then show up a few days later at some other settlement in order to trade with the Spanish.

One consequence of this increased predation by nomadic groups was a modification of Hispano settlement patterns. In contrast to the Pueblo Indians, who had long lived in compact settlements, Hispanos had always preferred dispersed settlements. The result was that most of the Hispano population lived in small ranchos scattered across parcels of land bordering the Río Grande or other waterways. This was true even for most of the Hispano settlers living in the so-called villas. In his account of the villa of Santa Fe, for instance, Domínguez first discusses the pueblo of Tlatelolco near Mexico City, whose "appearance, design, arrangement and plan . . . lifts the spirit by appealing to the senses," and then uses this community (whose plan conformed to the ideal envisioned in the Laws of the Indies[7]) as a baseline for establishing Sante Fe's deficiencies:

> This villa [Santa Fe] is the exact opposite [of Tlatelolco], for in the final analysis it lacks everything. . . . The Villa of Santa Fe (for the

most part) consists of many small ranchos, at various distances from one another, with no plan as to their location, for each owner built as he was able, wished to, or found convenient, now for the little farms they have there, now for the small herds of cattle they keep in corrals of stakes, or else for other reasons. (Adams and Chávez, 1956, 39–40)[8]

Domínguez's account of Santa Cruz de la Cañada (82) and Albuquerque (151), the other two settlements formally designated as "villas" in New Mexico, indicate that they too consisted for the most part of small ranchos scattered apparently at varying distances from the church associated with each settlement.

Although this predilection for dispersed settlement had always made the Hispano population vulnerable to attacks by nomadic raiders, something outside commentators had routinely pointed out, it was only with the intensification of these attacks that began in the 1740s that many settlers were finally convinced to abandon dispersed settlement in favor of the safety afforded by larger concentrations of population. Sometimes this meant abandoning outlying ranchos and moving within the jurisdictional limits of one of the three villas, where population concentrations were higher. In August 1747, for example, settlements in the Río Chama region west of the Río Grande were attacked by Comanches and a few Ute allies. Two people were killed (a woman and a girl) and twenty-three women and children were carried off. A group of settlers who set out to find the raiders came upon the bodies of three more women and a newborn. In response to these attacks, the settlers in Abiquiú, Pueblo Quemado, and Ojo Caliente petitioned the governor (successfully) for the right to move in with relatives living in the villa of Santa Cruz.[9]

Although these particular communities were resettled under the protection of a detachment of soldiers during the 1750s, the general pattern of settlers abandoning outlying areas and moving closer to the more populated villas continued. In 1782 Fray Juan Agustín de Morfi indicated that the number of families living in Santa Fe had more than doubled since 1744, going from 120 families to 270 families, mainly on account of settlers deserting the frontier on account of Comanche and Apache attacks (Thomas 1969, 91).

Other settlers sought the protection afforded by concentrated settlement by moving closer to the Indian pueblos, sometimes moving right into a pueblo itself. During his 1776 visitation, Domínguez found some Hispanos living inside Taos Pueblo (with the permission of the Indians) and says that they had moved there in 1770 in response to Comanche raids (Adams and Chávez 1956, 113). The closer contact between settlers and Pueblo Indians brought about by the increased Comanche/Apache predation is usually taken as one cause of the documented increase in racially exogamous marriages that occurred in the 1770s and 1780s (R. Frank 1992, 360–61; 1996, 775; Gutiérrez 1991, 288–89).

Demographic processes. Hispano population growth, both relative and absolute, was another process promoting change in late colonial New Mexico. Information on population in late colonial New Mexico comes from a variety of reports written over the period 1744 to 1820. These include several censuses as well as reports written by various ecclesiastical visitors (like Bishop Tamarón y Romeral, who toured New Mexico in 1760; and Domínguez, who came in 1776). Although these reports are problematic in a number of ways, separate analyses of the available data by different scholars (see, in particular, T. Hall 1989, 144–47; Gutiérrez 1991, 166–75; Jones 1996, 109–35) suggests that certain broad patterns can be identified. First, although some Pueblo communities gained in population and others lost, the overall Pueblo population was relatively constant during the latter half of the eighteenth century, fluctuating between 8,000 and 11,000 individuals.[10] The Hispano population, by contrast, grew steadily throughout the eighteenth century and experienced a particularly dramatic increase in numbers in the period between 1780 and 1820. Around 1750, the Hispano population of northern New Mexico (that is, excluding the El Paso district) numbered a little less than 4,000 individuals; by 1800, this number had increased to more than 19,000 individuals; and in 1817, it had increased to more than 27,000 (T. Hall 1989, 145). Although there was some in-migration into New Mexico during this period (including some artisans sent northward to help develop New Mexico's economy; see below), this dramatic increase in the Hispano population was fuelled primarily by natural increase.

One consequence of these two demographic trends (the relative stability of the Pueblo population and the dramatic growth in the Hispano population) was that Hispano settlers came to outnumber the Pueblo Indian population for the first time in the history of the colony. Ross Frank's analysis of the available evidence suggests that the turnover point fell somewhere around 1780 (1992, 70).

The Bourbon Reforms. Socioeconomic change in late colonial New Mexico was also fuelled by the various economic reforms initiated by the Bourbon kings of Spain over the course of the eighteenth century, in particular by the reforms initiated by Carlos III from the 1760s onward. In shaping their reforms, Carlos and his ministers quite consciously took certain tenets of Enlightenment thought as self-evident. In particular, it seemed self-evident that social progress was *facilitated* by the centralization of power into the hands of an enlightened monarch (like Carlos) and by the rationalization of economic and religious[11] activities, just as it was *hindered* by superstition and by the proliferation of special privileges associated with local elites and the Church. Ramón Gutiérrez provides a succinct description of how the Bourbon reforms played themselves out in the Spanish Americas: "The series of economic, administrative, political and military reforms, known collectively as the Bourbon Reforms, sought to recolonize Spanish America by increasing taxation, by industrializing, by increasing communications, by colonizing marginal areas, by fortifying defenses, and by stripping corporate bodies such as the Church, the nobility and sheep breeders of their special status and privileges" (1991, 299).

In northern New Spain, one of the first consequences that flowed from the pursuit of these goals was a renewed determination to eliminate the threat posed by nomadic Indians to the important mining communities of northern Mexico. Partly, this threat was addressed through a series of administrative reforms, such as the reorganization of Presidio defenses in 1772 and the establishment in 1776 of a new administrative unit, the Internal Provinces, that put the northern provinces (including New Mexico) under the authority of a commandante-general.

Still, as Thomas Hall (1989, 114–15) and others have noted, the Comanche / Apache threat in New Mexico and elsewhere receded mainly because government authorities increasingly adopted two interrelated pacification strategies. The first of these involved distributing food and other gifts to hostile Indian groups in order to make them dependent on Spanish goods. The general idea here was that as Indians acquired more and more Spanish goods, they would, simultaneously, become more "civilized" and more hesitant about cutting off the supply of such goods in the future through hostile actions. The second strategy encouraged Spanish commanders to form alliances with particular nomadic bands and then to require them (as a part of the alliance) to fight against other bands.

Although the administrative reforms and pacification policies of the late 1700s failed to end nomadic Indian attacks on New Mexican settlements once and for all,[12] these reforms did usher in a period of relative peacefulness that lasted for several decades. One result was that during the last two decades of the eighteenth century, Hispano settlers population could and did resume their traditional pattern of dispersed settlement.

The Bourbon Reforms also had a dramatic impact on the economy of New Mexico in the late 1700s. In part this was an offshoot of the pacification campaign. Although many of the gifts distributed to Indian bands under the first pacification strategy were imported from outside the province, others were purchased from craftsmen in the province. In particular, the purchase of woven items (blankets, capes, shirts, stocking, etc.) made wholly or in part from wool produced by local sheep was substantial stimulus to sheep production in New Mexico during this period (R. Frank 1992, 145–48). Even apart from the pacification campaign, however, the Bourbon reformers were concerned with promoting more trade between New Mexico and other areas under Spanish control. This led to the abolition of a number of restrictions on trade and travel, to tax exemptions on various New Mexican products, and to policies that had the effect of bringing various specialists in matters relating to agriculture, weaving, and animal husbandry to New Mexico in order make New Mexican products more appealing to export markets (Gutiérrez 1991, 301–2).

Ross Frank provides a succinct overview of the various forces working to produce change in late colonial New Mexico and the nature of the economic boom they produced:

> In the aftermath of the Spanish defeat of the Comanche and the subsequent alliance, trade between New Mexico and the rest of northern New Spain saw a quarter century of tremendous expansion and development [which], combined with strong population growth and the influence exerted by Bourbon officials . . . produced an economic boom. . . . The Vecino [Hispano] population increased their per-capita production of agricultural goods and livestock, for export and a growing internal market. From 1785 to approximately 1815, New Mexico developed an economy which created prosperity unparalleled during the earlier colonial period. (1996, 166)

Frank provides evidence for the economic prosperity associated with the end of the colonial period through a careful analysis of tithe rentals, that is, the amount individuals paid for the right to collect and retain the tithe on all increases in agricultural products and livestock that Hispano settlers owed to the Bishop of Durango. What he demonstrates is that the value of these tithe rentals increased steadily after 1786 even after corrections are made for inflation, for Hispano population increase, and for changes in the mechanics of letting tithe contracts and collecting the produce associated with the tithe. This only makes sense, he argues, if there was an increase in economic productivity (see especially R. Frank 1996). Gutiérrez had earlier found evidence of an economic boom in the late 1700s in a variety of reports from New Mexico that suggested an increased use of hard currency during this period (1991, 320–21; 1980, 378–81).

At least for certain segments of the Hispano population, however, the increasing economic prosperity of the late 1700s was counterbalanced by an increasing shortage of agricultural land. Although the primary cause of this shortage was the joint interaction of (1) a burgeoning Hispano population, and (2) the fact that the amount of arable land that could be irrigated by gravitational flow in northern New Mexico was limited, the situation was exacerbated by at least two other factors. First, the large land grants made by various governors during the first half of the eighteenth century had put much of the most valuable land in the hands of a relatively small number of families (Gamble 1988, 303–4). Second, the Black Legend notwithstanding, Hispano settlers were generally barred by law and legal precedent from encroaching on the large tracts of arable land held by the Indian pueblos—which is not to say that they did not sometimes try to do just that (see Gamble 1988, 239–61).

One response to this shortage of agricultural land was a geographical expansion of the Hispano population outward from the core Hispano settlements located in or around the Río Grande valley. The establishment of new communities outside this core area was facilitated by governing officials who increasingly awarded land grants in these new areas to entire communities rather than to individuals. Of the thirty "community" land grants that were made between 1692 and 1821, for example, the majority (twenty, or 66 percent of the total) were made between 1762 and 1816 (see Table 1 in Gamble 1988, 149). This outward geographical expansion of the Hispano population helps to explain why the number of inhabited settlements in New Mexico nearly doubled between 1776 and 1840 (Snow 1979, 48; see also Nostrand 1992, 70–97).

Unfortunately, establishing these new settlements did not fully offset the shortage of land among Hispanos. This was evident most of all in the fact that an increasing number of settlers became landless and consequently contracted out their labor to others. A one-third sample of the household census returns for 1790, for instance, indicated that only 60 percent of all household heads owned the land they worked; and a report by Governor Chacón in 1796 estimated that 1,500 household heads were landless (Gutiérrez 1991, 321).

In summary, then, New Mexico in the late colonial period was not at all the stagnant backwater that historians like Bancroft, Bolton, and others assumed it to be. It was a society in a state of economic and social flux as the result of a burgeoning Hispano population, increasing involvement with the outside world, increasing economic prosperity, an increasing number of settlements, and increasing social differentiation (most of all evident in the polarization of the Hispano population into those who owned land and those who were landless laborers).

Surprisingly, there has been relatively little concern among scholars interested in New Mexico with the question of how these dramatic social and economic changes would have affected the institutions that existed at the local level in Hispano communities. On the other hand, the little work that has been done suggests that these changes ushered in a period of cultural innovation. Charles Carrillo (1997), for instance, marshals much archeological evidence in support of the contention that many of the Hispanos who became landless during this period turned to the manufacture of pottery and that this accounts for much of the surge in craft specialization that developed in the late colonial period. More relevant to our concerns here, however, is Ramón Gutiérrez's account of the ways in which the Bourbon Reforms affected patriarchal authority.

In his final chapter, Gutiérrez (1991) notes that in Europe, and in most areas under European control, the late eighteenth century saw the rise (or at least the intensification) of a "romantic love" ideology that stressed the special importance of love or physical attraction, rather than the economic or status interests of a person's family, in determining marital choice. This new ideology proved especially popular with segments of the social elite in New Mexico because, Gutiérrez argues (330), it resonated with local Pueblo Indian traditions that had always celebrated sexual desire as something that promoted societal harmony.

Because this new romantic love ideology was perceived as a threat to familial authority, Carlos III issued a Royal Pragmatic on Marriage in 1776. This decree, which was extended to all of Spain's territories (including New Mexico) in 1778, sought to shore up familial authority by requiring parental consent to marriages involving persons under the age of 25. Gutiérrez's point, however, is that this attempt by the Bourbon regime to bolster parental authority was quite at odds with the thrust of the Bourbon economic reforms generally, which consistently worked to *erode* patriarchal authority.

Partly, the Bourbon Reforms eroded patriarchal authority (the authority vested in male heads of households) in areas like New Mexico because these reforms aimed at reducing the power of local elites and thus came to reduce the power of the males who held power in local elite families. But partly too, at least in New Mexico, the Bourbon economic reforms eroded patriarchal authority because such authority had traditionally been exercised in situations where males were linked to one another through ties of blood or marriage; and one consequence of the Bourbon reforms was that household heads were increasingly thrust into economic relationships with unrelated males. There was, remember, a dramatic increase in the number of landless heads of households in New Mexico during the late 1700s and early 1800s, and Gutiérrez argues that this group increasingly came to contract out their labor to nonrelatives: "The growth of an agricultural production sector tied to market forces on a land base concentrated in the hands of a few persons and with a large landless rural population, provided the basis for the development of service labour relationships in New Mexico" (1980, 394). As evidence of this increase in "service labour relationships," Gutiérrez points to the dramatic increase in composite households (households consisting of two or more conjugal families that were not linked by kinship, or households in which a conjugal family resided with one or more unrelated working-age males). While such households had comprised a mere 4.1 percent of all households in the 1790 census, they accounted for 10–30 percent (depending on the area surveyed) of all households by the early 1820s (Gutiérrez 1991, 325–26). Further evidence of a dramatic increase in such service labor relationships is seen in the census data on occupational structure that is available for the three villas for the years 1790 and 1827. Thus, in the case of Albuquerque, the proportion of the adult working population listing themselves as "day laborers" increased from 10 percent to 19 percent; while in Santa Fe, that same proportion increased from 8 percent to 31 percent (see Table 10.1 in Gutiérrez 1991, 322). There was no similar increase in Santa Cruz de la Cañada, but only because the proportion listing themselves as day laborers was already extremely high in 1790 (accounting for 27 percent of the population) and remained stable.[13]

Given the concerns of his book (marriage and sexuality in New Mexico), Gutiérrez does not speculate further on the effects of this erosion (both threatened and real) of patriarchal authority, except to say that the general loosening of social bonds occasioned by the Bourbon reforms and the associated shattering of traditional hierarchies likely created a climate favorable to political independence from Spain (1991, 336). Yet surely there is much more that needs to be said here. In particular, I suggest that if we put Gutiérrez's conclusions about the crisis in patriarchal authority that was taking place in late colonial New Mexico together with the conclusions that have been reached (independently) by another group of historians concerned with the social organization of Hispano agriculture in this same period, we are inexorably led to posit the existence of a previously unacknowledged crisis within Hispano communities that would have threatened in a fairly dramatic way the social institutions that permitted these communities to function on a day-to-day basis.

⚜ Patriarchal Authority and the Maintenance of Communal/Cooperative Forms of Agriculture

As already mentioned, Hispano settlements throughout the colonial period consisted mainly of small ranchos that were widely dispersed along the banks of the Río Grande or other rivers. For outside commentators of the time who confronted this pattern, it was clearly something that worked to erode cooperation at the local level and to erode as well the integration of local communities into a larger political structure. For example, in 1778 Fray Agustín de Morfi identified the Hispano preference for dispersed settlement as one of the five most serious "disorders" (read: problems) then existing in New Mexico. Dispersed settlement, Morfi argues, makes it difficult for priests to minister to Hispano settlers, makes individual households more vulnerable to Indian attack, and delays the organization of an effective pursuit group following a raid. But the most serious consequence of dispersed settlement, Morfi argues, is that it shields settlers from observation by other members of society and so permits them to engage in depraved behaviors:

> As they live isolated with no one to observe them there are those who have no inhibitions about running around stark naked. . . . Out of this, other moral disorders proceed which shock even the barbarous Indians, from whom such behavior cannot be hidden. As a result lewdness holds destructive sway here, more so than among animals. And even robbery is looked upon as a tolerable expedient that

does not diminish one's reputation, so that blatant violence is the rule. (Morfí 1977, 14)

A similar charge was levied by Viceroy Revillagigedo in 1793, when he suggested that "the settlements of the Spanish vecinos [in New Mexico] consist of dispersed houses or ranchos, where there are no witnesses that might discover the vices and the dissolution in which they prostitute themselves" (cited in Bancroft 1888, 277n).

Anthropological investigators doing fieldwork in Hispano villages in the twentieth century recurrently reached conclusions similar to those reached by Morfí or Revillagigedo almost two centuries earlier. Thus, Paul Kutsche's (1979) review of the relevant anthropological literature suggests that Hispano villages were routinely characterized as being pervaded by "familial atomism," that is, by a cultural ethos that encourages individual nuclear families to maximize their self-interest at the expense of other nuclear families and thus works against the formation of voluntary associations and against cooperation with other families or with higher levels of political authority. As Kutsche points out, the familial atomism found in Hispano villages was usually taken—by the investigators involved—as establishing a similarity between these communities and peasant communities in Mexico and elsewhere in Latin America.

It happens, however, that there are good reasons for setting aside both the conclusions reached by early commentators like Morfí and Revillagigedo and the conclusions reached by twentieth-century anthropologists when trying to assess the "ethos" that prevailed in Hispano communities during the colonial period. As a start, even granting that a certain amount of familial atomism did exist in Hispano villages during the twentieth century, this does not in itself mean that it was traditional. Kutsche (1979a), for example, after first noting that the familial atomism detected by twentieth-century anthropological investigators in Hispano villages has likely been exaggerated, suggests that what familial atomism did exist was a relatively recent cultural adaptation. In particular, he suggests that familial atomism is an adaptive cultural response to the progressive dispossession of Hispanos from their land following the American takeover in 1846.[14]

The conclusions reached by eighteenth-century commentators are also suspect. Morfí and Revillagigedo, after all, were outsiders with no firsthand experience of daily life in Hispano communities; and their perception of New Mexico was shaped by the view, common enough during the Enlightenment, that the natural depravity of human beings was only kept in check by the restraints of civilization. Given this view, it would have seemed obvious to such commentators that dispersed settlement and the consequent lack of surveillance by central authorities would free people from those restraints and allow free rein to their depravity. Sifting through the reports coming from resident friars, it would then not be difficult to find "evidence" of this presupposition in, say, the practice of Hispano settlers adopting the mode of dress of nomadic Indians (something attested in other contexts and likely the source of Morfi's "nakedness" reference).

With such caveats in mind, a number of historians[15] have tried to reconstruct Hispano social organization as it likely functioned in the late eighteenth and early nineteenth centuries without regard to the judgments made either by contemporary outsiders or by twentieth-century anthropological investigators. One of the consistent findings to emerge from their investigations is that while dispersed settlement may have (in fact, did[16]) allow settlers to evade control by the government authorities, it did not entail social isolation or familial atomism. On the contrary, it seems clear that settler households, despite being dispersed, were enmeshed in a complex set of social relationships with neighboring households that carried along with it a variety of behavioral constraints.

John Van Ness (1979; 1987; 1991), in particular, has argued that by the late 1700s Hispano settlers had adopted a subsistence pattern that was especially well suited to exploiting the ecological diversity and limited supplies of water that were characteristic of northern New Mexico. There were three core elements to this pattern. First, individual families engaged in a mix of subsistence activities that included both agriculture and animal husbandry (especially sheep raising). Second, many local resources were regarded as communal resources on which all local families had a claim. Water was probably the most important of these communal resources, but there were others. As Alvar Carlson suggests in his discussion of community land grants, "Bottomland [however] represented but a small fraction of the total grant. The adjacent meadows and surrounding uplands were designated as communal pastures for livestock. Additional communal pasturage was to be found on those grants with mountains covered by forests of piñon, juniper, and ponderosa pine, which could be used also as sources for fuel, building materials, and game" (1990, 25). Although these common areas were usually identified in a precise way in the grants made to entire communities (see Gamble 1988, 157–59), common areas also developed as a matter of practice even in the case of land grants made to particular individuals. Finally, and most importantly (given the argument I will be developing) the social system prevailing among the Hispano population, especially in the Río Arriba, was a system characterized by a high degree of cooperation between neighboring families.

Much of this interfamily cooperation centered on the exploitation of communal resources. A visible example of this sort of cooperation, and one which persists to this day in many communities, involved the *acequias* (irrigation ditches) that delivered water to individual tracts of land. Typically, Hispano settlers farmed relatively long strips of bottom land that were irrigated with water diverted using gravitational flow from one or more main canals. These main canals could be fed either by upland springs or (especially in upriver communities) from water diverted from sections of a river where the flow was especially plentiful and strong.[17] Because of the nature of the terrain, communities typically required a network of canals and ditches to deliver water to all the agricultural strips in the area. In the modern hamlet of Cañones, for instance, Van Ness (1991, 177–78) found seventeen *acequias,* seven of which seemed to be of considerable antiquity. Generally, families cooperated in maintaining and cleaning these ditches on a regular basis and in determining how much water could and should be diverted for the use of particular plots of land.

The maintenance of local *acequias* aside, interfamily cooperation was also evident in grazing practices. All stock (mainly sheep and goats) were removed to upland pastures in the spring. Since the maintenance of grazing herds in these pastures could be managed by a relatively small number of shepherds, families cooperated by rotating the relevant tasks among the younger males from different families (Van Ness 1991, 190–91). After crops were harvested, the resulting stubble was also regarded as a community resource, with the result that grazing animals (sheep, goats, and some cattle) were brought down from these hillside pastures and allowed to graze in the harvested fields.

Finally, communal concerns were evident in the distribution of lands owned by particular families. It was common, for example, for individual families to own segments of land in different locations. Partly this resulted from the irregular distribution of arable land and the effects of partible inheritance (Van Ness 1991, 24). Partly too, however, it resulted from a cultural emphasis on equity: the view that all families had a reasonable claim on access to some of the best land in an area. Certainly there is evidence in the decisions made by local magistrates in New Mexico that Hispano settlers did hold to the view that community harmony rested in part on maintaining *equidad,* that is, insuring that each person and group in the community received their fair share of the community's resources (Cutter 1994).

The land-use pattern that prevailed in northern New Mexico—a pattern that included individual families working separated strips of agricultural land, communal lands, movement of grazing animals to outland fields during the summer months, and a high degree of interfamily cooperation in exploiting communal resources—will be familiar to students of European history. It was a variant of the "open field" system of farming that prevailed in many, if not most, areas of Europe during the Middle Ages and early modern period (see Hopcroft 1994). In England this was the system of land-use that was brought to an end by the Enclosure Movement, which insured that all the land (including the common areas) in a particular area was consolidated into relatively large units, with each unit being put under the control of a single owner who could develop the land as he saw fit.

In the case of New Mexico, the impression that derives from the work done by Van Ness and others is that the cooperative/communal system prevailing among Hispano settlers functioned smoothly right up until the American annexation. It was only at that time—when this traditional system came into conflict with an Anglo-American tradition that emphasized precise boundaries, individual ownership of land, and the right of owners to dispose of their land as they saw fit—that the traditional system in New Mexico began to erode (see in particular Van Ness 1987, 192f). But that seems an unlikely scenario.

As indicated, the Hispano land-use pattern in late colonial New Mexico involved extensive cooperation both within and between families. How was such cooperation maintained? The answer has seemed so obvious to previous commentators that it is rarely discussed at length: cooperation was maintained through a patriarchal system in which authority was vested mainly in male heads of households. Van Ness deals with the matter in a single sentence—"The basic social unit was the patriarchal extended family, which served to coordinate most economic, political and social activities" (1991, 125)—and then moves on to other matters. The subject is ignored entirely in Jones's (1996, 109–65) account of Hispano life.

Typically, the only time that commentators call attention to the centrality of patriarchal authority in maintaining interfamily cooperation is when they talk about the close ties of kinship or affinity that bound together neighboring families. In discussing land transfers during the Mexican period, for example, Van Ness says, "The overwhelming majority of these land transfers were among relatives. Custom dictated that grant lands should not be sold to anyone other than kinsman. (This prohibition is understandable given the need for cooperative management and use of community irrigation system, pastures and woods)" (1987, 176). His parenthetical remark here takes it as self-evident that patriarchal authority functions best when the members of the cooperating families are linked by kinship or affinity.

In summary, then, all commentators take it as self-evident that patriarchal authority was central to the maintenance of the cooperative/communal system of agriculture that was in place in northern New Mexico. Yet as we have seen, the Bourbon economic reforms would have worked to *erode* patriarchal authority, both directly (by reducing the power of local elites) and indirectly (by forcing male heads of households to deal more and more with other males to whom they were not related by ties of blood and marriage). Putting these two observations together would seem to lead very straightforwardly to the conclusion that the Bourbon economic reforms should have worked to destabilize the cooperative/communal agricultural system prevailing in northern New Mexico—and yet we know from the work of Van Ness and others that that system functioned effectively at least until annexation. How are we to explain this?

One solution lies in suggesting that the Bourbon Reforms and other social changes taking place in late colonial New Mexico *did* pose a threat to the system of patriarchal authority relations that was central to Hispano agriculture but that Hispano communities responded to this threat by creating new authority relationships that both complemented and reinforced those that were being eroded. Furthermore, I believe that evidence attesting both to this crisis of patriarchal authority and to the cultural response it called forth has been hidden in plain sight for some time. That evidence is the emergence of Penitentes, so it is now time to revisit the matter of Penitente origins.

❧ One More Time: Penitente Origins

Cultural innovations like the emergence of the Penitentes do not come into existence simply because they are "needed" or "useful." On the contrary, it is always the case—and must always be the case—that cultural innovations come into existence in the first instance because they are shaped and promulgated by particular individuals. Although most of the individuals who set up and maintained the very first Penitente moradas are lost to history, there is one exception: Bernardo Abeyta (1771–1856) of Chimayó,[18] whom Thomas Steele has quite justifiably called "the most important individual in the first century of the penitential Brother of Our Father Jesus the Nazarene" (1993c, 48).

In retrospect, what makes Abeyta loom so large in Penitente history is that he appears to have been the person who formulated the rules and regulations that would come to appear in most Penitente constitutions. Thus, the earliest known Penitente constitution, which dates from 1853, ends with the line "I, Bernardo Abeyta, Principal Brother of the Holy Brotherhood of the blood of our Lord Jesus Christ, give this present rule to one of the Brotherhoods under my care." But the document is not written in Abeyta's hand; and in any event, an appended line says that "this is a copy taken from the original with complete and appropriate exactness" (Steele and Rivera 1985, 84). In other words, it appears that well before 1853, Abeyta drew up a model constitution for the Penitentes, which was passed along and copied in local communities throughout northern New Mexico. Indeed, paragraphs from the model constitution drawn up by Abeyta continued to show up in Penitente constitutions well into the early decades of the twentieth century (Steele and Rivera 1985, 18). Unfortunately, we know nothing about Abeyta's life that would explain why he drew up the rules he did for the Penitentes. The only possible clue we have lies in the observation that the Penitentes were not the only religious innovation with which Abeyta was associated.

In 1813, speaking in the name of several local families at Chimayó, Abeyta sent a petition (reproduced in de Borhegyi 1953, 93) to Fray Sebastián Alvarez, the priest at Santa Cruz de la Cañada, for permission to build a chapel (*una capilla*) dedicated to Our Lord of Esquipulas in the nearby plaza of Potrero. The petition was eventually forwarded to diocesan authorities at Durango, and the sanctuary was built over the period 1813–16. "Our Lord of Esquipulas" was a title originally associated with a miraculous crucifix enshrined in a church at Esquipulas in eastern Guatemala since the late 1590s. Since satellite sanctuaries dedicated to Our Lord of Esquipulas had subsequently been established in number of different locations throughout Mexico and Central America,[19] there are a number of ways in which Abeyta could have become familiar with the Esquipulas cult. De Borhegyi (1954, 397), for example, suggests that some member of the Abeyta family had made a pilgrimage to Guatemala or at least to one of the shrines dedicated to Our Lord of Esquipulas in Mexico. Angélico Chávez (1957, 66; 1981, 47) suggests that the Esquipulas cult may have been introduced by José Vibián Ortega, the secular priest who took charge of the parish at Santa Cruz and who in 1803 asked a fellow priest traveling to Chihuahua and Durango to pray for him before an image of "El Señor de Esquipulas." Possibly the link to the Esquipulas cult was even closer to home. A church dedicated to "Our Lord of Esquipula," for example, existed in a small Indian community near Tucson (Arizona) at least as early as 1772 (Salpointe 1898, 225)—which suggests that someone had already brought the devotion north from Mexico by that time.

However he came to know about the Esquipulas cult, there is evidence that by the early 1800s Abeyta and his relatives in the Chimayó area were becoming quite devoted to Our Lord of Esquipulas. Thus, starting in 1805, "Esquipulas" begins to appear with increasing frequency in the baptismal records at Santa Cruz de la Cañada; and in most of these cases, a member of the Abeyta family was either the parent or the godparents of the child being baptized (de Borhegyi 1953, 92). Similarly, in forwarding Abeyta's 1813 petition to build a sanctuary at Chimayó, Fray Alvarez mentioned that an image of Our Lord of Esquipulas had been venerated for three years (that is, since 1810) in a *hermita* (small chapel) annexed to Abeyta's house at Chimayó.[20]

Were the two religious innovations that Abeyta promoted, the Esquipulas cult and the Penitentes, linked in any way, at least in the mind of Abeyta himself and other Abeyta family members? Possibly. Certainly there is a common emphasis on the Passion of Christ in the two devotions. Then too, one of the (many) origin legends associated with the discovery of the image suggests that Abeyta was guided to the spot where the image was buried by a light that appeared to him as he engaged in various Penitente penances during Holy Week (de Borhegyi 1953, 98; Steele and Rivera 1985, 17). There is also a tradition, gathered from Penitente informants in southern Colorado, that the very first set of rules for the Penitentes was drawn up and approved at Santa Cruz de la Cañada in 1810 (Beshoar 1949, 2), which is, remember, the very same year in which Abeyta first established that small *hermita* dedicated to Our Lord of Esquipulas next to his house. Finally, there is the matter of Bernardo Abeyta's son, Tomás.

In March 1813, several months before he petitioned to build a church in honor of Our Lord of Esquipulas, Abeyta and his second wife had a son who was subsequently baptized in the parish church at Santa Cruz. De Borhegyi (1953, 92) reports that baptismal records indicate the son was given the name "Tomás de Jesús de Esquipulas." We know that in later life, however, that son identified himself as "Tomás de Jesús *Nazareno* de Esquipulas Abeyta" (Steele 1993c, 50). What is interesting here is that in Mexico and Central America, "Our Lord of Esquipulas" is not normally considered a "Jesús Nazareno" (see the discussion in Solórzano 1914), nor was the "Nazareno" title used in the various documents relating to the establishment of the chapel at Chimayó,[21] which refer only to "El Señor de Esquipulas." The fact that Tomás Abeyta, at least in later life, saw "Our Lord of Esquipulas" to be a "Jesus Nazareno," a title that is so intimately bound up with the Penitentes, is evidence—however meager—that Abeyta family members did originally see a connection between the Esquipulas cult and the Penitentes. Unfortunately, it seems likely that we will never know for sure what that connection might have been.

Acknowledging Abeyta's centrality in bringing the Penitentes into existence, of course, does not explain why the Penitentes became so popular. After all, although Abeyta may indeed have had a "personal authority" (to borrow Steele and Rivera's characterization [1985, 16]) that made him a man of influence in northern New Mexico, the fact remains that his two religious innovations were not equally successful. On the contrary, the immense popularity of the Chimayó sanctuary at the present time does not change the fact that for most of the nineteenth century that sanctuary drew only a very limited number of pilgrims, and even these were mainly from the Chimayó/Santa Cruz area. Just as importantly, devotion to "Our Lord of Esquipulas" at the sanctuary (which had been so important to Abeyta himself) did not survive his death. On the contrary, shortly after Abeyta's death in 1856, a cult centered on an image of the Santo Niño (Christ as a child) emerged at the Chimayó sanctuary and very quickly became (and remains) its devotional focus, eclipsing entirely the Esquipulas cult (see Gutiérrez 1995; Nunn 1993). So why did one of the religious innovations with which Abeyta was associated, the Penitentes, become immediately popular; while another, the Esquipulas cult, did not?

The hypothesis I want to offer here—and it is just that, a hypothesis— is that *Penitente popularity was in the first instance a response to the crisis of kin-based patriarchal authority facing Hispano communities in the late 1700s.* In short: the Penitentes became popular because their internal organization and the imagery their rituals evoked were well suited to establishing and stabilizing the male-to-male authority relations on which their communal/cooperative system of agriculture in northern New Mexico depended at a time when the older pattern of kin-based authority relations that had maintained this system in the past was being eroded by the Bourbon Reforms. This hypothesis has the advantage that it would explain the *timing* of Penitente emergence (i.e., the Penitentes became popular in the early 1800s because this was the period when local kin-based authority structures were being eroded by the social and economic changes described earlier in this chapter). It also helps to explain some of the patterns uncovered earlier in connection with the iconography of the "Nuestro Padre Jesús Nazareno."

In confronting that great iconographical sea filled with any number of Madonnas, saints, and Christ-figures that was part of the Spanish Catholic tradition, Hispano settlers would have found the "Nuestro Padre Jesús" title particularly appealing because it allowed the new system of authority to seem similar to the older and more familiar system that was being eroded. Thus, because a "father" (in the sense of "head of family") had been central to the older system, it was appropriate that a father— Padre Jesús—be made central to the new system. Furthermore, because real-life fathers were "suffering," in the sense that their authority was being challenged and eroded, it was also appropriate that this new "Padre Jesús" be a Jesús Nazareno, that is, an image of the suffering Christ on the way to Calvary. The fact that this new "suffering Father" was the metaphorical representation of the very real fathers whose authority was *still* being eroded in the early nineteenth century also explains, I suggest, why the Penitentes borrowed from the iconography of other "suffering Jesús" images (the Ecce Homo, the Man of Sorrows) in order to intensify the suffering of their Padre Jesús even further.

⚜ Is This All There Is?

At the end of the day, then, am I saying simply that the Penitentes were popular because they performed a number of community functions? And if that *is* what I am saying, hasn't the "community functions" argument been made before (e.g., Kutsche and Gallegos 1979)? In a very general sense, I will concede that the answers here are "yes" and "yes." On the other hand, previous scholars who have pointed out that Penitente moradas performed a number of community functions have made no attempt to link this "community functions" argument to the changes produced by the Bourbon Reforms in the late 1700s, to the erosion of patriarchal authority occasioned by these reforms, and/or to the threat that this posed to the communal/cooperative system of agriculture that was in place in northern New Mexico. As a result, these scholars have had no basis for explaining the timing of Penitente emergence or for explaining why the Penitentes coalesced around the image of a suffering "Padre Jesús" rather than around any of the countless other figures that were available to them in the Spanish Catholic tradition. And finally, all previous commentators making a "community functions" argument have accepted, either implicitly or explicitly, the standard contention that the Penitentes were an outgrowth of a deeply rooted Hispano religiosity; and, as we saw in Chapter 2, it seems unlikely that such a deeply rooted religiosity ever existed.

The Penitentes, then, were in the first instance a social response to a socioeconomic crisis that just happened to be dressed in a religious cloak. On the other hand, precisely because Penitente moradas did invoke religious imagery, they could and did become the core around which a Hispano religiosity might coalesce and develop. What I am suggesting, in other words, is that the Penitentes were less the *outgrowth* of a deep-seated Hispano religiosity than a seed that *gave rise* to such a religiosity. It is now time to tell the story of how that seed sprouted and grew. A good place to start, maybe the only place to start, is with someone whose name has already been linked several times to the Penitentes: Padre Antonio José Martínez of Taos.

FIVE

Padre Martínez of Taos and the Meaning of Discipline

Death Comes for the Archbishop (1999), originally published in 1927, has always been one of Willa Cather's (d. 1947) most popular books. In it, Cather
tells the story of two valiant and dedicated priests from France—Bishop
Jean Marie Latour and his friend and associate Father Joseph Vaillant (who
are only barely disguised representations[1] of the historical Bishop Jean Baptiste Lamy and his friend and associate Joseph Machebeuf)—as they struggle to bring civilization, order, and progress to the Vicariate (later, the Archdiocese[2]) of Santa Fe. The great appeal of Cather's book lies partly in the
fact that she uses the Latour/Vaillant story as a vehicle for introducing
readers to a variety of colorful locations and characters associated with
each of the three groups (Pueblo Indians, Hispanos, Anglos) who were
(and are) so important to New Mexico's cultural mosaic. But for many
Catholic intellectuals, *Death Comes for the Archbishop* has always been appealing as well because of the favorable way it depicts Catholicism and the
modern Catholic Church. In a review of Cather's book published in *Commonweal*, Michael Harris, who was the editor of *Commonweal* at the time,
told his readers:

> [The book] tells the story of one Jean Marie Latour [and] Father
> Joseph Vaillant. . . . And always, everywhere, they give all their pow-
> ers, their endurance, their courage, their strength, their culture, their
> riches of European experience, to the task . . . of extending the
> Catholic Church, the Faith; the task of saving souls. . . . Miss Cather
> is not a Catholic, yet certainly no Catholic American writer . . . has
> ever written so many pages steeped in spiritual knowledge and un-
> derstanding of Catholic motives. (Harris 1927)

In short, the Catholic Church that emerges from Cather's account is a progressive organization led by educated and compassionate clerics who bring order, morality, and "real" Catholicism (read: that variant of Catholicism, with its emphasis on papal authority and standardized rituals, that was favored by Catholic intellectuals in the early twentieth century) to a backward area of the world. Little wonder that Harris ended his review by suggesting that he "consider[ed] it the duty of Catholics to buy and read and spread Willa Cather's masterpiece" or that other Anglo-Catholic reviewers (see the examples cited in Murphy 2000, 360–65) were equally laudatory.

Hispano commentators, by contrast, have generally been less favorable (if not outright hostile) to Cather's work. Partly this is because of the overtly patronizing attitude that she has Latour adopt toward what he sees as the theatrical and superficial nature of Hispano piety. What Hispano commentators have always found most objectionable, however, is Cather's chapter on Padre Antonio José Martínez of Taos (who is not given a pseudonym in the text).

Cather scholars rightly see Latour's encounter with Martínez at Taos as climactic (see Woodress 1987, 398). Within the logic of the story that Cather is telling, Martínez epitomizes "the old order" (which is, in fact, the subtitle of her chapter on Martínez) that the progressive Latour is trying to eradicate. Cather's Martínez is a petty tyrant who dominates not just the laity in the Taos area but also most of the Hispano clergy in northern New Mexico. He is a ruthless and unprincipled man, who had a few years earlier fomented bloody rebellion among the Indians of Taos Pueblo and then betrayed these same rebels in order to gain control of their land. Finally, and worst of all, Cather's Martínez is a sexual predator.

Martínez (in real life and in the novel) had been married and widowed before joining the priesthood and had a daughter born of this marriage. But the Martínez who emerges in Cather's work is more than just a priest who had formerly been married; he is an unscrupulous monster, driven by an unbridled lust to despoil whatever woman happens to fall into his clutches. He was especially fond, it appears, of debauching virgins. Cather relates the story of a young girl who had been captured by Indians at age eighteen and who with great effort had managed to preserve her virginity until ransomed seven years later. Alas, a virginity that survived seven years among savage Indians did not survive the poor girl's encounter with Martínez. After his lust for the girl was spent, Cather tells us, he gave her to one of his peons as a wife.

Far from being embarrassed by his sexual debauchery, the Martínez who appears in Cather's book flaunts it. In dinner-table conversation with Latour, for example, he challenges the Church's position on priestly celibacy by arguing that a priest cannot appreciate repentance until he himself has fallen into sin. Just to make sure there is no doubt about just what Martínez represents, Cather writes the ugliness of his character onto his physical appearance. We are told that his head is overly large and set on a thick neck and broad shoulders, giving him the look of a bull buffalo; that his eyes and teeth have a yellowish cast; that his face, instead of being smooth like an Anglo-Saxon's face, was muscled in ways which ensured that his appearance changed as his emotions changed; and that his full lips reminded her of an animal charged with fear or desire (Cather 2000 [1927], 147). A photo of the historical Martínez (see gallery following p. 86) suggests that at least Cather got the "large head" right.

If Cather writes hedonism and sexual degeneracy onto Martínez's body, she writes disorder onto his household. Entering Martínez's study, Latour finds a dissolute youth lying about in a stupor (the boy, Latour is later told, is almost certainly one of the good Padre's illegitimate sons); books are piled so high on his desk that they come close to hiding the crucifix on the wall (simplistic metaphors of this sort abound in Cather's book); items of the Padre's clothing are piled here and there; and dust and dirt from outside are everywhere. Moreover, the house is overrun with yellow cats who are allowed to lie about wherever they want and even worse (at least as far as the fastidious French bishop is concerned), are allowed to feed at the dinner table. The final insult to Latour's delicate (and civilized) sensibilities occurs when he is shown to his room and finds hair from a woman's toilet in a corner. This discovery, we are told, greatly annoyed the good bishop (149).

The only compliments that Latour/Cather is willing to grant Martínez are that he did know his Latin and Spanish classics (a result of his training at the seminary in Durango); he did have a pleasant baritone voice; and he did seem possessed of a disturbing mysterious, magnetic power that, if he had been "rightly guided" (presumably by right-minded clerics like Latour), might have made him a great man.

Interestingly, Cather's decision to depict Martínez, on balance, in negative terms seems to have been deliberate. For example, while some of the published works on which she relied did indeed associate Martínez with sexual misconduct, this is not an element that appears in the discussion of Martínez in Howlett (1908), which, by Cather's own admission, is the source on which she relied most heavily in constructing her story (see the discussion of Cather's sources in Murphy 2000, 342–54, 454). On the contrary, although Howlett's account is full of disparaging remarks on the state of the Hispano clergy generally at the time of Lamy's and Machebeuf's arrival, he depicts Martínez in surprisingly positive terms, calling him "a man of great learning" (228) who did much to foster literacy in northern New Mexico.

In any event, modern scholars trying to rescue the historic Martínez from Cather's portrayal[3] point out that the real Martínez, far from clinging to an "old order" of things (as Cather's account suggests), was actively involved in promoting a number of progressive changes. Martínez, for instance, was indeed a champion of educational reform and literacy. In 1826 he founded a school at Taos for both boys and girls, and in 1833 he obtained permission from Bishop Zubiría (during the bishop's visitation of that year) to establish a "preparatory seminary" at Taos for the training of would-be priests. Martínez also brought a printing press (and a printer) to Taos during the early 1830s and oversaw the publication of a variety of books. Nor did the real Martínez cling stubbornly to a Mexican past in the face of American rule. On the contrary, during the 1847 rebellion at Taos, he actively opposed the rebels who had killed Governor Bent; and in the process, he saved the life of a man the rebels were on the verge of killing. Generally, Martínez played a constructive and leading role in the politics of the post-annexation period. In 1848, he served as president of the Convention at Santa Fe that petitioned the U.S. Congress for the establishment of a civil government in New Mexico; in 1850, he was president of a Constitutional Convention; in 1851, he served as president of the first Legislative Assembly; and in 1852 and 1861, he was a member of that same Legislative Assembly.

Martínez's modern supporters have also taken aim at Cather's characterization of him as a sexual predator. Some simply deny her allegations of sexual impropriety entirely (López-Gastón 1985, 306; Aragón 1988, 147–48). Others are willing to admit a bit, but *only* a bit, of sexual impropriety. Angélico Chávez 's reading of the evidence, for instance, leads him to conclude that Martínez likely fathered two (and possibly as many as five) illegitimate children as the result of his relationship with one woman (1981, 35–40). Mares (1988b, 39–40) tends to agree, though he is careful to point out that Chávez 's evidence is by no means incontrovertible. But the important point, implicit in both Chávez and Mares, is that even if we grant that this one relationship did result in several illegitimate children, that hardly makes Martínez the lustful monster who appears in Cather's work.

Also relevant to any assessment of Martínez's moral character, his supporters contend, is that during the 1820s and 1830s he was often singled out for special praise by his ecclesiastical superiors. In 1830 Vicar Rafael Rascón wrote that Martínez was the only priest in New Mexico against whom he had never heard any complaints (A. Chávez 1981, 33). Similarly, during his 1833 visitation, Bishop Zubiría chose Martínez as one of two priests in New Mexico who were authorized to administer the Sacrament of Confirmation (see Aragón 1978, 16; A. Chávez 1981, 33). It seems unlikely, so the argument goes, that Martínez would be singled out in these ways and entrusted with special responsibilities if any hint of scandal or immorality had attached to his reputation.

With the arrival of Bishop Lamy, to be sure, Martínez's relationship with his ecclesiastical superiors would take a turn for the worse. Martínez would come to struggle with Lamy over Church policy, especially in regard to tithing; and the matter would end with Lamy excommunicating Martínez, and Martínez continuing to perform his priestly functions at Taos. Even so, the (thick) file in the archives of the Archdiocese of Santa Fe that documents Martínez's struggle with Lamy contains nothing that hints at immoral conduct on Martínez's part (Vigil 1975, 128). The fact that Lamy never added immorality to the list of charges against Martínez takes on added significance, given that Lamy and Machebeuf did level this charge at other priests in New Mexico (see A. Chávez 1981, 101–3; Bridgers 1997, 92–108).

Another set of documents that has been mined by those seeking to defend Martínez against charges of immorality are the various accounts of the Taos "schism"[4] written by Jesuit authors shortly after Martínez's death. Bishop Lamy, it happens, had brought a small group of Jesuits into New Mexico in 1867, and in January 1869 a Jesuit mission was conducted at Taos by Donato M. Gasparri. As far as Jesuit commentators were concerned, it was the Gasparri mission that brought Martínez's "schism" to an end; so for this reason, a number of Jesuit documents written during the 1870s make a passing reference to the events that had created the schism in the first place. In his review of five such documents, Thomas Steele (1988) notes that all five tell the same basic story: there was some sort of dispute between Lamy and Martínez; Martínez resigned; Martínez and his successor, Father Taladrid, subsequently became embroiled in a dispute over Martínez's right to perform marriages; and as a result, Martínez refused to acknowledge Taladrid's authority and eventually turned the people away from Lamy. Steele (1988, 79–80) also points out that the Jesuit authors writing these accounts were generally negative in their "take" on Martínez, in the sense that they saw him as having provoked the split and *did* see the split as a true schism. Despite this, there is nothing in any of these Jesuit reports that associates Martínez with lascivious behavior.

Unfortunately, the matter has been complicated somewhat by Gerald McKevitt's (1992) discovery of a report written by Father Gasparri himself in the archives of the Jesuit order's Neapolitan Province in Naples, Italy. Gasparri's account of the dispute between Martínez and Lamy is much the same as would appear in succeeding Jesuit documents (not surprising, since it seems likely that his report was the model for these later documents), but Gasparri did have this sentence in his report: "Because of his behavior [the dispute with Taladrid, etc.] *and his scandalous life,* the bishop, after invoking the three canonical warnings or citations, saw fit to suspend him and then to excommunicate [him]" (McKevitt 1992, 386; emphasis added). There is nothing in Gasparri's text that tells us what the phrase "and his scandalous life" refers to, and at best Gasparri was repeating gossip. Still, as brief as it is, Gasparri's remark here raises the possibility that more scandal attached to Martínez's private life, at least in his later years, than some of his modern supporters would care to admit.

On balance, however, and even taking Gasparri's passing remark into account, it still seems evident that scholars like Aragón, Chávez, Mares, and Vigil have amassed much evidence suggesting that *Cather's* depiction of Martínez severely distorts the man's life. He was certainly in the forefront of promoting changes that even Cather herself would have to call progressive; and if he engaged in sexual improprieties, they were likely not as extensive as her account suggests. Indeed, the weight of modern scholarship lends strong support to the assessment of Padre Martínez that appeared in the *Santa Fe Weekly Gazette* on May 24, 1856. In commenting on Padre Martínez's letter of resignation, which was carried in that same issue of the *Gazette,* the paper's editor suggested:

> We have heard it said that it was better to be useful than popular;
> this may be so, but we seldom find a man who has been useful to his
> fellows, who is not also popular. This seems to be the case with Cura
> Martínez. He is among the few native priests of the country who
> while engaged in their ministerial duties, has at the same time la-
> bored to improve the condition of their parishioners. We have heard
> it said, and it is no doubt the case, that many young men in the valley
> of Taos are almost entirely indebted to the kindness and industry of

the Cura for excellent and useful educations. The Cura may have his faults, but who does not? We should speak kindly of them all, even of the errors, for it is but a little time that we have to remain here below, and life has enough to teach us that is sad and sorrowful, without harsh words from those around us.[5]

Martínez, in other words, had a few faults. But on balance, he worked hard, was a good priest, and greatly benefited those under his care.

And yet, as important as it is to rescue the historical Martínez from Cather's villainous depiction and to give him his due as one of the most important leaders in nineteenth-century New Mexico, I believe that both Martínez's supporters and his detractors have missed an element in the cluster of factors shaping his behavior. In particular, what I want to suggest in the remainder of this chapter is that if we read the story of Padre Martínez through a lens shaped by recent scholarship on "Catholic Reform" in early modern Europe, then not only do we catch sight of previously undetected themes in his life's work, but also, and more generally, we catch sight of processes operating to create a new variety of Hispano Catholicism in the early nineteenth century.

⚜ Changing Views of the Counter-Reformation and Catholic Reform

During the nineteenth century the term *Counter-Reformation* came into common usage among Protestant historians as a way of denoting the attempts at reform enacted by the Catholic Church over a period that stretched from the middle of the sixteenth century to the middle of the seventeenth century.[6] By the early twentieth century even some Catholic historians were beginning to use the term, although when they did, they were usually careful to disassociate themselves from the implication (latent in the word *counter*) that all attempts at Church reform in this period had been a reaction to the Protestant Reformation (see, for instance, Pollen 1913). In the special case of Italian historiography (which has always exerted a strong influence on the study of Church history during the early modern period), Adriano Prosperi (1994, 4) suggests that the idea of a repressive and coercive Counter-Reformation appealed to leftist intellectuals in Italy because it provided them with a convenient way of explaining the disappointing results that had followed upon the Unification of Italy during the late nineteenth century. The Counter-Reformation, being reactionary and coercive, so the argument went, had prevented the birth of a modern

state in Italy and so had prevented the development (in Italy) of the entre-
preneurial spirit and efficient social institutions that had emerged in other
European states and allowed them to modernize.

Whatever the source of its appeal, there is no denying that the term
Counter-Reformation has proven amazingly durable and is still routinely encountered in books and articles that discuss the religious history of modern
Europe. Nevertheless, although the term may still be in widespread use, our
sense of what the Counter-Reformation was has changed considerably.

In a particularly influential article on Reformation historiography published in 1929, Lucien Febvre (1973) argued that it was time to put aside the
view that the Reformation had been a reaction to abuses in the Church.
On the contrary, he suggested, the Reformation was fueled by a diffuse and
growing desire for a simpler and more individualized religion that had been
building throughout Europe for centuries. Although Febvre's article was
mainly concerned with the (Protestant) Reformation, he did suggest that
this diffuse demand for religious reform had also given rise to the many
movements promoting internal reform of the Church that had quite con-
fusingly been lumped together under the heading "Counter-Reformation."
Subsequently, under the influence of scholars like Hubert Jedin and
Giuseppe Alberigo, it became conventional to make a distinction between
the "Counter-Reformation" and "Catholic Reform." The Counter-Reformation continued to be conceptualized much as before, as a reactionary
and repressive reaction on the Church's part to the Reformation. Catholic
Reform, on the other hand, was something quite different.

Following Febvre's lead, "Catholic Reform" came to be seen as a continuation in the last half of the sixteenth century of a search for a more
deeply felt and interiorized religion that had been building within the
Church since the late 1300s. It was this search, so the argument went, that
had given rise to the Observant Reform of the various mendicant orders
in the fourteenth and fifteenth centuries; to new types of confraternal organization (notably including the Oratory of Divine Love founded at
Genoa in 1497 and a similar confraternity at Rome in 1517); to the dramatic
increase in mystical activity that occurred in the early 1500s; and to the new
religious orders that emerged in the 1520s (notably the Capuchins and the
Theatines). This same desire for a more interiorized religiosity was also the
common thread that linked the various individuals who had led the struggle to promote reform within the Church before Trent, a list that almost
always included Girolamo Savonarola at Florence, Cardinal Ximénez of
Spain, Erasmus of Rotterdam, and Bishop Gian Matteo Giberti of Verona.

Under this model, it was this building desire for a more interiorized religion that had led to many of the reform decrees passed by the Council of Trent.

One of the most important findings to emerge from studies of the individuals and traditions associated with Catholic Reform was that reform within the Church—both before, during, and after the Council of Trent—had been characterized by far more diversity than had previously been recognized. Donald Weinstein's (1970) study of Savonarola, for instance, made it clear that while previous commentators had portrayed Savonarola as having had a consistent vision over the entire course of his career, his message had, in fact, changed over time in response to changing political conditions. Dermot Fenlon's (1972) study of Cardinal Pole demonstrates that there was a divergence of opinion about what "being Catholic" meant even among the highest echelons of the Roman Church in the period just before Trent. Giuseppe Alberigo's (1966) review of then-recent scholarship on the Council of Trent suggested that the council's actions had been more ad hoc and unsystematic than had previously been acknowledged, and that partly this was due to the fact that the great majority of delegates had no clear and coherent vision of what the Church should be like. Similarly, Eric Cochrane (1970) drew attention to the diversity that continued to exist even after Trent, mainly because different bishops could be Tridentine in quite different ways (he singled out the contrast between Carlo Borremeo of Milan and Gabriele Paleotti of Bologna as being especially instructive in this regard).

Within the Italian scholarly community, this increasing recognition of the diversity that had existed within the Church after Trent gave rise to a distinctive research tradition that is still little known among English-speaking scholars. Gabriele De Rosa and his students are the central figures in this tradition, and the guiding premise of their research is that the history of Catholic piety in Italy since the Council of Trent is the story of how individual bishops, all committed to the Tridentine reforms, adapted those reforms to the peculiar conditions they encountered in their dioceses.[7] Studies of particular dioceses in France and in the Spanish Netherlands (reviewed in Harline 1990) revealed the same diversity among "Tridentine" bishops in these dioceses that De Rosa and his students had uncovered in Italian dioceses.

Simultaneous with this increasing emphasis on the diversity promoted by different bishops in different dioceses came a more nuanced understanding of the conditions under which the push for Catholic Reform had operated. Jean Delumeau's well-known book on the Counter-Reformation

(1977 [1971]) was especially influential in this regard. Starting with the now-standard view that both Protestant and Catholic reform in the sixteenth century had proceeded from the same roots, Delumeau developed three arguments. First, he suggested that the great mass of the people living in the European countryside had been only barely Christianized before Trent. Although Delumeau's remarks here are often taken as suggesting that rural Europeans were "pagan," in fact, his text indicates that he meant something different. In Delumeau's account, the European countryside was characterized by a "folklorised" Christianity, by which he meant a Christianity whose elements had been received by the local population and then "shaped" by the mode of thinking that prevailed in rural areas. What people in the countryside lacked, he argued, was that sort of interiorized Christianity favored by literate elites in both the Protestant and Catholic traditions.

Delumeau's second argument was that after Trent both Protestant and Catholic elites were engaged in projects that were more similar than different, mainly because both groups were trying to promote an interiorized Christianity among the masses. In discussing the Catholic campaign to promote this interiorized religiosity in the countryside, Delumeau laid stress on organizational innovations (the use of catechisms, educational reform, synods, pastoral visitations, seminaries).

Finally, using data from a variety of sources, Delumeau suggested that the Counter-Reformation had proceeded at different rates in different areas of Europe. Whereas in areas like northern Italy and Spain, a substantial number of reforms had been put in place very quickly after Trent, there were other areas where these same reforms did not arrive until the late 1600s. In short, while earlier investigators had pushed the roots of the Counter-Reformation back into the centuries before Trent, Delumeau's work very forcefully extended the Counter-Reformation beyond the limits (the early seventeenth century) favored by earlier commentators.

In summary, then, by the 1980s a new paradigm for the study of Catholic Reform was in place. Central to all summary statements of this new paradigm (see Mullet 1984; Cochrane 1988, Olin 1990) was the view that an increased emphasis on interiorized religiosity had been building within the Church since at least the late fourteenth century, and that during the sixteenth century it was this building desire for a more interiorized religion that would fuel both the Protestant Reformation and the various attempts to reform the Church from the inside. The new paradigm also suggested that sometime around the middle of the sixteenth century this desire for interiorized renewal had been fused, in both the Catholic and Protestant traditions, with a variety of organizational reforms that were at least as important as the doctrinal innovations of the period. There was also widespread recognition that the Church after Trent had been characterized by great diversity, mainly because bishops had had to adapt Tridentine reform to local conditions. Finally, it was now agreed that the reforms envisioned by Trent had not been implemented in many areas of the Catholic world until the late seventeenth century.

Even as it was establishing itself, however, this new paradigm was being challenged, not for what it said, but for what it left out. More specifically, a growing number of scholars began to criticize *all* analyses—old or new—that studied Catholic and/or Protestant reform in isolation from the more general transformation of European society that was taking place during the early modern period. Paolo Prodi (1989) and Wolfgang Reinhard (1989), in particular, suggested that Catholic Reform (and, for that matter, the Protestant Reformation) were simply manifestations in the religious sphere of that "rise of the modern" that was reshaping all aspects of European society. Central to this rise of the modern in all its manifestations, they argued, was an increasing emphasis on the "social disciplining" *(Sozialdiszi-plinierung* in German, *disciplinamento sociale* in Italian) of individuals through a simultaneous emphasis on (1) internalized mechanisms that caused individuals to monitor and control their own behavior, and (2) rules and regulations that were to be enforced by external agencies. In Prodi's words,

> Social disciplining appears in the early modern period as a phenomenon that cannot be seen only from one point of view (military, ecclesiastical, political, economic, professional, etc.) but must instead be seen as a process that permeated all these different aspects of social life as a function of the new society and new state that were coming into being and that regularized the public sphere in a variety of ways, ranging from the most external manifestations of police surveillance to the most internal regularization of ethical habits. (1989, 235)

One immediate advantage of conceptualizing Catholic Reform as part of a more general process of social disciplining is that it allowed investigators to see (or at least, to propose) connections between Catholic Reform and the rise of the modern state. Reinhard (1989), for instance, argues that during the sixteenth century both the Catholic Church and the various Protestant churches did the same thing: they transformed themselves into stable groups with well-defined boundaries, a process that he calls "confessionalization." For each group, this was accomplished by (1) settling on a clear statement of pure doctrine (as occurred for Catholics at Trent, and for Lutherans with the Augsburg Confession of 1530); and (2) eliminating elements in their rituals that might lead to confusion (i.e., any elements that might make Catholic rituals seem "Protestant," and any elements that might make Protestant rituals seem "Catholic"). These newly formulated doctrines and rituals were then spread as widely as possible, using both older methods (like preaching) and newer technologies (like printing).

But confessionalization had an unintended consequence. In Reinhard's words,

> Society after "Confessionalization" was certainly more modern than before: education was improved and more widespread, and the first media revolution in history had taken place, the victory of printing. By these means . . . churches had contributed to the further development of rationality. At the same time, they had trained their members in discipline and made them accustomed to the objects of bureaucratic administration—both essential preconditions of modern industrial societies. (1989, 397)

In short, Reinhard is suggesting that the various "social disciplining" measures introduced by Catholic and Protestant reformers in the pursuit of confessionalization had the quite unintended effect of creating social conditions (or better, of inducing a social conditioning of the populace) that facilitated the rise of the modern state in Europe. As Prosperi (1994, 9) points out, the suggestion that *Protestant* reform may have prepared individuals for life in a society that was becoming ever more rational and regulated was old hat, but the suggestion that *Catholic* reform may have performed a similar function is a significant new addition to our view of the Counter-Reformation.

The conceptual framework undergirding the "social disciplining" approach is not new. The term itself was first introduced by Gerhard Oestreich in the late 1960s in connection with his study of early modern Germany (see Prosperi 1994, 8–9; Hudon 1996, 788). Even earlier, Max Weber had written extensively on the increasing rationalization of Western society, and Norbert Elias (1978 [1939]) had talked about "the civilizing process." Michel Foucault (1990 [1976]) made reference to similar processes in his work on the history of sexuality and had even discussed, if only in passing (see 18–20), how a simultaneous emphasis on internalized and externalized control had reshaped the practice of auricular confession after Trent. What was different in the 1980s, as Gabriella Zarri (1996, 6) points out, is that ecclesiastical reform was now seen to be more central to the general process of "social disciplining" associated with the early modern era than earlier commentators like Elias or Foucault had recognized.

Daniele Montanari's *Disciplinamento nella Terra Veneto* (1987) is a good example of how scholars in the 1980s were using the social disciplining perspective to study Catholic Reform. Montanari's study looks carefully at the career of Domenico Bollani, who became bishop of Brescia (in northern Italy) in 1559 and who died in 1579. Bollani was a suffragan to Archbishop Carlo Borromeo of Milan and, like Borromeo, worked to promote Tridentine reform in the immediate aftermath of the Council of Trent. One of the important findings to emerge from Montanari's study is that Bollani did not implement the different Tridentine reforms with the same vigor in all areas of his diocese, mainly because he—like the bishops so favored by Gabriele De Rosa—took local conditions into account. In some communities, for instance, enforcing the Tridentine rules relating to matrimonial impediments would have deprived too many people of a potential mate, so in these cases Bollani was relatively tolerant of local practice even if they violated the Tridentine decrees.

Bollani recognized that promoting reform of the laity depended first of all on reform of the clergy, and this meant two things. First, it meant reform of the existing clergy. Toward this end, Bollani did two things: he worked to promote a more moral life among the clergy (which for the most part meant campaigning against priests who frequented prostitutes, who engaged in sexual abuse of local women, and who maintained common-law wives); and he had local priests examined to make to make sure that they could read and write, could recite their breviary and missal properly, and could properly administer the sacraments. But reform of the clergy had a second and ultimately more important meaning: it meant creating a new and more professionalized class of priests by means of a diocesan seminary. Bollani started work on establishing a seminary at Brescia in 1567, and it was brought to completion in 1570.

Clerical reform aside, Bollani worked to subject the laity in his diocese to an ongoing process of religious disciplining that would produce the sort of good Catholic envisioned by Trent—that is, someone who was, to use Montanari's words, "disciplined and animated by a conscious faith which had been shaped by a catechism learned early in life, reinforced through the constant reception of the sacraments, and fortified by collective prayer and by active participation in the liturgy of the Church" (1987, 157). This meant, among other things, promoting regular attendance at Sunday Mass, making the Eucharist more central to the Catholic experience, establishing schools of Christian doctrine in local parishes, suppressing many of the secular activities associated with particular feast days, and—something that was especially important to the process of disciplining the laity—increasing the number of people who confessed to their parish priest at least once a year.

The social disciplining of the laity also meant promoting forms of confraternal organization that reinforced Tridentine emphases, and reformers like Bollani and Borromeo saw *penitential* confraternities (so long as they were under episcopal control) to be especially useful in this regard. In Montanari's words,

> These [*disciplinati* confraternities] were seen to be the element that was most in accordance with their attempts to translate the dictates of the Council into practice and so to effect the spiritual revitalization of the diocese (of Brescia) and, more generally, the spiritual revitalization of the larger ecclesiastical province. Evidence of this can be found in the proceedings of the third provincial Council, which requested of all bishops in the ecclesiastical province of Milan that they found *disciplinati* confraternities in their dioceses, taking care to correct the ancient rules and to supervise the spiritual progress of these groups. (1987, 218–19)

In 1567 (which was only a year or so after his arrival at Milan), for example, Borromeo himself had proposed the creation of a new and prestigious *Compagnia dei Battuti,* whose members were to be drawn from Milan's leading families; and in the succeeding years he devoted much effort to both clarifying and expanding the role played by flagellant confraternities in the devotional life of the laity (Zardin 1987; 110–11; 2000, 197–98). For reforming bishops like Bollani and Borromeo, organized and strictly supervised penitential activity (which usually, though not always, meant flagellation) was something that expressed the disciplinary emphasis associated with Tridentine reform in a concrete and literal way and as such could be used to make this emphasis intelligible to local populations that had previously had little or no experience of the "disciplining" that the reformers were trying to establish in their dioceses. As already mentioned in Chapter 3, the support given to flagellant confraternities by bishops committed to the Tridentine reforms is one of the reasons that these confraternities proliferated in the century and a half after Trent.

Whether the social disciplining approach promoted during the 1980s by scholars like Prodi, Reinhard, Montanari, and others carry the day among scholars concerned with the history of Catholic Reform is by no means assured. John Bossy (1994, 676–77), for example, snidely dismisses attempts to associate the social disciplining of religious life in the early modern era with modernization as little more than a "sociological plot" that brings no particular insight into the materials being studied. By contrast, John O'Malley (2000, 136–40) is quite willing to give the "social disciplining" approach high marks for what it does do (notably, sensitizing investigators to the links between Catholic Reform and the more general processes working to reshape European society in the early modern period), but he has strong reservations about what it does not do. Specifically, O'Malley suggests, an emphasis on social disciplining leads investigators to ignore, or at least to minimize, that "yearning for the transcendent" (139) that is, he feels, so central to the experience of religion for a great many Catholics.

Certainly, it is true that some of those who used the new perspective when it first appeared have now set it aside and returned to more traditional approaches (compare, for example, Hsia 1989 with Hsia 1998). Even those who continue to use the new perspective are willing to acknowledge some shortcomings. Both Roberto Bizzocchi (1994, 496) and Gigliola Fragnito (1994, 532), for example, concede that seeing Catholic Reform as just one of many processes contributing to a process of social disciplining during the early modern era risks "flattening" historical discourse and "homogenizing" history itself. What this means, as I understand it, is that the social disciplining perspective can lead historians away from the emphasis on local diversity that was so much a part of the "new thinking" that revitalized the study of the Counter-Reformation during the 1970s and early 1980s.

Adriano Prosperi (1994, 222–24) has responded to this last criticism by suggesting that the study of European societies regularly oscillates between stressing similarity and stressing difference and that we should see the "social disciplining" approach as representing a historiographical swing toward "similarity," just as the traditional view of the Counter-Reformation as a coercive and repressive Catholic response to the Protestant Reformation represented a historiographical emphasis on "difference." So long as we recognize that these are simply emphases, Prosperi suggests, and in some measure pay attention to both differences and similarities, this sort of oscillation serves the useful function of enabling us to discern patterns that over-reliance on one emphasis or the other would otherwise hide. And certainly, a number of scholars continue to find the social disciplining perspective useful in the study of Catholic Reform (see for example the various essays in Prodi [1994] and Zarri [1996]).

So what does this romp through historiographical trends in the study of the European Counter-Reformation have to do with Padre Martínez of Taos? A great deal, if only because the social disciplining perspective (whatever its ultimate fate in the study of the Counter-Reformation in European societies) has never been applied to the study of Hispano Catholicism and yet seems so obviously suited to such a task. In particular, the social disciplining perspective allows us to see Padre Martínez for what, I believe, he was: an agent of Catholic Reform (1) who sought to effect that same merger of interiorized religiosity and exterior discipline that had been the goal of Counter-Reformation leaders in Europe two centuries earlier; (2) who used the same tools that these earlier leaders had used; and (3) who, just like them, had to do all this in connection with a population that had little or no experience of either interiorized religiosity or exterior discipline. The social disciplining perspective also allows us to develop a more nuanced understanding of Padre Martínez's relationship with the Penitentes, if only because this perspective permits us to see the Penitentes as having played a crucial role in facilitating the rise of the modern state in New Mexico . . . but here I am getting too far ahead of my story. First things first: rethinking just what Antonio José Martínez was about.

⁓ Padre Martínez's Pastoral Vision

At one level, the suggestion that Padre Martínez was associated with "modernization" is hardly novel. On the contrary, as mentioned earlier, Martínez's supporters have routinely pointed to the schools he founded at Taos, to his publishing activities, and to his active involvement in politics both before and after the American annexation as evidence that he was very much a modern and progressive leader and not at all the representative of the "old order" that Cather's account makes him out to be. Invariably, however, these same commentators explain Martínez's modernist concerns by suggesting that he was one of a long line of nationalist leaders scattered throughout Latin America who had been influenced by revolutionary Enlightenment-era ideologies and who, as a consequence, fought for the rights of the common people against the secular and religious elites who oppressed them. This is why it has become something of a convention in accounts of Martínez's life to compare him to Miguel Hidalgo and José María Morelos, both priests like Martínez and both important figures in the fight for Mexican independence in the period just before Martínez entered the seminary in Durango (see Francis 1956, 268; Bridgers 1997, 138; Lopez Pulido 2000, 46). Francis expresses what is still the dominant view among Martínez scholars when he suggests that "once the pastor of Taos is recognized as a Mexican nationalist and champion of the common people, both Spanish and Indian, his life and actions . . . show a remarkable consistency" (1956, 268).

There is no denying that this commonly encountered view of Martínez as a nationalist leader concerned with the plight of the poor and oppressed seems consistent with a number of mutually reinforcing historical facts. After all, Martínez *did* enter the seminary in Durango at a time when nationalist/revolutionary ideas were popular with Mexican intellectuals; he *was* enrolled in that seminary when Mexico gained its independence from Spain in 1821; and upon returning to New Mexico he *was* committed to progressive change and to relieving the poor of oppressive financial burdens. Finally, there is clear evidence that Martínez did admire Hidalgo, even going so far, in one of his sermons, as to compare Hidalgo to Jesus Christ (Steele 1997b, 54–75).

Even so, there is another and quite different way of making sense of Padre Martínez's commitment to programs and concerns that now strike us as modern and progressive, and the key to this new understanding of Martínez lies in something that is usually (and surprisingly) overlooked in most commentaries on his life: the good Padre's pastoral vision. Generally, I will argue that when Martínez returned to New Mexico from Durango, he brought with him the same pastoral vision that had guided reforming bishops in Europe two centuries earlier; and thus, if we want to find models that help us to understand Martínez's actions (and in particular, his commitment to progressive social change), we should look as much to Counter-Reformation bishops like Carlo Borromeo and Domenico Bollani as to nationalist leaders like Hidalgo and Morelos. Let me be clear: I am not suggesting that nationalist visions did not influence Martínez; on the contrary, they almost certainly did. What I am suggesting is that the pastoral vision that Martínez shared with Counter-Reformation prelates acted to reinforce many of the concerns derived from his nationalism *and* led him to undertake programs of action that would not likely have developed from his nationalism alone.

I recognize, of course, that all this runs counter to the usual story told about Catholicism in New Mexico. Bollani may not be widely known, but

Borromeo is still widely regarded as the "saintly, austere, well-organized archbishop of Milan [who is] the embodiment of the Tridentine reform bishop" (Bireley 1999, 60). And in the usual story, at least as popularized by authors like Cather, it is *Lamy* (not Martínez) who brings Tridentine Catholicism to New Mexico. Nevertheless, if we examine Martínez's early career without taking into account our foreknowledge of his eventual conflict with Lamy, then the similarities with those bishops like Borromeo and Bollani who worked to implement reform in the immediate aftermath of Trent are both obvious and plentiful.

For instance, although Carlo Borromeo sought to effect that interiorized renewal of the individual that had been the goal of all reformers since the late 1300s, what he rejected, as Paolo Prodi (1985) points out, were the methods of achieving this interior reform that had been popular before Trent. Thus, Borromeo rejected the attempts at engendering this interior reform by emotional appeals (often millenarian in their content) to large masses of people, and he rejected too the sort of individualized meditation on the life of Christ that had been popular with European intellectuals associated with the *devotio moderna* tradition. In Borromeo's view, interiorized reform was best achieved by systematic social disciplining, which included catechismal instruction at an early age, regular experience of the sacraments, constant exposure to Catholic doctrine as a result of public preaching by the clergy, and regular participation in the liturgy of the Church and in collective prayer. Like Bollani and other reforming bishops of the period, Borromeo also believed that the implementation of these social disciplining policies among the laity depended on reform of the clergy.

Now what about Martínez? What were *his* ultimate goals? In the very first sermon that he preached at Taos upon his return from the seminary at Durango (reproduced in Steele 1997b, 46–53), Martínez spent most of his time urging his audience to give thanks to God for the benefits he has bestowed on them, not the least of which is that he has raised up one of their own sons (i.e., Martínez himself) to the priesthood and given this minister to them "for their spiritual consolation." But toward the end of that sermon, he does say something about his pastoral vision, about the sorts of effects he wants to induce in those under his care:

> [God] has done what he has done so that you might have someone who can immolate and offer sacrifices of inestimable and even of infinite value [= celebrate Mass], someone to instruct you in God's

mysteries, laws and precepts, someone to be for you an accurate and thorough guide for the journey of your spirit. . . . Receive often with all fervor the sacrament of Penance and the Eucharist. These are those spiritual remedies which Christ our Life provided for our salvation and our inner consolation. (Steele 1997b, 53)

The emphasis here on instructing his parishioners in "God's mysteries, laws and precepts" and on encouraging them to receive the sacraments of Penance and the Eucharist—although impeccably Tridentine—is probably formulaic rhetoric of the sort that all young priests of the period would be predisposed to repeat. More significant, I think, are Martínez's references to "the journey of your spirit" and "our inner consolation." However brief these references are, they hint at that same concern with interiorized religiosity that was the hallmark of Catholic Reform.

In any event, if we look at what Martínez went on to do in the decades following this first sermon—and in particular if we look at what he did that was different and distinctive compared to what had previously been done by the clergy in northern New Mexico—then it certainly looks as if he was trying to induce the same interiorized reform of the individual desired by Borromeo and Bollani (and others) using the same methods.

Consider, for instance, the nature of the books Martínez published at Taos in the years immediately following his acquisition of a printing press in the early 1830s. In an unpublished biography of Martínez written in 1877 (see RITCH 8: RI 2211), Santiago Valdez[8] says that one of these books was a primer for those just beginning to read and that others dealt with Spanish orthography, arithmetic, rhetoric, and Christian oratory (202). Most of the books, in other words, were textbooks. But Valdez also says that Martínez printed a catechism, and the significance of this should not be overlooked.

Valdez identifies the title of the catechism published by Martínez as "El catecismo de la doctrina cristiana." As Angélico Chávez (1981, 49) notes, this suggests that Martínez's catechism was a version of the *Catecismo de la doctrina cristiana,* originally published by Jerónimo de Ripalda, a Jesuit, in 1591. Ripalda's catechism, in fact, was one of the most widely reprinted catechisms in the Spanish-speaking world. Juan Sánchez (1909) lists 155 different editions published between 1591 and 1836. Most of these editions were published in Spain or the Philippines, but a significant number were published in Mexico, and that is likely where Martínez obtained the copy that he used as the basis for the catechism he published.

As with catechisms generally, Ripalda's text (reprinted in J. Sánchez 1909, 1–46) consists mainly of questions to be asked by a tutor and answers to those questions to be memorized by a learner (identified as a "child"). The topics include the key articles of the Catholic faith; the Ten Commandments; the Commandments of the Church (attend mass on Sundays and holy days of obligation, confess at least once a year, receive communion during the Easter season, etc.); various prayers (the Apostle's Creed, the Pater Noster, the Ave Maria, the Salve Regina); the nature of each of the sacraments; the seven deadly sins; the works of mercy; and so on. Toward the end of the text, the Catechism also gives the Latin responses to be made by acolytes assisting a priest at Mass. Generally, the purpose of the catechism is to introduce the child, using plain and simple language, to the beliefs and activities that were defined as central by the Council of Trent.

Occasionally a modern reader comes across something that might seem a bit odd, but even in these cases the intent is quite clearly to "pull" the young child toward things considered important within the logic of Tridentine Catholicism. For instance, Ripalda lists nine things that can be done to effect the forgiveness of venial sin; these include (in order) hearing Mass, receiving communion, hearing the word of God, receiving an episcopal blessing, saying the Pater Noster, making a general confession, taking holy water (*agua bendita*) or holy bread (*pan bendito*), and striking one's chest (J. Sánchez 1909, 33). Whatever else might be said about these activities, they would have had the effect of bringing the child into closer contact with (1) the liturgy of the Church (Mass, confession, communion); (2) approved prayers (the Pater Noster); and (3) representatives of the official church (priests, preachers, bishops). In the end, then, Ripalda's catechism was designed to achieve one of the goals sought by all agents of Catholic Reform: to ensure that from their earliest years, Catholics would have their character shaped by a sound knowledge of core Catholic beliefs and by participation in the sacramental life of the Church. In making a catechism one the very first books that he published, it seems evident that it was a goal also sought by Padre Martínez.

Valdez's biography also says that Martínez published a variety of booklets, some of which contained devotional prayers and some of which contained advice on how to lead a moral life (RITCH 8: RI 2211, p. 202). Although Valdez himself provides no further clues as to the precise content of these booklets, we can get a sense of what they likely were from a list of books provided by Martínez himself. On the back of the title page for a book on politics that he published in 1839 (reproduced in Wagner 1937, 8),

Martínez indicated that his press had published twenty "useful" books that were all available for purchase at his office in Taos. He then gave the titles for nine of these works:

Manualito para Parrocos
Exercicios devotos cotidianos
Ortografías Castellanas
Retoricas
Cuadernitos de Arismetica ó de enumerar
Cuadernitos de Villacastín par encomendar el alma á los enfermos
Ortografías chicas
Cuadernitos del tramite judicial
Cartillas de primera letras
Catones Cristianos

Most of these are identifiable as the textbooks mentioned in Valdez's *Biografía*. The first, second, and sixth works, however, are religious works (none of which, incidentally, are Ripalda's catechism).

The only one of these three religious books to have survived is the first, whose full title is *Manualito de Parrocos, para los auto[s] del ministerio más precisos, y auxiliar á los enfermos. Tomado del de El P. Juan Francisco López* (Concise manual for parish priests, for use in developing a more precise conduct of their ministry and in ministering to the sick. Derived from the work of Padre Juan Francisco López"; see gallery following p. 86). The Jesuit Miguel Venegas (1680–1764) had published the original version of this manual in Mexico in 1731, and later editions had been brought out by Juan Francisco López (1699–1764), another Jesuit. The version of the Venegas/López manual published by Martínez is short (52 pages) and presents the prayers and rituals associated with a range of activities that a local parish priest might be called upon to perform (Venegas 1839). The manual, for example, instructs priests on how to properly administer the sacraments of baptism, extreme unction, and marriage; how to give holy viaticum to the sick; and how to bury adults and infants. It also gives the prayers and procedures to be used in blessing a range of objects—including baptismal fonts, the holy water used in aspersions, new crosses and images, scapulars, and burial shrouds. Although the prayers in this manual are in Latin, the instructions relating to ritual are always in Spanish.

No copy of *Cuadernitos de Villacastín para encomendar el alma á los enfermos*—another of the books printed by Martínez—has survived, but it is not difficult to make an educated guess as to what it was. Tomás de Villacastín

(1570–1649) was a Jesuit whose most famous work was his *Manuall de consideraciones y ejercicios espirituales,* originally published around 1600. This manual, which was based on the spiritual exercises of Ignatius of Loyola, presented a structured program of mental prayer that invited readers to meditate on a variety of subjects. These were either general concepts or, more usually, events from the New Testament. Each subject was associated with a series of "points," which explored the various lessons that might be learned by meditating on that subject. The book also explained the best way to create the conditions that would allow meditation to be most useful (e.g., reading the points before going to sleep at night, getting up early in the morning, and finding a secluded spot for meditation). The goal of these exercises (quoting from an English version of this manual published in 1618) was to help people "increase and go forward in the spiritual life . . . [by establishing] an interior and mutual communication with Almighty God" (Villacastín 1618, 1). It was, in short, a manual concerned most of all with promoting the sort of interiorized religion sought by all agents of Catholic Reform.

Villacastín's original manual was more than five hundred pages in length, and that was almost certainly beyond the capacity of Padre Martínez's printing operation. On the other hand, Villacastín had a section on "iaculatorie praiers," which were short prayers (usually consisting of a single line) that might be used, he said, "for such as have not health to pray or meditate" (1618, 48–51). Also, several of Villacastín's meditations on general subjects (e.g., Death, the Particular Judgment, the Last Judgment, etc.) would have been especially suited to those who were dying or in poor health. Likely, then, Martínez's *Cuadernitos de Villacastín para encomendar el alma á los enfermos* was a short booklet that included Villacastín's "iaculatorie praiers," along with those meditations that were especially well suited for those in danger of death. This gains plausibility from the fact that a 60-page book containing selections of just this sort from Villacastín's manual had been published by an anonymous editor in Mexico City in 1797 (see Villacastín 1797) and so might have been available to Martínez. It seems likely, in other words, that Martínez was publishing a handbook of mental prayer that those on the brink of death could use to establish that interiorized communication with God that was a central goal of the Catholic Reform movement.

Of course, if Martínez's pastoral vision was indeed propelling him to promote the sort of interiorized religiosity favored by agents of Catholic Reform, it is unlikely that he would have limited his efforts here to the sick and the dying. On the contrary, he would have been concerned with promoting such an interiorized religiosity with the laity generally. And in fact, it seems likely that this was the goal of *Exercicios devotos cotidianos* (Daily devotional exercises), another of the books that he published. Although no copy of this book has survived, the title alone suggests that it too was a structured program of daily meditation designed to promote interior renewal, and it was probably based on other sections of Villacastín's *Manual* (if not more directly on Loyola's *Spiritual Exercises*).

To understand the significance of the four religious books that Martínez published after he had established his printing operation, imagine that we were studying the history of some Italian (or Spanish or French) diocese and learned that sometime in the early 1600s that diocese had been flooded with (1) catechisms designed to insure that children came to have an understanding of Tridentine Catholicism and came to participate in the sacramental life of the Church at an early age, (2) books of spiritual exercises aimed at adults and designed to produce an interiorized communication with God, and (3) manuals designed to help parish priests perform their pastoral duties properly—all authored by Jesuits. How would we interpret this? In this case, the interpretation seems clear. We would almost certainly take the proliferation of such books as clear and unequivocal evidence that Church leaders in this diocese were making use of a modern technology (printing) to accomplish what all agents of Catholic Reform were trying to accomplish: the interiorized renewal of individual Catholics through the social disciplining of both the clergy and the laity.

The fact that in the New Mexican case such books proliferated only in a much later period (the 1830s) and that a single man (Martínez) was the driving force behind this proliferation should not blind us to the fact that exactly this same conclusion can (and should) be drawn here as well. What I am suggesting, in short, is that the social disciplining associated with the European Counter-Reformation, with its simultaneous emphasis upon interiorized religiosity and the control of external behavior, came late to New Mexico and that it came in the person of Antonio José Martínez.

Preaching, like printing, was another technology privileged by the early leaders of the Counter-Reformation in their pursuit of social disciplining. Preaching was to be the means by which parish priests would shape the character of the adults under their care just as catechismal instruction was the means by which they would shape the character of children. In a decree published early in its sessions (in June 1546), the Council of Trent said that parish priests should preach on Sundays and on all solemn festivals in order to "feed the people committed to them with wholesome words in proportion to their own and their people's mental capacity, by teaching them those things that are necessary for all to know in order to be saved, and by impressing upon them with briefness and plainness of speech the vices they must avoid and the virtues they must cultivate" (Schroeder 1950, 26). Though the mendicant orders, especially their Observant branches, had long been committed to popular preaching, Trent's insistence that bishops and parish priests preach to the people under their care was new.

Still, although popular preaching became routine in many Catholic dioceses in the century or so following Trent, it was missing from the Catholic experience in New Mexico. Remember that although the primary concern of the Franciscan missionaries had been to proselytize their Indian charges, these missionaries had not learned the indigenous languages. The net result was that the Franciscans in New Mexico were unable to preach to Indian audiences and not much interested in preaching to Hispano audiences. Angelico Chávez 's review of the information relating to the secular priests who began to take charge of New Mexico parishes from the late 1700s onward suggests that they too—like the Franciscans they were replacing—were little interested in preaching (1981, 31). It was only with Padre Martínez that this pattern changed.

Martínez was not simply committed to preaching; he preached widely and was good at it. By the early 1830s, Martínez was preaching not just in Taos but in a number of outlying communities that had been entrusted to his care by diocesan authorities. Santiago Valdez reports that more than seven thousand people had been entrusted to his care and that they were regularly impressed with the force and clarity of his sermons. "Never," says Valdez, "had they heard any native of New Mexico speak in such a fashion" (cited in A. Chávez 1981, 31).

Martínez's strong commitment to preaching remained with him to the end of his pastoral career. For example, in his letter of resignation, which was published in the *Santa Fe Gazette* on May 24, 1856, Martínez says that two things had caused him to resign: his conflict with Archbishop Lamy over tithing (which I will discuss below), and his advanced age. His age (he was almost sixty-four), he said, was a problem because he could no longer perform his duties as they ought to be performed. The only concrete example he gives of this inability to perform his pastoral duties, however, is that he can no longer preach even a *short* sermon that might last a half hour or so.

A strong emphasis on record keeping was another part of the of the general process of social disciplining that occurred during the early Counter-Reformation. In its decree on matrimony adopted in November 1563 (Schroeder 1950, 183–90), the Council of Trent mandated that parish priests should maintain a register in which they recorded the circumstances (e.g., date, names of the parties involved, names of the witnesses, etc.) surrounding baptisms and marriages. The same decree makes it clear that the purpose of such record keeping was to make it easier for Church authorities to enforce the regulations relating to impediments to marriage (regulations that themselves received renewed emphasis in the same degree).

We have already seen (in Chapter 2) that the Franciscan missionaries in New Mexico kept records relating to the baptisms, marriages, and burials performed at their missions at least from the time of the reconquest in 1692 (if not earlier) and that the secular priests who replaced them maintained this tradition. In addition, both the Franciscans and the secular clergy kept records relating to the *diligencias matrimoniales,* the matrimonial investigations that established the presence or absence of impediments to marriage. In the case of record keeping, then, there can be no claim that Padre Martínez was an innovator in the way that we can make that claim in regard to his publishing activities and his preaching.

On the other hand, there are degrees of zealousness in regard to record keeping as in everything else, and Padre Martínez seems to have had a commitment to record keeping that stood out among his contemporaries. In 1838, for example, Martínez published a short account of his own life, written in the third person, which has been translated and reprinted by Romero (1928).[9] In referring to the visitations made by Vicar Fernández San Vicente in 1826, by Vicar Rascón in 1830, and by Bishop Zubiría in 1833, Martínez took note of the positive evaluation that each of these visitors had made about his records:

> [During these] visits the entries in all his [Martínez's] books were approved, and all his marriage records, sentences copied and the fulfilment of his ministry, *all comparing so favorably with his predecessors, and even with other parishes visited,* that in the certifying entries made in the parish books [by these visitors] it was specifically stated in very special terms that he was given thanks and urged to continue in the same tenor. (Romero 1928, 338; emphasis added)

Bishop Zubiría again commended Martínez on the state of his parish records during his second visit (1845), and he took special note that the entries made by another priest while Martínez had been away in Durango (from August 1840 to February 1841) did *not* meet with his approval (A. Chávez 1981, 74–75). Even Bishop Lamy, during a visit to Taos in August 1854, made a note in the parish books commending Martínez on his orderly entries (A. Chávez 1981, 74; 123). Given Martínez's strong commitment to neat and orderly record keeping, it hardly comes as a surprise to learn that he used his printing press to create the first standardized forms for prenuptial investigations (A. Chávez 1981, 50).

Seeing Padre Martínez as an agent of Catholic Reform, committed to the same emphases and policies pursued by the likes of Carlo Borromeo and Domenico Bollani, also explains his position on the one issue that more than any other would bring about his downfall: tithing. Santiago Valdez says that sometime in the late 1820s Martínez authored an exposition that strongly condemned compulsory tithing (the collection of tithes by the civil authorities). This exposition was received favorably by the New Mexico Assembly in Santa Fe, which forwarded it to the National Mexican Congress. In Valdez's account, it was the opposition by Martínez and other patriots throughout the Republic that eventually insured the passage of a law abrogating compulsory tithing in 1833. Although Valdez is unquestionably exaggerating the effect of Martínez's opposition (since there are solid reasons for believing that the law would have been passed even without Martínez's contribution[10]), there is no doubt that Martínez did oppose compulsory tithing early in his career. The question is *why*.

For modern commentators anxious to construct Martínez as a nationalist leader, his opposition to compulsory tithing is assumed to derive from his persona as a champion of the oppressed. However, Valdez, summarizing Martínez's own justification for his actions (see RITCH 8: RI 2211, pp. 153–54), gives a slightly different answer: because of the financial burdens placed on the laity by the clergy, people were often unable to pay the fees charged for different religious services. In particular, he says, many people had to bury their dead in the desert because they could not afford the burial fees charged by priests; priests often refused to baptize children unless the fees were paid; and many people had to live together in sin because they could not afford the fees charged for a proper marriage ceremony. Another biography of Martínez, this one written in 1903 by Pedro Sánchez (who had been a student of Martínez and who had married one of his nieces), points to these very same conditions in his own account of why Martínez was opposed to tithing (see P. Sánchez 1978 [1906], 40). Taking Valdez and Sánchez at face value, then, it would seem that for Martínez compulsory tithing was objectionable most of all because it prevented the poor from participating in the sacramental life of the Church.

Martínez's opposition to tithing, more than anything else, brought him into conflict with Archbishop Lamy. All commentators agree, for instance, that Lamy's conflict with the Hispano clergy in New Mexico, including Martínez, escalated with Lamy's publication of a pastoral letter in 1852. What varies from commentator to commentator, however, is *why* that letter provoked conflict. Lynn Bridgers (1997, 102–3) says that in this letter Lamy reduced the fees charged for particular ceremonies (weddings, baptism, burials, etc.) by two-thirds, and that this action (reducing fees) provoked outrage from a number of Hispano priests. In other words, in Bridgers' account *Lamy* is the hero anxious to relieve the poor of oppressive burdens placed on them by a venal (Hispano) clergy. In fact, although Lamy did reduce the fees that priests could charge for marriages, baptisms, and burials in his 1852 pastoral letter, what Bridgers fails to mention (but what is central to an understanding of Martínez's conflict with Lamy) is that in that same pastoral letter Lamy insisted on the prompt payment of tithes and then went on to insist that in the case of those who did not pay their tithes, "we will be forced, though with much heavy sadness, to deny them the Sacraments and consider them as not belonging to the Catholic Church" (cited in A. Chávez 1981, 104). This threat was reinforced in January 1854, when Lamy issued a Circular to his clergy saying that priests were to exclude from the sacraments all household heads who refused to pay tithes and to demand triple fees for baptism from members of such families (the text of Lamy's letter is reproduced in Aragón 1978, 79). Lamy's rigid insistence on collecting tithes was sufficiently strong that he went to civil court on at least one occasion to secure collection (Francis 1956, 277).

Angélico Chávez's (1981) close reading of the correspondence that Martínez sent to Lamy establishes that Martínez was more than willing to compromise in regard to many of the issues associated with tithing. Martínez conceded that parishioners in New Mexico were often niggardly in contributing to the support of the church and that they might reasonably be expected to contribute more, just as he conceded that it was entirely appropriate to *ask* for tithes. What Martínez objected to, however, was the suggestion that those who did not pay tithes should be cut off from the sacraments or charged triple fees. Indeed, in his letter of resignation, published in the *Santa Fe Gazette* on May 24, this is the only aspect of Lamy's various policies that Martínez criticizes. The complexity of Martínez's position was lost on Lamy, who simply saw him as impeding the collection of tithes. In the very first letter by Lamy in which he says anything negative about Martínez (written in March 1857 to John Baptist Purcell, Bishop of Cincinnati and Lamy's former superior) Lamy identifies Martínez as one of three priests whose "tactic now is to try to cut us off from the little means we get from the people, such as the small part of *diezmos y primicias* [tithes and first fruits] our people are accustomed to give" (cited in Francis 1956, 277).

The conflict between Martínez and Lamy over the exclusion from the sacraments of those who did not pay their tithe would grow, spill over into other areas, and eventually end with Martínez being excommunicated— but the details of that story have been well told by Chávez and Aragón. The only point I want to make here is that Martínez spoke out against compulsory tithing throughout the entire course of his priestly career, and that the reason for this opposition—both at the very beginning and at the very end of that career—derived less from the revolutionary rhetoric of oppression than from the fact that he was opposed to any policy that cut Catholics off from the sacramental life of the Church. Like all agents of Catholic Reform, in other words, Padre Martínez had a deep and impassioned commitment to promoting participation in the sacramental life of the Church; and he maintained that commitment even if it brought him into conflict with those he would rather not have been in conflict with.

As already mentioned, the reform-minded bishops who operated in the aftermath of Trent saw clerical reform as central to the program of social disciplining that they envisioned for the laity. Partly, this meant reform and retraining of the existing clergy by getting them to lead more moral lives and by assessing their competence. But ultimately, reform of the clergy meant creating a new type of priest, since "only a new generation of priests, who were more prepared than previously, would be able to carry out the new program of pastoral care in a way that was fully effective" (Montanari 1987, 128). Moreover, following the guidelines laid down at the Council of Trent, these early reformers saw the establishment of seminaries as the most effective way of creating this new class of priests.

Now, although the preparatory seminary established by Padre Martínez at Taos in 1833 was really only a stepping stone to the seminary in Durango, it was clearly intended to achieve the same end envisioned by Trent, namely, the creation of a new class of clergy who were more educated than had previously been the case. Furthermore, if we compare Martínez's school with some of the seminaries founded in the immediate aftermath of Trent, especially in dioceses that lacked extensive resources, then he does not come off that badly. For instance, writing in 1573, the papal nuncio at Naples (cited in Borromeo 1997, 70) described the seminary in the small diocese of Aversa as consisting of "a house near the cathedral" where "ten or eleven children [*putti*]" gather to received instruction from three teachers (one who taught grammar, one who taught singing, and one who taught "ceremony," i.e., liturgy). The students received their education free; they also lived and took meals with their own families. On balance, this southern Italian "seminary" sounds a lot like Padre Martínez's "preparatory seminary."

The precise number of students who started out in Martínez's preparatory seminary at Taos and went on to become priests is not entirely clear. Certainly it is a matter of record that Bishop Lamy ordained three of Martínez's students in 1854 (A. Chávez 1981, 122). The number of students ordained by Lamy's predecessor, Bishop Zubiría, however, is less certain. In his 1838 autobiographical account (Romero 1928), Martínez himself says that of the ten students who had so far attended his seminary, three had already been ordained and returned to New Mexico, five were at the seminary in Durango, and the remaining two were still studying at Taos. In his 1877 biography of Martínez, Santiago Valdez (RITCH 8: RI 2211, p. 291) gives the names of seventeen priests serving parishes in New Mexico, all of whom, he says, had been ordained between 1833 and 1845 and all of whom had been educated in Martínez's seminary. Angélico Chávez 's (1981, 43–44) careful consideration of these names, however, suggests that two of them were likely natives of Mexico and that another three were from well-to-do families in the Río Abajo who had likely been educated locally and not at Taos. Pedro Sánchez's 1903 biography (1978, 64) reports that Bishop Zubiría ordained sixteen of Martínez's students and that Bishop Lamy had ordained another four, for a total of twenty. Thomas Steele (1997b, 42) reports that twenty-two of Martínez's students were ordained but gives no indication as to how he arrived at this figure. On balance, then, it seems likely that something like twenty, plus or minus two, of the students who started out in Martínez's preparatory seminary went on to become priests.

Although twenty (or so) priests might at first sight seem a small number, it probably compares favorably with the output of many early Continental seminaries, at least if we take into account the size of the Hispano population in northern New Mexico and the fact that Martínez's seminary operated for less than thirty years. We also need to remember that what Martínez *did* is in the end less important than what he was *trying* to do, and there seems little doubt that he devoted much of his energy (and personal fortune) in aid of producing a more educated clergy for northern New Mexico—and this establishes yet another commonality between Martínez and the agents of Catholic reform operating in the immediate aftermath of Trent.

Of course, Martínez wanted to do more than just create a more educated clergy; he wanted simultaneously to create a "local" clergy, that is, a clergy recruited from among the Hispano population of New Mexico and who would return to New Mexico after ordination. In his 1838 autobiography, Martínez boasts that the three students already ordained had returned to New Mexico and were now serving in local parishes (Romero 1928, 342): Don Juan de Jesús Trujillo was administering the parish at Santa Cruz de la Cañada; Don Eulogio Valdes was administering the parish of Santo Tomás de Abiquiú; and Don Mariano Lucero was assisting Martínez at Taos and Picurís. Furthermore, it also seems implicit in his discussion of the students who were still studying either at Taos or Durango that he expected them to return to northern New Mexico as well.

Why was it important to Martínez to create a class of priests recruited from the local Hispano population? Cather's novel seems to suggest that Martínez's emphasis on a parish clergy recruited from the local Hispano population was a way of building up his own power base. In the very first paragraph of her chapter on Martínez, for example, she identifies Martínez as a dictator who has control over all the native priests (Cather 1999 [1927], 145). Yet, as Tony Mares (1988b, 42) points out, there is absolutely no documentary evidence to suggest that Martínez acted as a "dictator" in his relations with other priests. On the contrary, the available evidence suggests that his relations with most of his fellow clerics were amiable and that Martínez quite often offered help when it was needed, both to priests who had been his students and to those who had not. So the question remains: Why was Martínez so concerned with establishing a "local" clergy? Here again the question seems easily answered if we view Martínez's actions against the history of Catholic Reform in the aftermath of Trent.

In his review of the various methods by which Carlo Borromeo sought to "discipline" his diocese, Paolo Prodi (1985, 282–84) calls attention to one that has often been ignored in official accounts otherwise concerned with extolling Borromeo's virtues: Borromeo sought to create a "form of ecclesiastical discipline that was particular to Milan and to Lombardia." In doing this, Borromeo relied heavily on a mechanism that had been endorsed by the Council of Trent: the convening of diocesan synods and provincial councils. During his tenure as archbishop from 1565 to 1584, Borromeo in fact convened eleven diocesan synods and six provincial councils (Bireley 1999, 61). These synods and councils gave the clergy of the Lombardian church a privileged role in the process of ecclesiastical disciplining and thus allowed them to use their understanding of local conditions to formulate policies that stood the best chance of effecting that interiorized reform of the individual and that shaping of external behavior that had been mandated by Trent. Borromeo, of course, was not alone in championing the view that Trent had to be adapted to local conditions. On the contrary, this was an emphasis embraced by bishops throughout Europe; and as noted earlier, it was precisely this widespread emphasis on adapting Trent to local conditions that produced the great diversity that came to exist within the Counter-Reformation church.

Over time this early emphasis on adapting Tridentine reform to local conditions and the local diversity that resulted would be less tolerated by Roman authorities. By the nineteenth century, certainly, Roman authorities were actively trying to *eradicate* local diversity in the Catholic world by promoting what Taves (1986) and others have called "romanized Catholicism": a standard set of beliefs and devotional practices that were meant to be put in place throughout the Catholic world. We need to remember, however, that these nineteenth-century attempts to standardize Catholic piety only succeeded (to the extent that they did succeed) because most local Catholic populations throughout the world had already been subjected to a certain amount of social disciplining. In other words, the romanizers of the nineteenth century succeeded only because reformers like Borromeo, working in earlier centuries, had been successful in implementing and implanting ongoing policies of social disciplining that had bound individual Catholics to Tridentine Catholicism in both thought and deed. The New Mexico that Padre Martínez confronted, however, was an area of the Catholic world untouched by the social disciplining policies promoted by the early agents of Catholic Reform.

We saw in Chapter 2, remember—romanticized reconstructions of the Hispano past notwithstanding—that there is little evidence that Catholic piety had ever run deep among the Hispano population of northern New Mexico and much evidence that it did not. Thus, the available evidence suggests that there was no strong tradition of going to Mass or receiving the sacraments; no strong tradition of devotion to the sacred beings (Mary and Jesus) most favored by the Tridentine Church; no great awareness of Catholic doctrine; and little if any concern with the usual elements (such as apparitions, pilgrimage, and image cults) so central to the Catholic experience elsewhere. Furthermore, there was a general aversion to ecclesiastical discipline among the Hispano population.

The net result, then, is that Padre Martínez was faced with bringing Tridentine reform to a population that was every bit as "non-Tridentine" as the populations that Counter-Reformation bishops like Borromeo and Bollani had faced centuries earlier. Like they had, he recognized that in this situation the implementation of Tridentine reform rested on adapting such reform to local conditions. For Padre Martínez that required a local clergy who were intimately familiar with local conditions by virtue of having been born and raised in New Mexico.

Martínez's concern with adapting to local conditions is also evident, I might add, in at least one other area. In 1830 he was elected to be the Taos representative on the seven-member Territorial Council of New Mexico, which met in Santa Fe. Unfortunately, this Council had no independent power (it could only make recommendations to the governor); and in 1831 Martínez lamented the council's powerlessness in an exposition addressed to the governor. This document (which is discussed and reproduced in Weber 1975) was read before the Council in that same year, and they in turn voted to send it on to federal authorities in Mexico. One of the arguments that Martínez makes over and over again in his exposition is that the Council's powerlessness prevents it from promulgating laws and policies that are adapted to the particular circumstances that exist in New Mexico, especially as regards climate and local customs. Although his suggestion that local legislators in New Mexico be given more power apparently came to nothing, Martínez's exposition provides evidence that the issue of adapting legislation to local conditions was much on his mind just two years before proposing his "preparatory seminary" to Bishop Zubiría.

❧ In summary, then, every single one of the emphases found in the "social disciplining" policies promulgated by the agents of Catholic Reform in early modern Europe—notably, a concern for a more interiorized form of religion; a belief that religious character is best shaped though catechismal instruction directed at the young and public preaching directed at adults; a willingness to utilize new technologies like printing; a commitment to public preaching by parish priests; the creation of an educated and professionalized clergy; an emphasis on the regular reception of the sacraments; a mania for record keeping; a concern with adapting Trent to local conditions—are evident in the pastoral activities of Padre Martínez of Taos. It seems clear that Padre Martínez worked hard on a number of fronts to produce precisely that same sort of Catholic that post-Tridentine bishops like Bollani and Borromeo sought to produce, namely, a Catholic who was— to use Montanari's words again—"animated by a conscious faith which had been shaped by a catechism learned early in life, reinforced through the constant reception of the sacraments, and fortified by collective prayer and by active participation in the liturgy of the Church" (1987, 157).

There is final aspect of Padre Martínez's career that can be brought into sharper focus by seeing him as an agent of Catholic Reform concerned with "social disciplining," and it involves the padre's relationship with the Penitentes.

✣ The Padre and the Penitentes

As mentioned in Chapter 1, the first certain documentary reference to the Penitentes occurs in a letter written by Padre Martínez to Bishop Zubiría in February 1833, in which Martínez indicates that he has suppressed the group's public rituals. This one letter aside, however, local tradition in New Mexico has always suggested that Martínez was a strong *supporter* of the Penitentes. Lorin W. Brown (Córdova 1972, 17), writing originally in the 1930s, recalls how his grandmother often told him about how Penitentes from moradas all over northern New Mexico had come to Padre Martínez's funeral (in 1867) and about how the night was full of their comings and goings as group after group sang their hymns and wielded their *disciplinas* while the padre's body lay in state. Certainly we know from Martínez's obituary, published in 1867, that more than three hundred Brothers did indeed take part in his funeral procession (Weigle 1976a, 47–49). The fact that Martínez was strongly associated with the Penitentes in the popular imagination probably explains why William Gillet Ritch, in describing Penitente practices at Abiquiu and Tierra Amarilla in 1878, says in passing that "Padre Martínez in his time was superior of the Penitentes in New Mexico" (RITCH 6: RI 1866). Willa Cather was tapping into these same local traditions when she caused her fictional Martínez to give his approval to the bloody rites staged by the Penitentes and had him warn the mild-mannered Latour against trying to eradicate such deeply rooted practices.

Most Martínez scholars have sided with local tradition in their assessment of Martínez's relationship with the Penitentes. Angélico Chávez (1981, 36–37), for instance, argues that Martínez was promoting himself as a Penitente leader as early as the 1820s. Marta Weigle (1976a, 47–49)—implicitly adopting Chávez's "late transplant" theory—suggests that Martínez may have "shaped" the evolution of the Penitentes by providing them with some of the organizational trappings associated with the penitential *cofradías* operating at Seville and elsewhere. Aragón (1998, 35) simply asserts that Martínez was the "spiritual leader" of the Penitentes and, presumably because the assertion seems so obvious (to him), provides no justification. William Wroth (1991) argues that although Martínez may have opposed the Penitentes at first, he eventually reversed his position and came to promote the Penitentes as a way of maintaining Hispano traditions in the face of the American annexation. The presumed association between Martínez and the Penitentes is sufficiently strong that for Larry Frank (1992, 200) the fact that an early *santero* like José Rafael Aragón admired Martínez is in itself evidence that Aragón was a member of the Penitente Brotherhood.

Martínez's association with the Penitentes has generally been explained in one of two ways. For Willa Cather and for those who have accepted her characterization of Martínez, the padre's close association with the Penitentes is yet another sign of his backwardness, that is, of his commitment to savage rites that have no place in the modern Church. In Cather's story, the only reason that the progressive Latour does not act against the extravagances of the Brotherhood is that he is confident that younger Hispanos are not being attracted to it, thus ensuring that it will die out as their older and more superstitious parents and grandparents pass away (1999 [1927], 163).

Martínez's modern supporters, by contrast, have tended to see his support of the Penitentes as a purely tactical move aimed at strengthening his position as a popular leader. "By assuming the leadership of the [Penitentes]," says Angélico Chávez, "Padre Martínez was finding another way of extending and solidifying his personal influence over the entire countryside north of the Capitol" (1981, 37).

Seeing Padre Martínez as an agent of Catholic Reform, however, provides us with a third way of interpreting his support of the Penitentes and one that has not been considered by previous commentators. Remember what the analysis so far has suggested: Padre Martínez sought to bring Tridentine reform to the Hispano population of New Mexico at a time when this population was every bit as "non-Tridentine" (read: undisciplined) as the populations encountered centuries earlier by Counter-Reformation prelates like Bollani and Borromeo; and in doing this, he made use of the same methods of social disciplining that these early reformers had used.

Recall too (from Chapter 3) that one of the ways in which Counter-Reformation missionaries in Europe secured the emotional involvement of their "non-Tridentized" audiences was through the "theatricalization of blood," that is, by staging rituals that produced a copious display of blood that was eminently visible to onlookers. Part of the appeal of the Penitentes to Padre Martínez, I suggest, is that Penitente rituals quite naturally lent themselves to this same "theatricalization of blood" and so could likewise be used to secure the emotional involvement of onlookers in the religious activities of the Brotherhood.

Here it is important to emphasize that the Penitentes did go out of their way to insure that their rites produced copious amounts of blood that would be visible to onlookers, and indeed, more visible to onlookers than to the Brother whose blood it was. This is evident, for example, in one informant's account of an initiation ceremony involving two new members:

> The boys were told to bend at their waist forward and hold their breath. They felt the glass cutting into their loins. . . . The older boy happened to turn a little to the left and as he turned the younger boy saw the blood flowing, running freely from each loin. The younger boy, wondering if his back looked the same as the other boy's, almost fainted but held on. Each was handed a whip . . . and told to whip themselves right on the cuts on their back. . . . The whips had been wetted in water beforehand and each time the whip landed in its mark it became wetter and heavier with the blood it absorbed. (Rivera, cited in Steele and Rivera 1985, 181)

More than anything else, it was the laceration of a Brother of Blood's back prior to flagellation, a practice described in the earliest Penitente documents, that insured that the amount of blood produced—and visible to onlookers—would be far in excess of what might have been produced by flagellation alone. Indeed, magnifying the amount of blood produced during flagellation seems to have been the *purpose* of this prior laceration.

The end result is that Penitente flagellations were often as bloody and as dramatic as anything encountered in the missions staged centuries earlier in southern Italy or Spain by Counter-Reformation missionaries. Writing in 1874, for instance, a Jesuit priest working in southern Colorado described Penitente flagellation in this way: "Every time that a brother disciplines himself, the scars [given to him at his initiation] are opened with a small sharp stone. When the blood begins to flow, the discipline commences. . . . I assure you that when such a spectacle of fifty, sixty, or two hundred men disciplining themselves is seen for the first time, it is shocking" (Vollmar 1954, 178).

Sometimes, this emphasis on bloody display in Penitente ritual combined both the visual and the tactile. During the flagellations which took place in the dark during Las Tinieblas, for example, it was common for spectators to be spattered with blood shed by the flagellants; and this tactile involvement of onlookers appears to have been intentional, especially in the case of flagellants who were trying to attract the attention of particular females in the audience (Henderson 1937, 44; J. Hernandez 1963, 222).

But securing the emotional involvement of onlookers through the theatricalization of blood was not the only function served by flagellation during the early Counter-Reformation. On the contrary, reforming bishops like Carlo Borromeo and Domenico Bollani also saw the establishment of flagellant confraternities as a particularly effective way of inculcating a "disciplinary emphasis" in populations unused to discipline. And here again, I suggest, Padre Martínez saw things in the same way. Another way of putting this is to say that in the case of reformers like Borromeo and Bollani, their policy of encouraging flagellant confraternities is not taken to be puzzling when set alongside their commitment to preaching, catechismal instruction, clerical reform, the use of printed materials, record keeping, and so on. On the contrary, in the case of these early reformers, all these things—including their support for public flagellation—are easily seen as manifestations of a general emphasis on social disciplining that was an integral part of Tridentine reform. I see no reason not to adopt the same view in connection with Padre Martínez. In the end, then, I am suggesting that Martínez was predisposed to support the Penitentes in northern New Mexico for exactly the same reason that Borromeo and Bollani promoted penitential confraternities in Lombardia: such confraternities were a highly effective way of promoting "discipline" among Catholic populations unused to discipline.

But wait. What about the letter that Martínez wrote to Bishop Zubiría in February 1833 in which Martínez says that he has suppressed the Penitentes operating at Taos? How does that letter square with the argument I am developing, which suggests that Martínez saw in the Penitentes a way of "disciplining" his non-Tridentized flock? First, we need to remember that scholars writing about Martínez *prior* to the discovery of that letter (in the early 1990s) in the archives of the Cathedral at Durango had consistently read the historical record (including, for example, the fact that hundreds of Brothers had taken part in his funeral procession) as indicating that Martínez had been a strong *supporter* of the Penitentes from the 1820s onwards. In retrospect, of course, we can read such evidence as suggesting only that there a strong tie (of some sort) between Martínez and the Penitentes in the *last* few decades of his life.

So did Martínez start his career disapproving of the Penitentes and then change his mind? William Wroth (1991) takes the contents of the 1833 letter at face value and says "yes." He argues that Martínez did originally oppose the Penitentes, but later (around the time of the American annexation) he reversed his stand and chose to support them. By contrast, other investigators, writing after the discovery of that 1833 letter, have simply ignored it and have continued to write as if Martínez's support for the Penitentes did indeed date from an early period (see Aragón 1998; Larry Frank 1992, 200). For myself, that 1833 letter must be confronted; but that does not mean that it has to be accepted at face value.

Consider a question that Wroth does not ask: If, as Martínez himself says in his letter, the Penitentes had been operating at Taos since he took charge of the parish (which was the mid-1820s), why did the good padre permit their activities for the better part of a decade and then suddenly, just a few months before Zubiría's official visit in July, decide to suppress them? Why, in other words, if Martínez truly disapproved so heartily of the Penitentes, didn't he suppress their public activities earlier, especially given that the Penitentes at Taos were obviously willing to submit to his authority? (His own letter, remember, suggests they suspended their public activities when he ordered them to.) To me, the most parsimonious way to explain all this is to suggest that Martínez's very public suppression of the Penitentes in 1833 was a *response* to the news of Zubiría's impending visit.

Martínez may have confronted a local population every bit as non-Tridentized as the populations encountered by sixteenth-century reformers like Borromeo and Bollani, but the fact is that he lived in the early nineteenth century. This means that Martínez, quite unlike Borromeo and Bollani, had to operate within an official ecclesiastical climate that defined public flagellation as emotional excess and in poor taste. Thus, even though Martínez himself may have seen the value of promoting flagellant confraternities, and did in fact (I suggest) promote such confraternities at an early date, he had to present the appearance of disapproval to his ecclesiastical superiors, especially when they came visiting. This would explain why Martínez wrote to Zubiría expressing disapproval of the Penitentes (a group whose extreme behaviors would almost certainly have come to Zubiría's attention) a few months before that bishop's official visit *and* why everything else in the historical record suggests that Martínez supported the Penitentes as soon as he encountered them in the 1820s.

The larger story that I am telling about Hispano Catholicism and the Penitentes (and remember, it is just that, a story) does not end here. As already mentioned, scholars like Wolfgang Reinhard and Paolo Prodi have argued that the social disciplining policies promoted by the Counter-Reformation church had the unanticipated consequence of facilitating the growth of the modern bureaucratic state in Europe. Their arguments, linking social disciplining in the religious sphere to the rise of the modern state, provide us with another reason why Padre Martínez would have supported the Penitentes and—more generally and more importantly—with a new basis for understanding why the Penitentes flourished in nineteenth-century New Mexico. This part of the story will be will be told in the next chapter.

෴ Modern visitors to Taos who want to find traces of Antonio José Martínez can visit his grave in a local cemetery, now enclosed within Kit Carson Park, which lies a few blocks north of Taos Plaza. Most of the graves in this cemetery are well kept, and the gravestones themselves are intact. Certainly that is true of Kit Carson's own grave, and it is true as well of the graves of other local luminaries like Mabel Dodge Luhan. Indeed, when I last visited the cemetery in the spring of 2001, I saw only one vandalized gravestone—the one that belonged to Padre Martínez. Both the original vandalism and the failure to repair the damage done suggest that Martínez has still not been given his due in the public imagination.

SIX

The Penitentes and the Rise of the Modern in New Mexico

It is common in accounts of colonial New Mexico to suggest that New Mexico's isolation gave rise to a society that was "medieval" in many respects. Art historians, in particular, have fostered this belief in New Mexico's medievalism. Thus Robert Shalkop (1967, 29) describes *santero* art as "an extraordinary anachronism—a final unexpected flowering of medieval Christian imagery." William Wroth (1979, 276) says that "nurtured in the medieval atmosphere of remote New Mexican villages, the indigenous *santeros* ignored the provincial baroque style of their Franciscan predecessors and produced, quite naturally, a simple art form surprisingly close in style and intention to the religious images of Romanesque Spain." More recently, Thomas Steele (1998a, 24) repeats the same argument: "The twists and turns of the art history of Europe and New Spain made less and less sense in the New Mexican culture, which was steadily settling back into medieval styles and repeating the iconography of centuries past."

Taken in a strong sense, that is, as suggesting that *santero* art was shaped by longstanding iconographical traditions that had existed in the colony since its foundation and that in turn were an inheritance from medieval Spain, the characterization of *santero* art as medieval must be rejected. The fact is that we simply do not know what iconographical traditions prevailed in northern New Mexico between 1598 and 1750, if only because there were so few (if any) artisans around to carry on those traditions.

On the other hand, at least as regards two-dimensional art, it is true that the art of early *santeros* and the art of the European Middle Ages seem characterized by a number of common emphases, including a lack of concern with perspective, an emphasis on frontal or three-quarter views, a concern with outline and strongly contrasting colors, and so on. This means that characterizing *santero* art as "medieval" has a certain heuristic value even if such usage lacks historical foundation. Unfortunately, this emphasis on "medievalism" in art historical studies has often been carried over into studies of the Penitentes, where it is neither historically valid nor heuristically useful.

Alice Corbin Henderson, for example, told her readers that Penitente ritual "represent[s] a genuine Old-World survival" that derives from "the gorgeous processions of Seville, when Seville relives its medieval past" (1937, 9). Lorayne Horka-Follick (1969) quite unabashedly built the "Penitentes-as-medieval" emphasis into the title of her book: *Los Hermanos Penitentes: A Vestige of Medievalism in Southwestern United States.* William Wroth (1979, 281) tells us that "the Penitentes became, as it were, the final preservers of the medieval folk culture of Spanish New Mexico"; while Oakah Jones (1996, 149) characterizes Penitente ritual as "reminiscent of practices in Medieval Europe, especially in the neighborhood of Seville." Ray John de Aragón (1998, 41) asserts that the Penitentes "were primarily responsible for the preservation of the medieval customs and heritages of Spain in New Mexico." Nor does this emphasis on Penitente medievalism show any signs of dying out. Thus, in the Foreword that Thomas Steele (1998b, viii) provided for a reissue of Henderson's book, he suggests that that book is still worth reading because Henderson's Romanticist views made her "alert for and sensitive to the medieval characteristic[s] of the villages, the santos, the passion plays, the alabados, and the Brotherhood."

The historical flaw evident in seeing the Penitentes as medieval has already been noted several times in this book: the Golden Age of penitential *cofradías,* including those at Seville, was the early modern era (the sixteenth century in particular), not the Middle Ages. But the more important point, I think, is that this deeply entrenched historiographical tendency to think of the Penitentes as medieval has blinded us to a conclusion that is really far more defensible: the Penitentes were in many ways a *modern* organization. Indeed, what I want to demonstrate in this chapter is that the internal organization of Penitente moradas was characterized by several emphases that made them qualitatively *different* from the traditional *cofradías* of Spain and the Spanish Americas and qualitatively *similar* to the "rational" organizations usually associated with the rise of the early modern state.

❧ Comparisons with Traditional Cofradías

In many ways, of course, Penitente moradas were similar to traditional *cofradías.* Certainly many of the functions performed by the Penitentes (staging processions on holy days, providing for the burial of deceased members with appropriate pomp and ceremony, aiding the sick, and so on) were functions that had long been performed by *cofradías* in both Spain and Mexico. Similarly, it was common for traditional *cofradías,* as for the Penitentes, to help maintain order in the local community by having members scrutinize the behavior of other members and bring immorality and other inappropriate behaviors to the attention of *cofradía* officers. In the midst of these undeniable similarities, however, there were differences.

Robert Sprott (1984) is one of the very few previous commentators to have looked carefully at the ways in which the Penitentes were different from earlier *cofradías,* and he identifies two differences, in particular, as being significant. First, under Canon Law confraternities must be subject to the guidance of designated ecclesiastical authorities, and this was generally not true of the Penitentes. Second, the members of any given confraternity in most areas of the Catholic world comprised only a relatively small proportion of the local population. By contrast, in most Hispano villages almost all the adult males belonged to the Brotherhood, and most females functioned as auxiliaries in some way.

Unfortunately, while Sprott must be given credit for swimming against the tide of Penitente historiography (which generally stresses similarity rather than difference), his first point is a good example of the dangers that follow upon substituting the position of the official church for historical investigation. Whatever Canon Law may or may not have said, it was, in fact, common practice throughout the Catholic world, and certainly in Mexico, for confraternities to be led by lay officials who functioned with a fair degree of independence from ecclesiastical authorities. Furthermore, when Spanish authorities, acting under the impulse of the Bourbon Reforms, did mount a campaign in the late 1700s to reduce confraternal autonomy, the effect of this campaign, when it did not result in simple suppression, was to bring *cofradías* under the control of civil (not ecclesiastical) authorities (see Brading 1983; 1994, 131–49; Taylor 1996, 301–23). That the Penitentes functioned with a high degree of independence from ecclesiastical authorities, in other words, may not have been what the Church wanted or what Canon Law required, but it did not in itself make the Penitentes much different from most other *cofradías* in Spain and Mexico.

Sprott's second point, that the Penitentes were inclusive of the local community, stands up somewhat better (but only somewhat) under scrutiny. In making his argument, Sprott notes that while there may have been a relatively large number of *cofradías* operating in a city like Seville, and while each of these *cofradías* might have up to three hundred or so members, it would still have been the case that in a city as large as Seville *cofradía* members would only have constituted a small proportion of the overall population (14–15). Penitente inclusiveness, Sprott concludes, made the Penitentes different from earlier *cofradías* and simultaneously allowed them to have an importance in local communities that these earlier *cofradías* did not have (15). Unfortunately, the simple fact that the Penitentes were inclusive of the local community does not make them as unique as Sprott's account suggests.

While it may be true that *cofradía* membership might have accounted for only a small percentage of the population in large cities like Seville, the situation in smaller communities could be quite different. In his study of Counter-Reformation Catalonia, for example, Henry Kamen (1993, 165–70) found that in many villages, and even in some medium-sized cities, it was often the case that most of the local population belonged to a single confraternity. Similarly, William Taylor (1996, 303) reports that virtually all adults in most villages in colonial Mexico were members of the *cofradía* dedicated to the Holy Sacrament. In short, the fact that the Penitentes were so inclusive of the local community may have differentiated them from some, but hardly all, preexisting *cofradías*.

On the other hand, even though *cofradías* in Spain and Mexico might sometimes boast a technical membership that included a large proportion of the local population, it was relatively rare for these confraternities to acquire the social importance that Penitente moradas came to acquire in New Mexican villages. Obviously, while Penitente "inclusiveness" may have been a necessary condition for this importance, it was not sufficient. Something else was operative as well, and an understanding of that "something else" depends on a consideration of the other ways in which the Penitentes differed from traditional *cofradías*.

❧ Shedding Light on the Brothers of Light

In proposing his "late transplant" theory, Angélico Chávez (1954) made much of the similarities that existed between the Penitentes and the early Passion Week *cofradías* of Seville. The most striking of these similarities, he argued, was "the important division of the brethren into those of Light and those of Blood" (118). As evidence that this "important division" had in fact existed in the early penitential *cofradías* of Seville, Chávez cites José Ortiz Echagüe's *España Mística* (1950). Although this book consists for the most part of black and white photographs of various religious subjects that were taken in Spain during the early twentieth century, Ortiz Echagüe does provide an introductory essay in which he describes the Holy Week processions staged by early Sevillan *cofradías*. After describing the immense *pasos* (platforms) that *cofradía* members carried in procession, he says:

> Then came the penitentes, who were "of light" and "of blood."
> Those "of blood" went first. They were naked from the waist up, disciplined themselves with whips [*látigos de rodelas*] and wore a loose hood that covered their faces. The penitentes of light carried heavy candles. [Next came] the nazarenos wearing purple tunics tied at the waist with a rope, who went barefoot and carried heavy crosses. Their faces were hidden by the wigs they wore, which fell to their shoulders and enveloped them in front. Without a doubt, the disciplinantes and nazarenos—with their lashings, their vestments and their wigs—were the most outrageous elements [in the procession].

The fact that Ortiz Echagüe mentions *three* categories here (Brothers of light, Brothers of blood, and nazarenos), and not just the two that appear in Penitente processions, was a bit problematic for Chávez, and he handled the problem by saying that the "nazareno" and "Brothers of Blood" categories had been collapsed in the case of the Penitentes (1954, 118). Chávez relied too heavily and quite unnecessarily on this one source; for, in fact, we know from many other sources that penitential processions in early modern Spain quite often consisted of "Brothers of Blood" and "Brothers of Light" only. Christian (1981), for example, quotes from a report written in 1578 that describes a *cofradía* that existed at that time in the town of Carrascosa del Campo (Cuenca): "There is another brotherhood of the holy True Cross, in which there are more than five hundred brothers of candle and discipline, with a few women. On the night of Holy Thursday, a procession is held and the brothers go out, those of candles with their candles lit and those of discipline flagellating themselves and shedding much blood" (188–89). Accounts of penitential processions staged in the Spanish Americas indicate that here too such processions routinely included some *cofradía* members who flagellated themselves and others who carried torches (see, for example, Dunne 1944, 71; Wroth 1991, 21).

There seems little doubt, then, that at least in a purely visual sense, the structure of the processions staged by penitential *cofradías* at Seville and elsewhere in the late 1500s and early 1600s would have seemed similar to those staged by the Penitentes in New Mexico in the early 1800s. Though the earlier processions might have included more participants, in both cases observers would have seen two clearly demarcated groups: one consisting of flagellants, and the other consisting of *cofradía* members carrying torches or lanterns.

Nevertheless, while a visual and linguistic distinction between "Brothers of Blood" and "Brothers of Light" may have existed in the penitential *cofradías* that emerged at Seville and elsewhere during the sixteenth century, what Chávez and those sympathetic to this theory have always glossed over is that the relationship that existed between these two categories in these early *cofradías* was not at all what it would become in the case of the Penitentes. In his account of Passion Week celebrations in Jaén, López Pérez provides a succinct account of what these two categories "meant" in the fifteenth and sixteenth centuries:

> In times past . . . various types of penitentes existed. Generally though, they were divided into two groups: penitentes de sangre and penitentes de luz. The penitentes or hermanos de sangre were brothers who disciplined themselves along the processional route by whipping themselves with *ramales* [scourges made from strands of rope] such that they often ended up with serious wounds. . . . The penitentes or hermanos de luz were those who walked in procession with candles in order to light the way. Usually these were brothers who, on account of their age or health, were not able to undergo the rigors of discipline. Over time, and certainly by the eighteenth century, most penitentes took part [in these processions] as "hermanos de luz." (1984, 193)

José Bermejo y Carballo (1882, 22) says much the same thing, suggesting that the *hermanos de sangre* were those brothers who "struck themselves until they shed blood, or who engaged in other penitences" while the *hermanos de luz* "carried torches that illuminated the Sacred Images . . . and dispelled the darkness [surrounding] those who disciplined themselves." In short, a Brother of Blood in these older *cofradías* was simply a member who wanted to engage in discipline during the course of a procession; a Brother of Light was someone who wanted to participate in the procession without engaging in discipline and who—quite literally—provided "light" by carrying candles or torches.

Although flagellation is no longer a feature of Holy Week celebrations in Spain (save in one or two communities), the old distinction between Brothers of Blood and Brothers of Light survives in the distinction between *nazarenos* and *penitentes* (cf. Mitchell 1990, 40f). Nazarenos are members who walk alongside the ornate *pasos* that are carried in procession and that hold a statue or group of statues that depicts some passion event. These modern nazarenos wear long flowing gowns and stiff conical hoods with masks that hide their faces; the color of their robes and hoods varies from *cofradía* to *cofradía*. Sometimes nazarenos do carry long candles, but often they carry a staff or nothing at all. A penitente is simply a nazareno who decides in some particular year, often in response to having been granted some special favor (cf. Mitchell 1990, 40), to engage in penitential exercises. A penitente wears the same robe and hood as the nazarenos of his *cofradía* but removes the cardboard frame in his hood so that it falls across his back instead of standing upright. His penitential exercises consist for the most part of carrying wooden crosses made of planed lumber and/or walking barefoot. As with the older distinction between Brothers of Light and Brothers of Blood, then, penitentes and nazarenos are merely labels referring to two different ways of participating in a Holy Week procession, and individual members can move back and forth between these two categories at their own discretion.

In the case of the Penitentes (of New Mexico), by contrast, there is a hierarchical relationship between the "Brothers of Blood" category and the "Brothers of Light" category that has no counterpart in either the penitential *cofradías* that emerged in the early modern period or in the modern *cofradías* currently functioning in cities like Seville. Within the logic of Penitente practice in New Mexico, remember, a Brother of Blood was not simply a member who decided to engage in penitential practices during some particular year. On the contrary, a Brother of Blood was a relatively new member who had been marked with the seal of the Brotherhood and who was *required* to engage in a series of carefully supervised penitential practices during a probationary period that could last up to five years. Only after a novice had passed successfully through this probationary period did he become a Brother of Light. A Brother of Light might request to engage in discipline, but he was not required to discipline himself since he had already passed through his probationary period. More important, as a Brother of Light he was eligible to become one of the officials of the morada. The net effect, then, was that the Penitentes had a *graded system of membership categories,* with passage from one category to the next being dependent on the performance of closely supervised ritual activities and with the final category being associated with power and status within the organization.

In traditional *cofradías,* to be sure, those applying for membership were screened very carefully to insure that they possessed certain characteristics. Ulierte Ruiz's study of early Jesús Nazareno *cofradías* at Jaén and elsewhere, for example, suggests that potential applicants had to demonstrate that they had no Jewish or Moorish ancestors nor any ancestors who had been punished by the Inquisition; that they were the legitimate offspring of a legitimate marriage; that they were honest and lived a good life; and that they were "old Christian" (i.e., that their family had been Christian for more than four generations) (1991, 170). Similar criteria were used by the penitential *cofradías* at Seville (Webster 1998, 38–39). On the other hand, if applicants passed this initial screening process and paid the entrance fees, they were admitted as members and were entitled to all the privileges of membership, which included the right to speak and vote in the General Assembly and the right to be elected to positions within the organization (Ulierte Ruiz 1991, 170). Once admitted, in other words, there was no long probationary period during which members were supervised by senior members and no distinction between members who could hold high office and members who could not.

It happens, however, that the graded system of membership found among the Penitentes is not the only organizational feature that distinguished Penitente moradas from traditional *cofradías*.

❧ Penitente Moradas and Organizational Rationality

Cofradías in Spain and the Spanish Americas during the colonial period fell into three broad categories: (1) burial societies, whose members regularly paid fees in return for which the society would bury the individual with appropriate pomp and ceremony; (2) associations whose members gained special indulgences for saying various prayers; and (3) organizations that organized and sponsored a variety of liturgical functions (mainly processions and Masses) in honor of some particular image of Christ, Mary, or the saints. Whatever functions they performed, traditional *cofradías* tended to have the same tripartite administrative structure.[1]

First, each *cofradía* had a chief steward, who might be called a *mayordomo, hermano mayor,* or *prioste.* The chief steward was charged with managing the economic assets of the *cofradía* over the course of the year and organizing the various events that the *cofradía* sponsored. In some *cofradías,* chief stewards were elected at an annual meeting of the general membership; in others, they were appointed by the governing council (see below). In larger *cofradías,* the "chief steward" category might be expanded by electing two chief stewards or by providing the chief steward with lieutenants who could substitute for him on particular occasions. In the Padre

Jesús Nazareno *cofradías* studied by Ulierte Ruiz (1991, 167), for instance, the *prioste* was assisted by two *alcaldes,* one of whom was the preceding *prioste.*

Second, the chief steward aside, *cofradías* typically had a number of other officials who were each charged with performing a specialized set of tasks. Such officials commonly included a *celador* (supervisor), who collected dues and generally kept track of whether members met their obligations; a *secretario* or *escribano* (secretary), who kept minutes and other records; a *fiscal,* a quasi-legal officer charged with determining if the orders of the council were being carried out and/or if the obligations specified in the *cofradía*'s constitution were being met; a *tesorero* (treasurer), who maintained the financial records of the organization (although in many *cofradías* it seems that the treasurer's function was given over to the secretary or the *fiscal*); and a *muñidor,* who informed members of upcoming activities and who often walked at the head of the *cofradía*'s public processions ringing a bell. In addition, there were often a number of minor functionaries who attended to a variety of different tasks. During the processions mounted by penitential *cofradías* in Spain, for example, Brothers called *conserveros* provided food and water to the flagellants so that they could maintain their strength during the exercise; while other Brothers, called *confortadores,* were on hand to apply unguents and medicines to the wounds caused by the scourges (Mitchell 1990, 41; López Pérez 1984, 193). Similarly, the Constitution of the Brotherhood of Nuestro Amo Jesús El Nazareno at Cuencamé (Mexico) provided for the annual selection of officers who would act as bearers during processions, ring the church bells, sweep the church, and provide water from a barrel on those days when the Brothers engaged in their penitential exercises (AHAD 212: 664).

Finally, most *cofradías* had a governing council (variously called a *junta* or *mesa)* that held regular meetings *(cabildos)* throughout the year. At least in the case of larger *cofradías,* these councils consisted of the more important officials of the *cofradía* (usually the chief steward, the treasurer, the secretary, and the *fiscal*) along with a number of elected deputies. In colonial Peru, such governing councils might have up to twenty-four members (Meyers 1988, 11); whereas in colonial Mexico, councils with twelve deputies, presumably in imitation of the twelve apostles, were common (Lavrin 1988, 86). As a collectivity, the governing council was responsible for setting general policy and, in particular, was responsible for ensuring that the different officials—including the chief steward—met their obligations. This meant that such councils functioned as a collective constraint on the authority exercised by individual officials within the organization.

Now: what about *cofradías* in pre-Penitente New Mexico? How were they structured? Generally, the available evidence suggests that the *cofradías* that existed in New Mexico just before the documented emergence of the Penitentes conformed to the traditional pattern; that is, these *cofradías* exhibited the same tripartite administrative structure described above.

In the report of his 1776 visitation of northern New Mexico, Fray Francisco Antanasio Domínguez identifies and describes nine confraternities. Five of these were based in Santa Fe, two in Santa Cruz de la Cañada, and two in Albuquerque. One of these, the so-called Confraternity of the Poor Souls at Santa Fe, Domínguez says, was not really a confraternity at all since there were no members, just a majordomo who administered various devotional activities that had these Souls as their focus.[2] All of the rest, however, were legitimate confraternities (i.e., they had a formal list of members).

Domínguez himself makes mention of a majordomo or *hermano mayor* in seven of the eight confraternities, but refers to a governing board only in connection with the third order chapter at Santa Fe. Likely, however, this is because he assumed his readers would take the presence of both a majordomo and a governing board to be self-evident in the case of all the confraternities he was describing. We know, for example, that the Cofradía of Our Lady of Light at Santa Fe, which had been established in 1760 by Governor Marín del Valle and which Domínguez mentions, had a *hermano mayor* and a governing council consisting of the *hermano mayor*, two counselors, a secretary, an accountant (*contador*), a treasurer, three deputies (charged with organizing fiestas, attending to sick members, and attending to the suffrages for the souls of deceased members), two other deputies, and a servant of the congregation (*criado de la congregación*) who acted more or less as a sacristan (see *Congregación de Nuestra Señora de Luz*, 1766). Surviving archival records associated with the Cofradía of the Rosary at Santa Fe, another confraternity mentioned by Domínguez, suggest that it was administered by a majordomo and a council of four deputies (see A. Chávez 1948a).

On the other hand, Domínguez's description of the smaller confraternities he encountered does create the impression that it was common in New Mexico for the "majordomo" and "officials" categories to be collapsed, that is, for the majordomo to do everything. The fact that these two administrative categories were so often collapsed in New Mexico is likely why Adams and Chávez (1956), in the Glossary they provide as a supplement to the Domínguez report, chose to define a majordomo as "in church societies, the head of the governing board, who usually served as president, secretary and treasurer" (357).

So how does the tripartite administrative structure typical of traditional *cofradías* in Spain, Mexico, and pre-Penitente New Mexico compare with the administrative structure associated with the Penitente moradas? Table 1 lists the administrative offices that are described in several early Penitente constitutions. Looking over these offices, it seems evident that the Penitentes did borrow much from the traditional model. Thus, Penitente moradas had a *hermano mayor*, a *tesorero*, a *celador*, a *secretario* and a *mandatario* (comparable to the Spanish *muñidor*), and these officials performed functions that are obviously similar to those performed by their counterparts in traditional *cofradías*.

Still, the sheer *number* of officials found in Penitente moradas was generally larger than what was typical in most traditional *cofradías*. Thus, although some traditional *cofradías*, notably those sponsored by local elites (like the Cofradía of Our Lady of Light described above), might sometimes have a large number of officials, most—including most of those found in smaller communities and/or those not sponsored by local elites—did not. In part, the relatively large number of officials associated with Penitente moradas is due to the fact that Penitente constitutions created a number of highly specialized offices (e.g., the *maestro de novios*, the *rezador*, the *pitero*) that had no counterpart in earlier *cofradías*. Furthermore, the fact that only Brothers of Light could occupy any of the offices named in Penitente constitutions insured that these offices were associated with high status within the organization in a way that was not true for many of the specialized roles (the sacristans and *confortadores*, for instance) found in traditional *cofradías*. The net result, then, is that Penitente moradas, in contrast to most traditional *cofradías*, were characterized by a *relatively elaborate set of differentiated administrative offices, each of which is associated with precisely defined duties and relatively high status*.

Something else that makes the Penitentes different from most traditional *cofradías* is that the Penitentes laid greater stress on the need for all Brothers to obey the written rules of the morada and thus, by implication, on the need for members to obey the officials (notably the *hermano mayor*) responsible for enforcing those rules. Thus, in the confraternities established in early modern Europe, members were not asked to swear an oath

TABLE I Officials Mentioned in Some Early Penitente Constitutions and the Usual
Functions Associated with Each Office

Title	Usual Functions	1853 Cochiti Rules	1860 Cenicero (Colorado) Rules	1890 Mora Rules	1915–16 Cochiti Rules
Hemano mayor	Overall leader	x	x	x	x
Reconciliador	Assists and advises the *hermano mayor,* especially on occasions when members engage in their devotional exercises	—	—	x	—
Mendatario	Notifies members of meetings and times at which exercises are to be performed; sometimes collects dues	x	x	x	x
Colector	Collects delinquent dues and special assessments	—	—	x	—
Tesorero	Maintains account book; dispenses funds when authorized to so do by *hermano mayor*	x	—	x	x
Secretario	Maintains records; reads from rule book when requested	x	x	x	x
Celador, Zelador	Maintains order during the course of activities conducted inside the outside the morada	x	x	x	x
Enfermero	Visits the sick, makes their needs known to *hermano mayor*	x	x	x	x
Maestro de novios or de novicios	Supervises and instructs novices applying for admission into the morada	x	x	x	x
Hermano de caridad; Sangrador; Picador; Rallador	Inscribes the seal of the order on backs of new members; helps members with their disciplinary exercises	x	x	x	x
Coadjutor, Cuajutor	Attends to wounds incurred during discipline; washes the scourges	x	x	x	x
Hermano de morada	Keeps the furnishings of the morada in good order; prepares the morada for use by the *maestro do novicios*	—	—	x	—
Hermano do maderos	Makes sure that timber crosses are arranged for use and that *calvarios* are set up properly outside morada	—	—	x	—
Rezador; Resador	Reads prayers and rituals during ceremonies	x	x	—	x
Pitero	Plays flute during ceremonies	x	x	—	x

Sources: Steele and Rivera 1985, 77–125; Aranda 1974, 48–58; Weigle 1976a, 146–48.

of loyalty or obedience in order to avoid having members fall into mortal sin for breaking such oaths (see Weissman 1982, 97). Penitente constitutions, by contrast, were usually quite explicit in demanding the strictest obedience from their members. The earliest such constitution that we have, which dates to 1853, says, for instance: "Brothers, since our vow is humble and prudent, no dissension will be tolerated in this holy house of the morada. . . . All the Brothers will obey in whatever is asked of them according to the rulebook which is kept by the Elder Brother, noting that if we do not execute what we have promised to do, our efforts will be in vain" (Steele and Rivera 1985, 85). A somewhat later constitution, dated 1915–16, specifies that one of the questions to be asked of all novices should be: "Do you bind yourself to lose your life first rather than disclose the secret of the confraternity, and to do what you are commanded?" (Steele and Rivera 1985, 108). That the Penitentes required that members to take an oath of this sort was one of the things that made the organization especially objectionable to Church leaders like Archbishop Salpointe (cf. Weigle 1976a, 62).

This emphasis on obedience aside, the authority of Penitente officials, the *hermano mayor* in particular, was further enhanced by what is missing: there is no governing council of the sort that was commonplace in traditional *cofradías*. On the contrary, Penitente constitutions are quite clear in saying that ultimate authority resides in the hands of the *hermano mayor* and that he is responsible only to the written rules of the organization (see Steele and Rivera 1985, 78, 95). The absence of a governing council is significant because, as mentioned, in traditional *cofradías* this was the administrative unit to which all administrative officials (including the *hermano mayor*) were accountable and which thereby functioned as a check on the authority of individual officials.

In summary, then, by eliminating the general council, by making the *hermano mayor* (and the *hermano mayor* alone) ultimately responsible for enforcing the written rules of the morada, and by stressing strict obedience to the *hermano mayor* and other officers, Penitente constitutions created an organization characterized by a centralization of authority that was far in excess of what had been typical in earlier *cofradías*.

⚘ To anyone familiar with the "social disciplining" tradition discussed in Chapter 5, the sum total of all the things that made the Penitentes different from earlier *cofradías*—the division of members into graduated categories; the proliferation of specialized administrative offices, whose duties were specified by written rules, and which could only be filled by members who had passed through a period of spiritual and physical disciplining; a centralized authority structure; and an emphasis on obedience—will seem familiar. They are, quite simply, the cluster of emphases that social disciplining theorists have taken as indicating the "rise of the modern" in many of the Catholic organizations that emerged during the Counter-Reformation. The simplest way to demonstrate this is to (once again) dip into a body of scholarly literature that at first sight might seem unrelated to late colonial New Mexico but that in the end enables us to fashion a theoretical lens that permits us to see the Penitentes in a new light. That literature deals with the Jesuits.

❧ A Jesuit Interlude

The Jesuit order coalesced around the activities of Ignatius of Loyola and his associates in the late 1530s and was given official recognition in 1540 by Pope Paul III. In traditional accounts of the Counter-Reformation, the Jesuits, with their strong emphasis on obedience and their pervasive use of military imagery, were seen to embody the sort of repressive and reactionary emphases that were the hallmarks of the Counter-Reformation. Under this view, Paul III's establishment of the Jesuits in 1540 could be (and usually was) seen as deriving from the same impulse that led this same pope to reactivate the Roman Inquisition in 1542.

This older historiographical view of the Jesuits was captured perfectly in the entry for "Jesuits" in the first edition of the *Oxford Dictionary of the Christian Church,* which said that the order's purpose was "to support the Papacy against prevalent heresy" (Cross 1957, 722). The second edition of this same work said, somewhat more generously but still very much in the same vein, that the order's purpose was "to foster reform within the Church, especially in the face of the problems posed by the Reformation" (Livingstone 1977, 271). Seen in this way, as the pope's personal army in the battle against Protestantism, even the strong Jesuit commitment to education could be seen as a reactionary enterprise. Thus, talking of the Jesuit educational program, Henry Brinton could say that "by educating the princes in the old tradition, reform was held in check, and then, in places, the tide was turned back" (1968, 160). It happens, however, that the same historiographical revolution that has revised our thinking about the Counter-Reformation generally (see Chapter 5) has also forced a revision in scholarly thinking about the Jesuits.

As John O'Malley (1991; 1996) points out, it is misleading to see Loyola, and the early Jesuits generally, as being concerned with "reform of the

Church" at all. The Jesuits had little to say about the organizational reforms passed at the Council of Trent since most of these had to do with diocesan organization and so were of little relevance to the Jesuits, who existed outside the diocesan system. Furthermore, although the Jesuits were certainly active in the struggle against Protestantism, this was not their main concern. On the contrary, they directed most of their energies to educational and missionary activities in Italy, the Iberian peninsula, and various overseas locales like India, Japan, and Brazil. When the early Jesuits spoke of "reform" (as they undeniably did) what they were talking about mainly was that "change of heart effected in individuals through [Ignatius's] *Spiritual Exercises* and the other ministries in which the Jesuits were engaged" (O'Malley 1991, 182). In short, the Jesuits were less a reaction to Protestantism than a continuation within the Church of that same drive for interiorized religiosity that had been the driving force behind both the Protestant and Catholic Reformations.

Furthermore, and more importantly, given our concerns here, the early Jesuit order is now seen as being very much a "modern" organization by virtue of the strong emphasis on organizational rationality that they incorporated into their administrative structure. Indeed, for a social disciplining theorist like Wolfgang Reinhard (1989, 387), the Jesuit emphasis on organizational rationality is one of the best examples of "modern tendencies within the supposedly reactionary Counter-Reformation." Reinhard singles out the graded system of membership categories established within the Jesuit order, in particular, as indicative of this emphasis on organizational rationality. Thus, all entrants planning to become priests within the order spent two years in a novitiate at the (successful) completion of which they took vows of poverty, chastity, and obedience. This was followed by another five years or so of education (depending on the background of the individual), then a period during which they gained practical experience of one sort or another, and finally another four years or so of theological training during which they were ordained priests. Only at the end of all this were they allowed to take their final vows and become full-fledged members of the organization. For Reinhard, such an elaborate system of graduated membership categories, with passage from one category to another being dependent upon the successful completion of a carefully supervised program of study, denotes an emphasis on organizational rationality and thus modernity.

Another example of the organizational rationality of the Jesuits, as compared to earlier religious orders, is evident in the centralized nature of their authority structure. Ultimate authority within the Society was vested in a superior general, who was elected for life by a General Congregation and who was the only elected official in the organization. This superior general, in turn, was at the apex of a well-defined administrative pyramid in which provincials (i.e., the administrative heads of the different Jesuit provinces[3]) were responsible to the superior general, and in which rectors of local Jesuit communities were responsible to either a provincial or to the superior general. The centralization of authority evident in such a hierarchical system was further enhanced by two other organizational innovations.

First, the Jesuits demanded obedience far beyond what had been typical in earlier orders. As Loyola himself said, "We may allow ourselves to be surpassed by other religious orders in fasts, watchings, and other austerities . . . but [not] in the purity and perfection of obedience" (cited in Martin 1988, 30). Furthermore, while much of the extreme imagery used by the Jesuits in talking about obedience (e.g., the suggestion in the Jesuit Constitutions that obedience should be blind) may indeed be medieval in origin, says O'Malley, "there is no getting around the fact that the general teaching contained in [Jesuit letters] and in the [Jesuit] Constitutions reflected, sometimes in exaggerated form, the prevalent sixteenth-century worldview in which the universe was ordered from the top downward, in which the benefit of every doubt was enjoyed by persons in authority, and in which both religious and secular authority was invested with a sacral character" (1993, 353).

The second organizational innovation, which also contributed to the centralization of authority within the order, was the abolition of chapter meetings at the provincial and local level. Indeed, as O'Malley (1993, 52) notes, the abolition of chapter meetings is likely the organizational change that most of all differentiated the Jesuits from the mendicant orders.

Among the mendicant orders, notably the Dominicans and the three main Franciscan groups (the Conventuals, the Observants, and the Capuchins), two types of chapter (council) meeting had always been especially important.[4] The first was a General Chapter, which met every two to three years or so, and which functioned as the ultimate legislative body of the order. In addition to the General Chapter, chapters also met every two to three years in each of the order's different provinces. Although a provincial chapter lacked the authority to alter the order's constitution, it was otherwise the supreme authority within each province; and it could (and did) review the actions taken (or not taken) by the official in charge of the province and by the guardians in charge of each local convent. Although the precise rules for selecting the membership of these provincial chapters varied from order to order, it was usually the case that provincial councils included the guardians of local convents and/or deputies empowered by the friars in a local convent to represent their interests. Provincial chapters, then, were quasi-democratic bodies associated with a diffuse authority that enabled them to serve as a "check" on the authority of the important administrative officials of the order.

Although the Jesuit Constitutions did provide for a General Congregation that was in some ways similar to the General Chapter of the mendicant orders, this General Congregation met only infrequently (usually just upon the death of a superior general) rather than with the regularity of the General Chapters of the mendicant orders. More importantly, the Jesuits eliminated provincial chapters entirely, and in so doing eliminated an administrative structure that (in the mendicant orders) had functioned to constrain the authority of officials.

✺ In summary, then, it would appear that exactly the same organizational elements that made the Jesuits different from earlier religious orders—the division of members into grades, with passage from one grade to another being dependent upon closely supervised training; centralization of authority in the hands of a single leader; an especially strong emphasis on obedience; the elimination of councils that had served as a check on the authority of officials—are the very same organizational elements that made the Penitentes different from traditional *cofradías*. Indeed, the organizational similarities between the Jesuits and the Penitentes are so numerous and so striking that it is tempting to suggest that they are not entirely accidental.

After all, if the purely *visual* similarities between the Penitentes and the penitential *cofradías* of Seville (and those visual similarities alone) have been enough for decades now to give legitimacy to Angélico Chávez's suggestion that someone familiar with those Sevillan *cofradías* had a hand in shaping Penitente organization, then could we not say much the same thing here—that someone familiar with the Jesuits had a hand in shaping Penitente organization? We might even plausibly suggest that Padre Martínez himself was that person. Martínez entered the seminary in Durango in 1817, which was just around the time that the Bishop of Durango invited the Jesuits back into the country[5] to help in the management of the seminary (cf. Gallegos 1969, 254), and we know from the list of books that

Martínez eventually published (discussed in Chapter 3) that he had a high regard for Jesuit authors.

In the end, however, I will resist the temptation. Chávez and his school notwithstanding, similarities alone are never a good basis for inferring historical origins. So I am not going to posit a historical link between the Jesuits and the Penitentes; that is, I am not going to suggest that the Penitentes were modeled on the Jesuits. The theoretical significance of the organizational similarities between these two groups, however, is another matter.

In the case of the Jesuits, social disciplining theorists studying early modern Catholicism have taken the organizational elements listed above as indicative of an emerging and very "modern" organizational rationality—and I can see no reason not to draw precisely the same conclusion in the case of the Penitentes. In other words, the Penitentes may not exemplify all of the traits associated with modern rational-legal bureaucracies (cf. Weber 1958, 196–244), but in their organizational design, the Penitentes—like the Jesuits—were much closer to that rational-legal bureaucratic ideal than what had gone before.

Seeing the Penitentes as a modern organization may be a reversal of the usual historiographical view (which sees the Penitentes as medieval), but it is a view that is perfectly consistent with the evidence and also one that allows us to envision some likely consequences of Penitente membership that have previously been overlooked.

✼ Social Disciplining and Padre Martínez, Once Again

Although Padre Martínez may not have played as central a role in inventing the Penitentes as Bernardo Abeyta, he did (as mentioned in the last chapter) become one of the Brotherhood's most important supporters. I have already given one possible explanation for this: like Carlo Borromeo and other early leaders of the Counter-Reformation, Martínez saw in the practice of public flagellation an effective way of promoting the "disciplinary" emphasis that was central to the implementation of Tridentine reform. We are now in a position to advance a second reason for Martínez's support of the Penitentes. Simply this: the same organizational elements that made the Penitentes "modern" in comparison to traditional *cofradías*—their system of graded membership and the accompanying system of close supervision, and their emphasis on strict obedience to the *hermano mayor* and the written rules of the organization—would have functioned to produce in Penitente members two additional elements that were central to

Tridentine reform: (1) a deeply interiorized religiosity, and (2) an internalized willingness to accept behavioral scrutiny. I am suggesting, in other words, that there was a rough "fit" between the personality type on which Tridentine reform depended and the personality type engendered by Penitente membership, and that this was another reason why Padre Martínez would have been drawn to support the Penitentes.

At first glance, my suggestion here—that there was a fit between the Penitentes and the implementation of Tridentine reform—might seem problematic, given the well-publicized conflicts between the Penitentes and prelates like Zubiría and Lamy. The problem resolves itself, however, by keeping in mind what has already been mentioned in Chapter 5: the Hispano Catholics that Padre Martínez faced in New Mexico in the early nineteenth century were non-Tridentine in the same way that the populations faced by Counter-Reformation leaders like Carlo Borromeo in the late sixteenth century had been non-Tridentine. In both cases, reformers faced officially Catholic populations whose religiosity (to the extent it existed at all) was not strongly interiorized and whose members were not used to having their behavior scrutinized by external authorities. In the case of New Mexico, I suggest that Padre Martínez, by virtue of his intimate familiarity with the Hispano population there, recognized this; while outsiders like Zubiría and Lamy, being more used to populations that were *already* influenced by Tridentine reform, did not. As a result, Martínez saw in the Penitentes a mechanism that could be used to induce in Hispano (male) Catholics the interiorized religiosity and willingness to accept external scrutiny on which Tridentine reform depended, whereas Zubiría and Lamy saw only emotional excess and a secret society.

⚜ Setting Padre Martínez (gently) aside, the more general and somewhat surprising conclusion that emerges from the analysis developed so far is this: if Tridentine Catholicism established itself in New Mexico, this is in part due to the fact that the Penitentes shaped the psychology of Hispano (male) Catholics so as to engender in them the personality type on which Tridentine Catholicism depends. This means that the Penitentes, far from being an organization fueled by a religiosity inherited from a distant and fanciful medieval Spanish past, was instead an organization that worked to lay the foundations for a Tridentine religiosity that had not previously existed in New Mexico.

But there is more. As mentioned in Chapter 5, one of the more innovative arguments advanced by social disciplining theorists like Wolfgang

Reinhard and Paolo Prodi is that the policies and practices of the Counter-Reformation church facilitated the rise of the modern state by "conditioning" populations to discipline themselves and to accept being made the object of rule-governed bureaucratic administration. If we grant the hypothesis being advanced here—namely, that Penitente membership worked to produce a personality type characterized by a dual emphasis on internalized control and a willingness to accept external scrutiny—then the Prodi/Reinhard argument leads us to the somewhat counterintuitive conclusion that *Penitente membership would have functioned to facilitate the rise of the modern state in New Mexico.* I think this is exactly what happened, and the evidence that it happened is to be found in the tragedy that overtook the Hispano population following American annexation.

❧ Penitentes, Personality Formation, and the Prerequisites of Oppression

On August 15, 1846, General Stephen Watts Kearny entered the town of Las Vegas, New Mexico. Along with his staff and the local *alcalde,* he climbed onto the roof of a building and read a proclamation to the assembled crowd that marked a new phase in the New Mexican history. That proclamation began with these words:

> Mr. Alcalde, and the people of New Mexico: I have come amongst you by the orders of my government, to take possession of your country, and extend over it the laws of the United States. We consider it, and have done so for some time, a part of the territory of the United States. We come amongst you as friends—not as enemies; as protectors—not as conquerors. We come among you for your benefit—not for your injury. (Emory 1848, 27)

Kearny went on to release New Mexicans from their allegiance to Mexico and to make a series of reassuring promises. Thus, he promised the crowd that he would seize no foodstuff without just recompense; that the U.S. Army would protect them from the excursions of Apaches and Navahos; and that they would be secure in their religion ("At least one-third of my army are Catholics," he said, "and I respect a good Catholic as much as a good Protestant"). Finally, Kearny promised that local *alcaldes* could continue in office so long as they took an oath of allegiance to the new government. Four days later, Kearny was in Santa Fe and made a similar announcement.

Unfortunately, and despite the promises made by General Kearny, annexation was a disaster for the Hispano population; and the central element in this disaster was dispossession. Slowly but surely, Hispano farmers lost control of the land that had sustained the communal/cooperative pattern of agriculture described in Chapter 4. Sylvia Rodriguez (1987, 138) reports that by the early 1900s Hispano farmers had lost 80 percent of the land they had controlled at annexation—and the situation only got worse over the course of the twentieth century.

How was Hispano dispossession on such a scale possible? In answering this question, previous commentators have usually stressed a lack of fit between the system of establishing land claims that had traditionally existed in New Mexico, which emphasized "use of the land" over formal deeds and in which common areas and communal right were clearly recognized, and the American system that came into existence with annexation, which saw written documents to be central in establishing land claims and which was unused to dealing with communal rights. This lack of fit between the two systems, so the usual argument goes, made it relatively easy for unscrupulous Anglo businessmen and politicians to seize control of Hispano land. This was the argument, for example, that informed George Sánchez's account of Hispano dispossession in his *Forgotten People* (1996 [1940]):

> The opening of the area to American commerce opened the door to economic competition of a scale, and on a basis, far beyond the comprehension of the natives. Business relationships, legal technicalities, and sharp practices soon began to take their toll. . . . Ruthless politicians and merchants acquired their stock, their water rights, their land. The land grants became involved in legal battles. Was a grant genuine, was it tax free, was it correctly administered, was it registered? Who were the grantees, who the descendants, where the boundaries, and by whose authority? Defenseless before the onslaught of an intangible, yet superior force, the economic foundations of New Mexican life were undermined and began to crumble. As their economy deteriorated so did the people, for their way of life was based on, and identified with, the agrarian economy which they had built through many generations. (18–19)

Certainly, there is no denying that Hispanos fared poorly in the Anglo legal system. For example, two-thirds of all the Hispano land claims brought before the Court of Private Land Claims (which operated from 1891 to 1904) were rejected because they failed to meet the standards required by American law (Knowlton 1973, 116).

But a lack of proper documentation was not the only thing that contributed to Hispano land loss. As Sylvia Rodríguez (1987, 338) points out, dispossession also occurred because of forfeiture caused by a failure to pay back taxes, credit foreclosure, lawyers requiring land for fees, outright purchase, swindle, the complicated nature of the land claims process, and the loss of the lands that had been held in common.

It was this last element, the loss of common lands, that proved especially catastrophic to the Hispano community, given the centrality of these common lands to the communal/cooperative system of agriculture that prevailed within Hispano communities. To some extent, Hispanos were made complicit in this loss of their common lands. Thus, a 1876 New Mexico law established a procedure by which any one of the owners of jointly owned land could request its division or sale. Forced to defend their land claims in court, land grant heirs often had no choice but to make use of this law to pay their legal fees, either through the sale of common land or, more simply, by transferring title of such land to their lawyers in lieu of fees (Ebright 1994, 151–54). Even so, in the end it was the American court system itself that most of all insured that these common lands would pass out of the hands of land grant heirs. In 1897 the U.S. Supreme Court ruled that in the case of community land grants, ownership of common lands had rested with the Spanish government (and later the Mexican government) and not with the local settlers, with the result (the Court reasoned) that such ownership passed to the U.S. Government after annexation. From 1897 forward, then, this ruling guided every case involving community land grants that came before the Court of Private Land Claims, with the result that millions of acres of common land passed into the public domain and are now enclosed within the confines of the Santa Fe and Carson National Forests (Ebright 1989, 5).

Not surprisingly, perhaps, contemporary descriptions of these two National Forests in most tourist guides (see, for example, King 1999; Knight 1999) stress the scenic wonders to be found in the area, the abundant wildlife, and the availability of hiking trails and campgrounds. The impression given to the hordes of mainly Anglo tourists who descend on northern New Mexico, in other words, is that these are relatively unspoiled wilderness areas, when in fact they are lands that were an organic part of a communal/cooperative settlement pattern that long predated the coming of the Americans.[6]

Coincident with this assault by the Anglo judicial system on communal ownership of land was a similar assault on communal water rights, something else that had been central to the agricultural system in place in Hispano communities. In a relatively short period of time, mainly from 1890 to 1920, a series of judicial decisions (reviewed in G. E. Hall 2000) transformed water rights into property rights. Water rights, in other words, were detached from corporate bodies like community ditch associations, and were associated with individual property owners. These same judicial decisions established the view that any new allocations of water in particular areas would be regulated by the state of New Mexico (G. E. Hall 2000, 97), not by the older—and local—community associations that had previously performed this function.

The dispossession of Hispanos from their land—and, more generally, the broad Anglo assault upon their communal/collective system of agriculture—did not go unresisted. On the contrary, acts of resistance occurred throughout the territory. The most well known of these, and certainly the most well studied (see Larson 1975; Rosenbaum 1981; Schlesinger 1971), involved *las Gorras Blancas* (the White Caps), a Hispano vigilante group that operated in and around Las Vegas and other parts of San Miguel County. Nevertheless, what is most striking about Hispano resistance is how limited and sporadic it was, given the scale of the dispossession that was taking place. The night-riding activities of las Gorras Blancas, for example, were concentrated mainly in a two-year period (1889–90). Furthermore, even though las Gorras Blancas were relatively successful in removing barbwire fences that prevented access to common lands, and even though local juries generally did not convict when las Gorras Blancas members were brought to trial, the organization quickly died out in San Miguel County and did not inspire much imitation elsewhere in New Mexico.

Most commentators trying to explain the relative absence of Hispano resistance to dispossession have attributed it to "withdrawal." The basic idea here is that, faced with a system they did not understand and in which they were clearly at a disadvantage, most Hispanos simply gave up and decided to avoid Anglos and the Anglo legal system while simultaneously clinging even more tightly to their own traditions. Knowlton provides a succinct expression of this view: "Many Spanish-Americans, caught in the web of a . . . system they found impossible to understand, frequently surrendered their lands without a struggle when their rights were challenged. Bitter, resentful, and unable to defend themselves, they shrank from all Anglo contacts. To them the entire legal process seemed like a giant Anglo conspiracy to steal their property without possibility of escape or redress" (1973, 116). Rosenbaum (1981, 146) advances more or less the same argument, adding only that class position needs to be taken into account. Thus, he argues, while Hispano *ricos* (the wealthy) often responded to Anglo domination by adapting to Anglo culture, the great mass of *los pobres* (the poor) rejected adaptation in favor of clinging more tightly to Hispano traditions. Rosenbaum's point, in other words, is that withdrawal was a response associated with poor Hispanos.

Unfortunately, the problem with all versions of this "Hispano withdrawal" argument, quite apart from the fact that it feeds into essentialist stereotypes about Hispanic passivity, is that the argument borders on tautology. Thus, Hispanos did not actively resist dispossession because they gave up and withdrew from the Anglo world—where part of what "giving up and withdrawing from the Anglo world" means is that they did not actively resist their Anglo dispossessors.

Tobías Durán (1984) has offered a second explanation for the relative absence of Hispano resistance to dispossession—and it, I think, has to be taken more seriously. Durán suggests that the key lies in recognizing the legitimacy that most Hispanos accorded U.S. law. The system of law introduced into New Mexico by U.S. authorities may indeed have functioned to promote the interests of ruling elites (both Anglo and Hispano), but the Hispano population nevertheless perceived that system to be impartial and just. Durán argues that such a view of Anglo law as impartial and just was fostered by the fact that although "the law was used directly as an instrument of class power, [it was used] within limits, so as not to arouse deep dissatisfaction which could develop into sustained mass protest" (1984, 4). Using U.S. law "within limits," according to Durán, meant that Hispanos were occasionally allowed to win a legal battle or two and that, when abuses became particularly blatant, "reformers responded by investigating the fraud involved and by changing unimportant procedural aspects of the law, yet arguing for continued deification of the law" (1984, 6).

While I believe that Durán is correct in seeing the legitimacy that Hispanos accorded U.S. law as something that facilitated dispossession, and correct as well in saying that using this law within limits (broad though those "limits" were) helped to maintain the legitimacy of the U.S. legal system, his argument begs a very fundamental question: Why did the Hispano population come to accord legitimacy to the U.S. legal system in the first place? After all, quite apart from the fact that the U.S. legal system used standards for judging land claims that put Hispanos at a disadvantage (something that would have been obvious to the Hispano population from the very beginning of the American administration), it was more generally a system whose underlying philosophical foundations were quite different from those associated with the legal system that had prevailed previously in New Mexico.

The administration of justice in colonial New Mexico was mainly in the hands of the governor and a network of local *alcaldes*. In rendering their judicial decisions, as Charles Cutter (1994; 1995) has demonstrated, these officials—like similar officials throughout the Spanish Americas—paid attention to a mix of elements that included: (1) the formally enacted and written laws of the empire, (2) *doctrina* (the opinions of other jurists), (3) local custom, and (4) *equidad* (a community-defined sense of fairness). The important thing here is that elements (3) and (4) could be taken into account and used as the basis for judicial decisions independently of elements (1) and (2). As Cutter (1995, 35) points out, the fact that local jurists could and did render legal decisions that were shaped by local conditions and local practice, even if those decisions were technically inconsistent with written law, has probably been the most overlooked feature of the Spanish legal system during the colonial period. Moreover, there is also some evidence that jurists in New Mexico gave even more weight to "local custom" and "community-set standards of fairness" (in contrast to formal law) in rendering their decisions than jurists elsewhere in the Spanish Americas (Ebright 1994, 68). In New Mexico, then, the net result was a legal system that was qualitatively different from the system established after the American annexation.

In the Anglo-Saxon tradition, from which the U.S. system derives, jurists pay attention most of all to formal legal codes and judicial precedents. Custom can be taken into account, but it is given far less weight than in the Spanish system, especially as that system operated in New Mexico. More importantly, the popular ideology underlying the Anglo-Saxon tradition assumes that the impartial administration of the law by fair-minded jurists *will lead to* community harmony. In the Anglo-Saxon tradition, in other words, the maintenance of community harmony is not something that is supposed to be considered independently of the law, but rather is something seen to be a *natural consequence* of upholding the law and judicial precedent. While it would be foolish to say that U.S. jurists never took community harmony into account when rendering their decisions, this popular ideology would have certainly predisposed U.S. jurists to ignore community-defined standards of fairness if such standards were in conflict with written law or with judicial precedents.

The legitimacy that the Hispano population accorded this new and quite different legal system cannot be explained by pointing to some traditional and preexisting predisposition among Hispanos to submit to a central authority. On the contrary, we have already noted that eighteenth-century commentators like Agustín de Morfi (M. Simmons 1977) recurrently called attention to the "independence" fostered among Hispano settlers as a result of their predilection for dispersed settlement. Moreover, these same commentators recognized that this independence made settlers resistant to the demands of state authorities. Thus, for example, a government report written in 1788 recommended against trying to concentrate Santa Fe's population for purposes of defense, even though this would have been useful, on account of "the churlish nature of Santa Fe's inhabitants" and the "perfect freedom in which they have always lived" (cited in M. Simmons 1969, 18).

So the puzzle remains: Why did the bulk of the Hispano population in the late nineteenth century, which a century earlier had been characterized by an independence that predisposed them to *resist* the dictates of state authorities, come to accord legitimacy to a legal system whose underlying philosophy was quite unlike the one with which they were familiar; which used standards for assessing land ownership that worked against their land claims; and which from the very start took away their land on a massive scale? While we are undoubtedly a long way away from a full and complete answer to this question, I want to suggest that part of the explanation derives from the same thing that made the Penitentes so appealing to Tridentine reformers like Padre Martínez, namely, the sort of personality to which Penitente membership gave rise.

As already mentioned, the Penitentes differed from earlier *cofradías* by virtue of an especially strong emphasis on obedience, which meant obedience to those officials charged with enforcing the written rules of the morada, and by virtue of the fact that the Penitentes eliminated the Governing Boards that had functioned as a source of communal constraint on the authority of particular individuals. I have already suggested that these emphases functioned to produce a personality type that was consistent with the emphases on interiorized religiosity and external surveillance upon which Tridentine reform depended; I am now suggesting that Penitente membership functioned to produce a personality type that was far more at ease with the Anglo-Saxon legal tradition than would otherwise have been the case. In other words, although it was purely unintentional, Penitente membership functioned to produce "law-abiding citizens" in post-annexation New Mexico not only because (as earlier investigators have so often noted) local moradas exercised surveillance over the behavior of their members, but also because Penitente membership *engendered a strongly internalized compulsion to obey authority figures charged with enforcing written rules*—and in so doing, it helped to change the "churlish" and "independent" settlers of the previous century into citizens who quite willingly accorded legitimacy to a U.S. legal system even when that system so obviously worked against their interests.

But all this in turn leads to another (apparent) puzzle: If Penitente membership worked to produce a Hispano population who for the most part accorded legitimacy to a legal system that was depriving them of their land, why were the Penitentes so popular? Here we need to distinguish between manifest and latent functions, and consider the possibility that in particular historical circumstances these two types of function might work at cross-purposes.

There seems little doubt, for example, that annexation was associated with an increase in Penitente membership. Most commentators have explained this—correctly, I think—by suggesting that Hispanos clung to the Penitentes as something that was familiar and reassuring in the face of an Anglo culture that was both alien and threatening. This was the view, certainly, that Dorothy Woodward articulated toward the end of her well-known work on the Penitentes: "American civilization was aggressive; it had changed the government, dominated civil life, and dictated religious reform, but under the shield of the *cofradia* the Spanish-American could continue the familiar *mores* that he had for generations. He clung to his religious brotherhood for, in it, he preserved his integrity as a Spaniard, amidst the bewildering pressure of an alien culture" (1935, 309).

Decades later, E. Boyd said the same thing, arguing that Hispanos "took refuge in their confraternities [the Penitentes], which served as baffles against the foreigners, the new laws, the new language, and as it then seemed, new religious rulings and economic devices" (1974, 451). This view, that the Penitentes functioned to preserve Hispano culture and a distinctive Hispano identity in the face of Anglo threat, is still standard in most scholarly commentaries (see, for example, M. Gonzales 1999, 105–6).

Why the Penitentes were able to function as the basis for a reassuring Hispano identity is not hard to fathom. As Sylvia Rodríguez (1987), following Fredrik Barth, suggests, ethnic solidarity generally—and Hispano solidarity in particular—depends more on boundary maintenance, that is, on distinguishing between "us" and "them" using differences that exist at the moment, than on continuing traditions. While Rodríguez herself is primarily concerned with grassroots organizations that contributed to the maintenance of Hispano solidarity in the 1970s and 80s, her theoretical argument can easily be extended to the nineteenth century and to the Penitentes. Unlike, say, a more general "Catholicism," which Hispanos shared to some extent with Pueblo populations and with the new French clergy, the Penitentes were something that differentiated Hispanos from both of the other two ethnic groups (Anglos and Pueblo Indians) with whom they were competing for scarce resources. The Penitentes, in other words, were a distinctly *Hispano* phenomenon and thus obviously available for the sort of "boundary maintenance" that builds ethnic solidarity.

In short, then, the *manifest* function of Penitente membership was the development of a distinctively Hispano identity that was reassuring to ordinary Hispanos in the face of Anglo domination. This, I suggest, explains why the Penitentes became popular in the late nineteenth century. The *latent* function of Penitente membership, however, was the proliferation of a personality type that accorded legitimacy to the U.S. legal system and thereby made it that much easier for that system to transfer control of Hispano land to Anglo opportunists.

◆ In a well-known and often-cited article, John Bodine (1968) argues that during the twentieth century Hispanos found themselves caught in a "triethnic trap" (see also Rodríguez 1992, 112). Basically, what this means is that Hispano dispossession increasingly forced Hispanos to take on subordinate positions within a tourist-oriented economy that was dominated by Anglos and that depended on the glorification of Pueblo Indian culture. But this tourist-oriented glorification of Pueblo Indian culture, plus the protective role that the federal government has always exercised in regard to the Pueblo Indians, meant, in turn, that Pueblo Indians were able to hold onto their land, or even gain land, often at Hispano expense. In the end, then, Hispanos are "trapped," because dispossession forced them into an economic system that, while it may provide some limited economic benefits in the short term, has the long-term consequence of worsening their plight relative to the two other ethnic groups with whom they must compete for scarce resources. In the end, what I am suggesting is that a similar dynamic was operative in the nineteenth century.

However the Penitentes came into existence, they were available after annexation as a resource that could be and were used to foster a reassuring Hispano identity in the face of Anglo domination. But what has not previously been acknowledged, I argue, is that Penitente membership also shaped the personality of Hispano males in ways that in the end *facilitated* the very domination that was depriving them of their land. Life is not always fair, and neither are the sociological processes set in motion by particular concatenations of historical circumstances.

⁓ The main outlines of the argument I want to present are now complete, and I am tempted to end this book here. The problem is that there are still a few bits and pieces associated with the Penitentes that cry out for further explanation. For example, if Hispano Catholics were not particularly religious before 1800, as I have claimed, how do we explain the emotional intensity that so obviously characterized Penitente ritual and that fueled their bloody activities? Then there is the matter of Doña Sebastiana. How does she fit into the logic of Penitente ritual? And why is she called "Sebastiana" anyway? In answering these and other questions, I will be drawing on the one theoretical perspective that has always been at ease in explaining the joint association of intense emotion and religious rituals (especially the bloody variety), and in explaining, as well, juxtapositions of apparently unrelated elements. That tradition is *psychoanalysis,* and I will eventually be linking psychoanalysis to the Penitentes via the discussion of personality formation found earlier in this chapter. Still, be forewarned: anyone for whom a good cigar is *always* and under *all* circumstances only a good cigar might want to skip the next chapter and go directly to the Epilogue.

SEVEN

Stories That Connect to Guilt and Rage

Freud's most extensive analysis of religious belief and ritual appeared in *Totem and Taboo* (1913) and *Moses and Monotheism* (1939). Both works, unfortunately, have always been something of an embarrassment even to his most ardent admirers. Partly, this is because in each case he posited an "it-really-happened-in-history" scenario that strikes most readers as unlikely. In *Totem and Taboo*, Freud's unlikely scenario was that in prehistory a band of brothers had risen up and killed their powerful father, who had monopolized sexual access to their mothers and sisters; that this act of parricide had engendered a sense of guilt; and that, driven by this guilt, the brothers had sought to atone for their misdeed by establishing the incest taboo and by venerating the dead father under the guise of a totemic ancestor. In *Moses and Monotheism*, the unlikely scenario was that the historical Moses had been an Egyptian follower of the heretic pharaoh Akhenaten (and so not an Israelite at all); that following Akhenaten's death, this Egyptian Moses had established himself as leader of the Israelites and had led them out of Egypt in search of a land where he and they could practice the now-forbidden monotheistic religion of the dead king; and that for his troubles, Moses had been killed by his Israelite followers.

On the other hand, at least for psychoanalytically inclined investigators, it was never really Freud's account of historical events that has proved most unpalatable. After all, however unlikely and unsubstantiated Freud's historical claims about primal fathers and Egyptian Moseses might be, nothing he says is absolutely impossible. What psychoanalytic investigators did object to, however, was Freud's psychological Lamarckism: his claim that the memory of the primal parricide (and in the case of the Israelites, the memory of the Moses killing as well) was transmitted unconsciously from generation to generation and continued (and continues) to exert an influence on religious thinking.

Robert Paul (1996) has sought to rescue Freud's historical scenarios from the scholarly dustbin to which they have been relegated, even by psychoanalytic investigators, by suggesting that these scenarios are less a reconstruction of what actually happened in history than an unwitting reconstruction of an important narrative structure that underlies the core myths of the Judeo-Christian tradition. Along the way, Paul develops a theory that links the rituals associated with these core myths (mainly, the Passover ritual for Jews and the Mass for Catholics) to the rise of Western bureaucracies. For reasons that will become clear as this chapter proceeds, Paul's theory seems directly applicable to the rituals constructed by the Penitentes, that very real band of brothers who lacerated themselves in honor of their soon-to-be-dead Father Jesús.

⚜ Judeo-Christian Mythology and the Creation of the Conscientious Personality

Most of Paul's (1996) text is taken up with his close reading of two stories: the story of Moses, both as it is told in the biblical text and as it has been expanded and fleshed out in midrashic comment, and the story of Jesus as it appears in the Christian New Testament. The general theoretical argument that guides Paul's discussion, however, can be reduced to a few elegantly simple claims.

The first is that there is a "Core Narrative" (Paul's term) lying beneath several key Judeo-Christian myths and that this Core Narrative tells a three-part story about the evolution of human society. It suggests that human society in the first instance was a society in which power was held by a senior male, where one manifestation of this male's power was a monopoly on sexual access to all the females, and in which all actors were guided by self-interest rather than by a common commitment to agreed-upon rules. Movement into the second narrative stage occurs when the junior males unite and cooperate to overthrow the senior male. Having eliminated the senior male, however, these junior males face two problems. The first is logistical: if they allow one of their own to assume the senior male position, then nothing will have changed. The second is emotional: their feelings toward the father had always been ambivalent: he had been hated on account of his power and his sexual monopoly, but loved simply because he was their father. Once their hatred has been dissipated by the act of patricide, their love for the father comes to the fore. This produces guilt, and it is this guilt that propels the narrative into its third and final stage.

In the final stage of the Core Narrative, as reconstructed by Paul, the junior males seek to atone for their guilt by renouncing the very thing that had led them to parricide (namely, sexual desire for their mothers and sisters) and by venerating a father substitute. Although this father substitute can take many forms, it almost always includes submission to a set of impersonal rules associated with an omnipotent god who must be obeyed, just as the original father had had to be obeyed. On the other hand, since these new impersonal rules define murder to be a crime, justice demands that the murdering sons must themselves be killed. Within the logic of mythic thought, this is done by splitting the junior male category into two subcategories: the junior male who is primarily responsible for the rebellion and who is punished, and the junior male(s) who enforce the impersonal rules for the benefit of society.

Sometimes, Paul argues, one or more of the elements that define this Core Narrative will appear in a myth in a clear and explicit way. Both the Moses story and the Jesus story, for example, do indeed end with a set of new laws that are associated with a fatherly god and that must be obeyed by all members of the group (the Israelites, in the case of the Moses story; Jews and Gentiles together, in the case of the Jesus story). More usually, however—and this is probably Paul's most important contribution—the defining elements of the Core Narrative are only *implicit* in particular myths. What Paul means here is that the elements of the Core Narrative are implied when the manifest content of the myth interacts with the cultural presuppositions held by the individuals confronting that myth. For example: how does the Moses story conform to the events supposedly associated with "stage one" of the Core Narrative?

Following other investigators—and here Paul cites my own work on the Moses myth (Carroll 1987; 1988)—Paul sees Moses' rebellion against Pharaoh as an oedipal drama, that is, as a story about a son (in this case, an adoptive son) who rises up and replaces an authoritative father. But if Pharaoh is to be a father-figure (senior male) in "stage one" of the Core Narrative, then he should be associated with unregulated sexual access to females—and there is nothing in the biblical text that suggests this explicitly. What we must remember, says Paul, is that the Moses story was in the first instance addressed to the Israelites living in the ancient Middle East, and in that ancient world one of the things that made the pharaonic rulers of Egypt distinctive was that they routinely married their sisters and daughters. In other words, in the minds of those hearing the Moses story, there would have been a preexisting association between "pharaoh" and "unregulated marriage choices." This preexisting association would have meant that a story that casts a "pharaoh" in the role of a father being confronted by a rebellious son would conform to the Core Narrative; that is, it would be a story in which a junior male seeks to overthrow a senior male who is associated with unregulated sexual access to women.

Another example: how does the story of Jesus contain the "junior males kill the senior male" element that is a defining feature of the second stage of the Core Narrative? Here, Paul expands on Freud's own analysis of Christianity. Freud (1939) noted that it has been a central element in Christian thinking, at least after the theological innovations introduced by St. Paul, that Christ was the Son of God and that he had willingly died on the Cross in order to redeem human beings from the effects of Original Sin. And what was the "Original Sin"? Strictly speaking, at least in Pauline Christianity, it is supposed to have been Adam and Eve's disobedience of God's injunctions. But, Freud argued, the "eye-for-an-eye" mentality that prevailed in the ancient Palestinian world would have *implied* something quite different. Within the logic of this eye-for-an-eye mentality, the only "crime against a *father*" that would reasonably require the death of a *son* is parricide, that is, that the son had killed his father. For Freud himself, this was an only barely disguised expression of unconscious memory of the primal parricide.

Paul modifies Freud's argument by suggesting that the stories of Moses and Christ are myth (not history), and as such they must be read as a unified whole. Within the logic of mythic thought, "Moses" and "Jesus" are simply two personifications of the same junior male role (which is why, Paul suggests, the New Testament so often associates Jesus with Moses). More important, when the two stories are read as a unified whole, they do conform to the Core Narrative since they suggest that (1) a junior male (personified first as Moses) leads a rebellion that results in the death of an authoritative father (Pharaoh); and (2) this junior male (personified now as Jesus) must atone for this murder through his own death.

For Paul, the fanciful historical reconstruction that Freud developed in *Totem and Taboo* should be read as yet another manifestation of the Core Narrative—with one important difference: whereas most of the elements that define the Core Narrative are only implied in the stories of Moses and Jesus, these same elements are fairly explicit in Freud's version of the story.

Indeed, Freud's account of the primal horde—with its emphasis on a powerful father and his sexual monopoly, on the band of brothers who rise up and slay the father, and on the rules that these brothers subsequently establish—matches the Core Narrative almost on a point-by-point basis. For Paul, this is not accidental. Freud analyzed the stories of Moses and Jesus using the same psychoanalytic techniques that he had developed to ferret out the hidden structure lying beneath dreams and neuroses, and Freud's great skill in using these techniques led him to uncover an implicit narrative that does undeniably underlie these biblical accounts. Freud's only mistake, Paul argues, was in assuming that the underlying narrative he had uncovered reflected a historical reality.

Paul's final theoretical claim is that the Core Narrative found beneath the Moses/Jesus story has performed an important psychological function in Western culture. In developing his argument here, Paul first notes that Western bureaucratic organizations function most effectively when staffed by individuals who are driven by an inner compulsion to obey and enforce rules and regulations established by legitimate authority. But what gives rise to a personality type of this sort? Here Paul borrows from the literature on the obsessional personality and, in particular, from discussions of why this personality type is often (if not usually) associated with a compulsion to engage repeatedly in some private ritual or ceremony.

Most contemporary psychoanalytic investigators see the obsessional personality as an extreme response to the emotional ambivalence all children feel toward their parents. On one hand, children love their parents; on the other, they experience rage and hostility in response to the demands for subordination that their parents impose on them. In the usual case, these hostile impulses come to be repressed, and their continued presence in the unconscious generates guilt. Investing the rules that define a private ritual with the authoritativeness of the parent, and then obsessively carrying out these rituals, can function as a way of atoning for these unconscious hostile impulses and also as a way of relieving (but never eliminating) that guilt.

But there is a second defense mechanism that is usually also at work in these situations: the emotional affect associated with the unconscious feelings of rage and hostility directed against the parent can be split off from its content and attached to those same private rituals. This means that compulsively carrying out these rituals becomes a way of *discharging* that emotional affect, which means that performing the ritual allows for the disguised gratification of the original hostile impulses. The net result, in the case of the obsessional personality, is that the compulsion to engage in a particular private ritual is fueled both by the emotional intensity of the original hostile impulse and by the guilt that impulse engendered.

When the compulsiveness of the obsessional personality is too intense, or when this compulsiveness is attached to rules and ceremonies that serve no rational purpose, the result is a pathological condition. Paul's point, however, is that in certain bureaucratic settings an obsessional personality type can be useful if (1) the intensity of the compulsiveness involved is relatively mild, and (2) the compulsiveness itself is attached to the rules and regulations of the organization (rather than some purely idiosyncratic ceremony). In this case, such a personality type facilitates the smooth functioning of the organization and so is probably best described as "conscientious" rather than "obsessional."

Paul's claim, then, is that the stories of Moses and Jesus have been so central to Western civilization because the Core Narrative underlying each story does three things. First, the emphasis on oedipal rebellion in this narrative "connects" to the unconscious feelings of infantile rage and hostility directed at authoritative parents that are buried in the unconscious of those hearing the story. The Core Narrative, in other words, does not *create* these infantile feelings (such feelings, after all, are found to some extent in many, if not all cultures), but it does activate them and thus make them available for use in the same way (as Freud argued in his study of dreams) that the memory of a recent event can activate a repressed infantile desire in the mind of someone sleeping. Second, and simultaneously, the Core Narrative provides the mind with two defense mechanisms that can be used to manage these reawakened hostile impulses. First, these hostile impulses engender guilt, and the Core Narrative suggests that compulsive adherence to a set of impersonal rules associated with paternal authority is a way of relieving this guilt. And second, if the affect associated with these hostile impulses is split off and attached to this same set of rules, adherence to these rules becomes a way of gratifying those hostile impulses in a disguised manner.

The net result, Paul argues, is that the circulation of stories (read: myths) containing the Core Narrative within a society *creates* the conscientious personality needed by bureaucratic organizations, first by "connecting" to the ever-present feelings of rage and hostility against parental imagoes that lie buried in our unconscious, and then by "organizing" these feelings so that they fuel a compulsion to administer the impersonal rules of the organization.

To be effective, of course, the myths that embody the Core Narrative must be presented anew to each new generation. Partly this is done by disseminating these myths orally or in writing. Mainly, however, it is done through ritual. For Paul, the primary function of rituals (the Passover ritual in the case of Judaism; the Mass in the case of Catholicism) is to reenact the events that define the Core Narrative and so insure that the narrative has the opportunity to "connect" with feelings of oedipal rage and hostility in each new generation.

❦ A Revised Theory: Taking Degrees of Bureaucratization into Account

Although I find Paul's theoretical argument to be both elegant and compelling, there seems to be one glaring weakness: his remarks tying the "conscientious personality" to "Western bureaucracies" are relatively vague and seem to apply with equal force to any and all Western bureaucracies that have emerged at any point over the past two thousand years. Certainly, his discussion is devoid of any concern with degrees of bureaucratization in European societies over the past two thousand years. This apparent lack of concern with historical context becomes especially problematic when set against the scholarship that has now accumulated within the "social disciplining" tradition that was discussed in Chapter 5.

As has been mentioned, scholars working in the social disciplining tradition have argued that a necessary precondition for the rise of the modern state in Europe was the creation of publics who were predisposed to obey the rules and regulations emanating from centralized political authorities, not simply because they felt coerced to do so, but because they felt an inner compulsion to obey such rules and regulations. It is precisely because so many of the policies of the Counter-Reformation church had the effect of producing an "inner compulsion to obey" of this sort that social disciplining scholars were able to argue that the Counter-Reformation *facilitated* the rise of the modern European state. It seems obvious (to me) that scholars working in the social disciplining tradition are talking about the proliferation of a personality type in the early modern period that seems more or less congruent with Paul's "conscientious personality." In short, it would appear that Paul's "conscientious personality," while found to some extent in all Western societies over the past two thousand years, became far more common in the early modern period—and Paul's original theory takes no account of this. As a start toward revising that theory so that it does accord better with the historical data, it will be useful to confront an assumption implicit in Paul's argument that is almost certainly incorrect.

For Paul, the Catholic Mass recreates the Core Narrative because it is the ritual re-enactment of Christ's Passion and *is seen to be such* by those in attendance. The problem here is that while the story of Christ's Passion may be both widely known and central to the Catholic experience at this point in time, there is much evidence that this has not always been the case. Depictions of Passion events, including the crucifixion, for instance, are virtually absent from Christian art produced during the first few centuries of the Christian era (see Carroll 1986, 86–88). Similarly, studies of popular religion in medieval and early modern Europe routinely come to the conclusion that cults organized around saints and Madonnas were far more important to ordinary people than cults organized around Christ-figures. Indeed, when Counter-Reformation missionaries went into the European countryside after Trent, they regularly found that people were generally *ignorant* of core Christocentric doctrines and often did not know who "Christ" was, let alone the story of his Passion.

The first systematic (and only mildly effective) attempts to promote a greater public awareness of key Christocentric doctrines in Europe occurred during the fifteenth century with the revival of popular preaching by the Observant branches of the various mendicant orders; and even then, the Observant message was addressed mainly to urban audiences. It was really only in the sixteenth century, under the impact of the systematic campaign by Catholic authorities after Trent to promote a greater awareness of Christocentric doctrines and beliefs—including those relating to the Passion—that we can detect the beginnings of a sea change that introduced a strong Christocentric emphasis into popular Catholic religiosity. The already-mentioned proliferation of flagellant confraternities in the wake of Trent is one (but only one) manifestation of this sea change.

None of this is to deny that the Passion story has probably always been known and understood by intellectual elites within the Church; the claim is only that it was not until the sustained campaign on behalf of Christocentrism that began in the sixteenth century that this story came to be known and understood by a sizable proportion of the populations living in European societies. What all this means is that if the Passion story, as related in the Gospels and/or as recreated during the Mass, does indeed create the conscientious personality in the way that Paul suggests, then it is only in the modern period that this would have occurred to any significant extent among European populations.

In the end, then, Paul's argument and the argument put forward by scholars in the social disciplining tradition are consistent with one another and mutually reinforcing. Social disciplining theorists have suggested that many of the policies of the Counter-Reformation church had the effect of inducing in local populations that "interiorized compulsion to obey rules and regulations emanating from a central authority" that is a necessary prerequisite for the rise of the modern state. Paul's argument allows us to understand how the increasing Christocentrism of the Counter-Reformation church, and in particular its successful campaign to promote a wider awareness and understanding of the Passion myth, was one of those policies.[1]

❧ Penitente Passions

I suspect that the discussion to this point—with its talk of primal hordes, Moses killings, Core Narratives, and conscientious personalities—may lead many readers to feel I have (once again?) drifted far from the Penitentes and, more generally, from the matter of Hispano religiosity. In fact, we have ended up back where we need to be. Remember: it is one of the central claims of this book (articulated most of all in Chapter 2) that prior to 1800 the Hispano population of New Mexico was not an especially religious one in any sense of the word. There is no evidence that Hispanos went to Mass with any frequency, no evidence that they knew and understood core Christocentric doctrines, and much evidence that the forms of popular Catholicism that bound local populations in most other areas of the Catholic world to the Church—apparitions, pilgrimage, cults organized around miraculous images of Madonnas and saints—were absent from Hispano experience. In this context, the Penitentes represent the first documentable appearance of anything that even remotely resembles the sort of popular Catholicism found elsewhere.

I have argued (in previous chapters) that the proximate cause of Penitente emergence was the erosion of those patriarchal authority relations upon which the communal/cooperate system of agriculture that prevailed in Hispano communities in northern New Mexico had depended. But what still needs to be explained, as noted at the end of the last chapter, is the emotional intensity so obviously associated with Penitente practice. The explanation implicit in all earlier discussions—that this emotional intensity is simply the continuation of an ongoing and intense "Spanish" religiosity that was present in the colony since its inception—just won't work, since such an intense religiosity did not exist among the Hispano population in New Mexico. Nor does it seem reasonable to suggest that emotional intensity associated with Penitente rituals could derive solely from the utilitarian benefits of Penitente membership. What *can* explain that emotional intensity, however, is the revised version of Paul's argument that we have just developed. The key lies with the observation that Penitente ritual recreates the Core Narrative identified by Paul in a particularly effective manner.

Thus, just as stage one of the Core Narrative requires, the figure who lies at the center of Penitente ritual is a powerful father-figure (Padre Jesús) who is the object of hostile impulses, as evidenced by his being beaten, mutilated, and ultimately killed. Paul's argument permits us to see this emphasis for what, I suggest, it was: a way of connecting to the feelings of infantile rage toward an authoritative father that lie buried in the unconscious of all sons. Then too, Penitente ritual splits the "brother" category into precisely the same two subcategories that the logic of the Core Narrative requires, namely, those brothers who must be punished (the Brothers of Blood) and those brothers (the Brothers of Light) who are charged with administering an impersonal set of rules associated with the Father who was attacked (Padre Jesús). Finally, Penitente ritual provides Penitente members with the same two defense mechanisms that the Core Narrative always provides. First, precisely because the rules of the morada are associated with Padre Jesús, strict adherence to these rules provides Hispano sons with a way of atoning for the oedipal rage directed at their fathers and thus works to relieve them of the guilt that such rage generates. Second, the affect associated with this oedipal rage can be separated from its content and attached to these same rules, thus allowing strict adherence to these rules to function as the disguised gratification of that rage.

Furthermore, in at least one regard, Penitente ritual recreates the Core Narrative more effectively than the rituals analyzed by Paul. After all, for a limited period of time, all new members must subject themselves to the same sort of painful experiences experienced by their Padre Jesús. This is a fairly literal way of atoning for oedipal guilt that has no counterpart in, say, the Mass or the rituals associated with Passover.

In the end, then, my claim is that because Penitente ritual *connected to* and *organized* the oedipal rage and guilt of Hispano males in the manner just indicated, the logic of Penitente ritual itself could and did bring into existence an emotionally intense religiosity that had no counterpart in earlier Hispano experience. The intense emotionality associated with Penitente rituals, in other words, is not an inheritance stretching back to dim medieval mists; it is a *consequence* of the rituals, which is why that intensity, like the Penitentes themselves, is very much a creation of the early nineteenth century.

One advantage of the theoretical argument just developed is that it helps us to understand several other patterns associated with the Penitentes that would otherwise seem puzzling.

❧ Why Punish the Younger Brother?

Within Penitente logic, the Brothers of Blood, who are the only Brothers required to discipline themselves, are clearly a *junior* category. This is partly because they are chronologically the most recent members of their morada, and partly because they have less authority and prestige than the Brothers of Light. What should seem at least mildly problematic about this, at least for anyone familiar with the Catholic tradition, is that it is so easy to imagine the reverse pattern: a situation in which those who systematically disciplined themselves in imitation of Christ had a *higher* status than those who did not. After all, one of the defining characteristics of the mystics, both male and female, who proliferated during the late medieval and early modern periods, was their strong Christocentric emphasis. In particular, what such mystics sought was union with Christ; and quite commonly, they tried to achieve this union through bodily mortifications in imitation of Christ's Passion. This is why these mystics willingly embraced the stigmata, extreme fasting, flagellation, and so on.

But in the case of these late medieval/early modern mystics, such mortifications (which were not all that different from what the Brothers of Blood experienced) conveyed *high* status, that is, it was precisely the willingness of these mystics to mortify their flesh that set them apart from ordinary Catholics and made them objects of respect. This, in turn, is why these bodily mortifications were always given prominence in the hagiographical literature that grew up around individual mystics after their death. So again: why were the Brothers of Blood associated with relatively *low* status among the Penitentes?

A clue to what might be going on here lies with Paul's observation (1996, 107–10) that in most versions of the Core Narrative it is usually a *younger* brother who leads the rebellion against the father and who must therefore be punished. This is true in the case of the Moses story, since Moses is explicitly identified as the youngest of three siblings (his older siblings being Miriam and Aaron), and it is true as well in the story that Freud told in *Totem and Taboo*, since Freud suggested, for a variety of reasons, that it would likely have been the youngest brother in the band who would have first envisioned rebellion against the primal father. In any event, the logic of Penitente practice would seem to conform to the pattern that Paul identifies: among the Penitentes it is indeed the *younger* Brothers (the Brothers of Blood) who are punished. Paul himself never really explains *why* the logic of the Core Narrative requires that it be a "younger brother" who instigates rebellion against the father and so must be the one punished, but it is not difficult to fill that lacuna by once again going back to Freud's own work.

In analyzing fairy tales and myths, Freud suggested (see in particular Freud 1939, 7–16) that the different characters or groups that appear twice in these stories often reflect a child's perception of the same thing at different developmental stages. In hero myths, for example, the transition from the hero's "real" family (which is usually noble, kingly, or divine) to the hero's adoptive family (usually associated with relatively low status) reflects the young child's perception of his or her family at two different stages: an early stage, in which children greatly overvalue the authoritativeness of their parents, especially the father; and a later stage, in which they are more detached from their parents and more critical of their parent's abilities. What happens if we apply Freud's general argument here to the Core Narrative identified by Paul?

Remember that in the Core Narrative the "brother" category is split into two subcategories: the brother who is responsible for the imagined attack on the father and who must be punished, and the brother(s) charged with enforcing the impersonal rules of the father. There is already an implicit developmental sequence here, given that a son's oedipal rage (which leads to fantasied attacks on the father) emerges first in early childhood and then comes to be repressed in later childhood. The most straightforward way to represent this developmental sequence within the logic of the Core Narrative, then, would be to associate a *younger* brother with the imagined attack on the father and so with the associated punishment, and to charge *older* brothers with enforcing the father's rules. The transition from "younger brother" to "older brother," in other words, reflects only the developmental shift from the "younger child" who first experiences oedipal rage to the "older child" in whom this rage is repressed. This, I suggest, explains why the younger brother is identified as leading the rebellion against the father in the myths that Paul studied *and* why it is the younger brothers, not the older brothers, who were required to punish themselves in Penitente moradas.

This same argument also explains something that was at least mildly puzzling to Protestant commentators in the nineteenth century: why the Penitente Brother who played the Cristo during the mock crucifixion staged on Good Friday, a role that would otherwise seem to be prestigious, was invariably a Brother of Blood, not a Brother of Light (see Mills and Grove 1956, 36–38). Because the logic of the Core Narrative suggests that the *younger* brother be punished for the hostile attacks on the father, it is only fitting that a *younger* Brother (a Brother of Blood) re-experience in a precise and literal way the events that caused Padre Jesús to suffer during his crucifixion—and that is precisely what happens when a younger Brother is made to play the role of the Cristo.

✦ From Saint Sebastian to Doña Sebastiana

In July 1881 U.S. Army Lieutenant John Gregory Bourke visited the community of Las Trampas and wrote in his diary:

> The town was now in its decadence, but still "muy bonito" and boasted a church, which few Americans had ever seen. . . . In a room, to the right of the door [as you enter the church] was a hideous statue, dressed in black, with a pallid face and monkish cowl, which held in its hand a bow and arrow in position. "Es la Muerte" whispered my guide in awestruck tones. I recognized the fact that I had stumbled upon paraphernalia of some little band of Penitentes. (Bloom 1936, 272–73)

What Bourke is describing is a Doña Sebastiana image of the sort that is pulled along in the Death cart during Holy Week by one or more Penitentes. As we saw in Chapter 1, such images are a defining feature of Penitente moradas.

Most previous commentators have explained Doña Sebastiana using a purely art-historical approach, that is, by seeking out earlier images in the European tradition that the Penitentes might have used as a model in constructing their Doña Sebastiana. Stark (1971), for example, suggests that Doña Sebastiana was modeled on the "dejected" skeleton that often appeared at the base of an empty cross during the Holy Week processions staged in Mexico City. Somewhat more prosaically, Boyd (1974, 463) suggests that Doña Sebastiana was modeled on the image of Death that appears in the tarot deck. Another possibility, though as far I know it is not one previously mentioned by historians concerned with the Penitentes, is to be found in Bennassar's account of the female figure associated with Lenten practices in Spain: "Some of the representations of Lent were very expressive. Almost everywhere Lent was depicted as an old woman of card-board or paper whom some anthropologists have wrongly identified with Death. . . . [H]owever, there is no room for doubt: at Madrid, in the eigh-teenth and nineteenth centuries at least, the old woman was provided with seven thin legs that symbolised the seven weeks of Lent" (1979, 35). It is en-tirely possible, of course, that the Penitentes drew upon all of these images (as well as others) in constructing Doña Sebastiana.

Once again, however, purely art-historical explanations like the ones just reviewed, even if accepted at face value, do not really explain very much. Certainly, they do not explain why the Penitentes chose to focus on a figure like Doña Sebastiana rather than on any of the thousands of other images, secular or religious, that appear in the Catholic tradition. Just as importantly, because these purely art-historical explanations of Doña Se-bastiana are shaped by that same driving emphasis on "continuity" that is the hallmark of traditional Penitente historiography, they pay little or no attention to the details that make Doña Sebastiana different from earlier images associated with Death or with Lent. Why, for instance, is she called "Doña *Sebastiana*"?

Occasionally, commentators have noted that Doña Sebastiana's name and the fact that she usually holds a bow and arrow suggests some sort of association with St. Sebastian, the early Christian martyr. Wroth (1991, 150), for example, says that "since these figures often carry a bow and arrow, this name [Sebastiana] is apparently a reference to St. Sebastian, who was pierced by arrows." Stark (1971, 305) attributes it all to a confusion in iconog-raphy, that is, to the fact that "the naked Saint Sebastian, riddled with ar-rows, was confused with the naked skeleton holding a bow and arrow." Just what Stark means by "confusion" in this case is unclear. In any event, nei-ther Wroth nor Stark (nor anyone else) devote much attention to the Se-bastiana/Sebastian connection, and certainly do not explain how or why images depicting a *male* who is *pierced* by arrows would become a *female* who *shoots* arrows. On the other hand, the fact that the transformation from Sebastian to Sebastiana does seem to involve a double reversal ("male" becomes "female"; "pierced by arrows" becomes "shoots arrows") should ring a few bells with those readers familiar with the anthropologi-cal literature on myth.

During the 1960s, the study of myth was revolutionized by the struc-turalist studies of Claude Lévi-Strauss. One of Lévi-Strauss's most impor-tant findings was that there was an underlying logical structure to partic-ular myths, and that the logical structure of one particular myth could be related to the logical structure of other myths using a series of transformation rules. These transformation rules were comparable to the more familiar dreamwork processes identified by Freud (e.g., displacement, condensations, negation, etc.), so for a while, monographs comparing Lévi-Strauss and Freud became something of minor genre in anthropological theorizing. Over the intervening decades, the structural analysis of myth à-la-Lévi-Strauss has faded from fashion, and it seems now generally recognized that there was less value in the literally thousands of pages of myth analysis that Lévi-Strauss published than at first seemed to be the case. That Lévi-Strauss did uncover some rules governing mental transformations in mythic thought, however, has never been seriously challenged—and one of the most important of those rules involved a *double reversal*.

In his very first programmatic statement on myth, Lévi-Strauss suggested that this double reversal "is defined . . . by an inversion of *terms* and *relations,* under two conditions: (1) that one term be replaced by its opposite . . . [and] (2) that an inversion be made between the *function value* and the *term value* of two elements" (1963, 228; italics in original). His statement here is hardly a model of clear expression; and in any event, a review of sorts of double reversal that Lévi-Strauss actually uncovered in different myths (see Carroll 1977) suggests that the rule defined in this passage is really just an overly general formulation that subsumes several types of double reversal. One of these, however, reduces to something very simple: given a set of characters (in a myth), negate an inherent characteristic associated with one of the characters and reverse one of the functions (or more simply: one of the activities) associated with one of the characters. In fact, this is precisely the sort of transformation rule that seems operative in the Penitente case. In other words, if we start with "St. Sebastian" and then (1) negate an inherent characteristic (change "male" to "female"), and (2) reverse an associated activity (so that "being pierced by arrows" becomes "shooting an arrow that pierces"), the result is the Doña Sebastiana. Still, while this might explain the *how* of Saint Sebastian's transformation into Doña Sebastiana, it doesn't answer the *why*—and for that we must leave Lévi-Strauss and return to Freud.

For Freud, the transformations effected by displacement, condensation, negation, and so on, were processes of disguise: they functioned to transform images and ideas that had been repressed into images and ideas that could safely be allowed into the conscious mind without causing anxiety. Although Freud made this argument most forcefully in connection with his study of dreams, he detected these same processes of disguise in connection with jokes, neurotic behavior, myth, and religious ritual. If we operate on the hypothesis that the transformation of "Saint Sebastian" into "Doña Sebastiana" is also an attempt to disguise imagery associated with a repressed impulse or desire, then what might that impulse or desire be? Given that the base image is Saint Sebastian, the most likely possibility is homoeroticism.

According to hagiographical traditions that emerged in the fifth century A.D., the historical Saint Sebastian was a Roman soldier who had been a member of the emperor's Praetorian guard in the late third century. Secretly a Christian, Sebastian visited his imprisoned coreligionists and encouraged them to remain steadfast in their faith even if it meant death. Eventually denounced as a Christian himself, he refused to renounce his faith and was condemned to death. Taken to a field, he was pierced with arrows but recovered through miraculous means. Arrested once again, Sebastian was beaten to death and his body tossed into a sewer.

Although medieval images of St. Sebastian usually show him as a bearded older man in Roman garb, his iconography changed dramatically during the Renaissance. Increasingly, Sebastian came to be depicted as a beautiful youth who was naked except for a loincloth. In the usual case, he was standing upright, often against a tree or stake, with his hands tied behind his back and with a variety of arrows piercing his body.[2] Everything about these later images of Saint Sebastian—his beauty, the soft curves of his naked body, his contented expression, and his lack of evident pain (justified, presumably, by the tradition that he survived this first execution by miraculous means)—conveys homoerotic imagery. The fact that he is also a beautiful young boy in the process of being *pierced* by arrows loosed by other men reinforces this sexual imagery. I take it as evident that it would have been this later homoerotic Saint Sebastian, not the grizzled old Roman soldier, who is more likely to have been the Saint Sebastian familiar to Hispanos in New Mexico. I am suggesting, then, that the Penitentes' Doña Sebastiana is a transformation of this homoerotic Saint Sebastian and so can be regarded as a *disguised expression of homoerotic desire.*

What makes this interpretation all the more plausible is that Penitente ritual is pervaded by a great many elements that seem ideally suited to the gratification of homoerotic desire. These would include the strong emphasis on male solidarity, the seclusion of males in tightly confined quarters, and the exclusion of women from all important Penitente activities. Then there is the strong emphasis on male physicality and the male body.

Penitente members, after all, routinely stripped themselves naked to the waist in order to allow themselves to be scourged. Most moradas also had a bathing tub in which members washed away the blood occasioned by their penitential activity (Ahlborn 1986). Given the small size of the morada, such ablutions would have had to be taken, if not in sight of other males, at least with other males nearby. What needs to be explained, of course, is *why* Penitente ritual would be pervaded by so many elements that seem oriented toward the gratification of a diffuse homoeroticism.

Although Freud recognized that homosexual desire could be produced by a variety of conditions, including biological predisposition,[3] one of those conditions is something very familiar: the repressed feelings of rage and hostility directed against an authoritative father (or father-figure) found in the unconscious of almost all sons. Freud's (1922) argument, which is more or less the same argument advanced by Paul, is that the content of these repressed feelings is inverted (so that hatred becomes love) but that the intensity of these feelings remains unchanged. "Rage and hostility" directed against an authoritative father, then, become an "exaggerated love" of the father; and one manifestation of exaggerated love is a desire for the father as an erotic object. In Freud's account, this homoerotic desire for the father did not preclude heterosexual activity, and in fact only occasionally led to overt homosexual activity. Most often, this exaggerated love for the father produces in males an intense admiration for other males, a desire to be in the company of males, and—by extension—a strong commitment to work (with other males) for the benefit of the community as a whole. What Freud's argument suggests, then, in the case of the Penitentes, is that a diffuse homoeroticism can function as yet another defense mechanism against the unconscious feelings of oedipal rage and hostility that are activated by the Penitente emphasis on the intense suffering of their Padre Jesús.

Let me be clear: I am not suggesting that Penitente males were predisposed to overt forms of homosexual behavior involving genital penetration. This is not required by Freud's argument, and, in any event, there is a great deal of ethnographic evidence suggesting that a diffuse homoeroticism that is gratified by ritualized contact with unrelated males can coexist with overt heterosexuality. Indeed, Paul (1999) has argued that the coupling of overt male heterosexuality and the ritual gratification of a diffuse homoeroticism born of a son's erotic attachment to his father is in some ways a "default" option in human societies. Just as importantly, at least in the specific case of New Mexico, overt (male) homosexuality would have been prevented by any number of cultural factors. The most important of these would have been (1) the fact that phallic homosexuality was sinful in the eyes of the official church, and (2) the view, commonly found in Hispanic areas (see Trexler 1995, 38–63) and certainly found in New Mexico (Gutiérrez 1991, 208–15), that the sexually passive male (the one penetrated) in homosexual encounters was "feminized" and for that reason an object of ridicule.

But a puzzle remains: even granting that a diffuse (and nongenital) homoeroticism lies beneath so much of what the Penitentes did, why transform "St. Sebastian" into "Doña Sebastiana"? Wouldn't devotion to St. Sebastian himself be sufficient for the covert expression of latent homoerotic desire? The answer is likely "no." If the diffuse homoeroticism that pervades Penitente were combined with the explicit image of a beautiful and nearly naked young boy being pierced by arrows, I suggest, this homoeroticism would have become too explicit (read: too phallic) and would have run afoul of the cultural barriers mentioned above. Transforming Saint Sebastian into Doña Sebastiana is thus a compromise: it allows for a visual expression of the diffuse homoeroticism that pervades Penitente practice, but in a manner that does not generate the anxiety that would be provoked by the overtly phallic homoerotic imagery evident in most depictions of Saint Sebastian.

❧ The Protection Offered by Bloody Burial Shrouds

As mentioned in Chapter 1, one of the elements that the Penitentes added to the traditional Tenebrae service in constructing their version of Las Tinieblas was the practice of saying *sudarios,* or prayers for the dead, after the candles on the *tenebrario* had been extinguished. Interestingly, the word *sudario* is not used as denoting a prayer for the dead in any other part of the Spanish-speaking world, nor is there any evidence that it was ever used in this way in New Mexico before the emergence of the Penitentes.

Steele and Rivera (1985, 198–200) note that *sudario* (or, more precisely, its Greek equivalent, *soudarion*) is used four times in the New Testament, twice (Luke 19: 20; Acts 19:12) in the sense of "napkin" (a cloth used to wipe a person's face) and twice to refer to the cloth that was put on the face of a dead person (Lazarus in John 11:44, and Christ in John 20:7). By the Middle Ages, the term had acquired two additional (but complementary) meanings. First, in all areas of Europe, including Spain, it came to refer to the entire burial cloth in which Christ had been wrapped. Second, in its Latin version (*sudariolum* or *sudárium*) it referred to a cloth that was used to wipe away sweat. These two meanings converged in the case of the famous Shroud of Turin, the so-called Santo Sudario, which was supposed to be the burial shroud of Christ and which carried an image supposedly produced by contact with Christ's dead body.

So in light of this history, why would *sudario* come to denote a prayer for the dead in New Mexico? Steele and Rivera themselves say simply, "We suspect that the prayer fulfils, in relation to the departed soul, the function of comforting [which is the same function that] the shroud of cloth may be imagined to fulfil in relation to the dead body" (1985, 199). Such an explanation seems weak for at least two reasons. First, there is nothing in the preexisting associations surrounding *sudario* (as burial shroud) that suggests that it was seen as something that "comforted" the dead person. Second, given that suffrages for the dead are a routine part of Catholic ritual in all parts of the Catholic world, Steele's explanation fails to explain why *sudario* came to refer to a prayer for the dead only in New Mexico and—more precisely—*only* with the emergence of the Penitentes. Finally, Steele and Rivera's explanation glosses over the fact that *sudario* was used to refer specifically to the burial shroud of Christ, not to shrouds used to cover dead bodies generally. In New Mexico, the term used for the burial shroud wrapped around (ordinary) corpses was *mortaja* (Weigle 1976a, 177). What this suggests, I think, is that there was something about the association between *sudario* and Christ's burial shroud in particular that made it appropriate to use the term *sudario* to refer to a prayer for the dead within the logic of Penitente ritual—and we need to figure out what that something might have been.

As a start, it will be useful to note that although most discussions (including my own to this point) describe a *sudario* as a "prayer for the dead," this is not entirely correct. A *sudario* could be said for (1) the holy souls in Purgatory (in general); (2) for some specific named individual who was deceased, without regard to whether that person was in Purgatory; or (3) for a living person who was away from the community and possibly facing danger, for example, someone away at war (A. Henderson 1937, 44; Steele and Rivera 1985, 198–200). The common link between these categories is that they all involve people who were once members of the local community but who are now absent. Furthermore, there was prioritization evident in the *sudarios* recited during Las Tinieblas: *sudarios* were recited first of all for the benefit of men who were or are members of the morada, and only after this for relatives and friends of members and/or for anyone else (Lea 1953, 222).

In summary, a *sudario* is said for members of the community who are absent (either because of death or some other reason), and the primary concern seems to be with members of the morada who are absent. The implication thus seems to be that absent members of the morada are vulnerable (and so in need of protection) in a way that members present in the morada are not. But vulnerable to what? What dangers threaten absent members? At one level, the dangers being addressed seem obvious: the flames of Purgatory and the dangers that are part of a wartime situation. But since none of this would explain why prayers for the safety and comfort of these absent members would be called a *sudario*, we need to consider the possibility that the perceived danger proceeds from another source.

The suggestion that "danger" is indeed critical to understanding what a *sudario* is all about is reinforced by considering something else: the fact that each *sudario* is preceded by a general round of noisemaking. Here again, as already noted in Chapter 2, we are dealing with a Penitente innovation, since the traditional Tenebrae service only had a single round of noisemaking at the very end of the service. What would such noisemaking have connoted to Hispano Catholics? In another context, Thomas Steele (1993b) has pointed out that well into the late nineteenth century, it was common in New Mexico (as in many other cultures) to think of night as a time when evil and hostile forces, including those associated with demons and witches, were active and to believe that such forces could be warded off with loud noises of the sort produced by drums, bells, or guns. For instance, in an 1896 case that Steele (1993b) discusses in detail, a participant at a nighttime prayer vigil organized in honor of St. Joseph, unable to find a drum, loaded a bullet marked with a cross into his rifle and discharged it into the darkness, where it happened to hit and kill someone sitting on a fence nearby. Steele himself does not think to connect his remarks on noisemaking and unseen dangers to the Las Tinieblas ceremony, but the connection seems clear: the noisemaking at Las Tinieblas would have connoted a "warding off of danger" to the audience gathered in the morada simply because they routinely used making loud noises to ward off unseen dangers circulating in the darkness.

A clue to understanding what particular danger was being warded off by a *sudario* lies in remembering the literal (and preexisting) meaning of the term: a cloth soaked in the blood and sweat of the dead Christ. What the logic of the Las Tinieblas ceremony is suggesting, then, at least at the level of visual imagery and metaphor, is that by "covering" absent members of the morada (and by extension, absent members of the community) with a cloth soaked in the blood of the dead Christ, these members are protected from danger. But *what* danger? If we keep firmly in mind that we are dealing, not with the Tridentine Christ who appears in official Catholic pronouncements, but with the fatherly Padre Jesús of the Penitentes, then the psychoanalytic argument developed earlier provides an answer: it is the danger posed by the father's retaliation against sons who, fueled by oedipal rage, would depose him.

Remember: in the Core Narrative posited by Paul, the band of brothers only succeed in overcoming the father by uniting and acting as a cohesive whole. Since all brothers experience rage and hostility directed at the father and so come to fear retaliation from the father, the implication is that any brothers who are *not* part of this cohesive whole are most vulnerable to such retaliation. At one level, then, the Las Tinieblas ritual is recreating this part of the core narrative by suggesting that "absent" (read isolated) Brothers are more vulnerable, more likely to be in danger, than Brothers who are not absent. But mainly the Las Tinieblas ritual is recreating what is really the most important element in stage two of the Core Narrative: only by eliminating the father is the danger posed by the father's retaliation eliminated. This is why, I suggest, a word denoting what is—in effect—*evidence* of the father's death (namely, the blood-soaked burial shroud of Padre Jesús) is used to denote a prayer whose purpose is to protect absent Brothers from danger.

❧ Conclusion

I know all too well that professional historians often respond to psychoanalytic arguments by suggesting that such arguments are unprovable. This has always struck me as strange, given the ease with which these same historians embrace hypotheses of the Doña-Sebastiana-derives-from-tarot-card-images that are equally unprovable and—even worse, given their tolerance for arguments of the flagellant-confraternities-as-medieval variety —that are falsified by the historical evidence. Equally disturbing is the tendency of professional historians to ignore important patterns that do not seem explainable using conventional arguments. That there is some sort of link between Doña Sebastiana and St. Sebastian, for instance, has always seemed evident, and yet no previous commentator has explored the nature of that link in any detail, presumably because this particular iconographic element cannot be assimilated to any of the "cultural continuity" theories that see Doña Sebastiana as having been modeled on earlier European Death figures.

The great advantage and great appeal of psychoanalytic reasoning is that it so often makes comprehensible the juxtaposition of apparently unrelated elements—and doing just that has been one of my goals in this chapter. The result is an argument that allows us to understand why flagellation is associated with younger Brothers; why Doña Sebastiana is called that; why she holds a bow and arrow; and why prayers said for the benefit of the dead and other absent members of the morada are called *sudarios*. Still, I must close this chapter by emphasizing again that my primary goal here has been to explain something that has never been defined as problematic in earlier scholarship, namely, the emotionally intense compulsion to engage in religious ritual that so obviously fuels Penitente practice and that was absent in earlier generations of Hispano Catholics. What I have suggested, following Paul, is that this compulsion was a by-product of the particular imagery that pervaded Penitente ritual and that allowed Penitente ritual (like all versions of the Core Narrative) to connect to and organize the unconscious feelings of oedipal rage and oedipal guilt that lurk in the unconscious of all sons.

EPILOGUE

The Stories We Tell about Subaltern Groups

I started this book by suggesting that much of what has been written about New Mexico is storytelling and that certain stories have always been privileged over others. I now want to pursue the matter of "privileged stories" further and also to confront a related issue, one that I have until now avoided—that in matters relating to New Mexico, the storyteller is often as important as the story being told. A useful starting point here, if only because it is a work that is routinely cited in discussions of Southwestern historiography, is Edward Said's *Orientalism* (1994 [1978]).

Said was concerned with the "Orient," by which he meant mainly the Middle East; and he argued that Western discourse about the Orient had traditionally depicted Oriental culture as having a stable content that was simultaneously "different from" and "inferior to" Western culture. *Difference* was established most of all by focusing on those aspects of Middle Eastern culture that struck Westerners as exotic. *Inferiority,* by contrast, was established in variety of ways. Oriental culture, for example, was seen to be pervaded by timeless and unchanging traditions, and thus very unlike the "progressive" West; and Oriental populations were seen as being driven primarily by emotion rather than by (Western) rationality. But most commonly, Oriental inferiority was established through the use of an implicit sexual metaphor. What Said meant by this is that Western discourse about the Orient had long been pervaded by images that implicitly cast the West and Western actors in the role of an aggressive and assertive male, while simultaneously casting the Orient and Oriental actors in the role of an appealing but ultimately subordinate female.

Borrowing directly from Said's work, a number of scholars writing on Southwestern historiography (see in particular Babcock 1990, 1997; Hinsley 1990; Rodríguez 1994; Weigle 1994; Weigle and Babcock 1996) have suggested that Anglo discourse has long "orientalized" the Southwest, using the same distortions and metaphors found in Western discourse about the Orient. Sometimes this orientalization of the Southwest has been literal. During the late 1800s, for example, Charles Lummis described New Mexico as "a land of swart faces, of Oriental dress, and unspelled speech" (1952 [1895], 30), just as others writing in the same period (the late 1800s) compared Navaho males to "keen-eyed Bedouin" and Pueblo settlements to "Palestinian villages" (see the examples cited in Weigle and Babcock 1996, 6). Similar sentiments can be detected in a remark made by D. W. Griffith in 1912, suggesting that Isleta Pueblo was "the best setting he had ever seen for the enactment of Biblical . . . plays" (cited in Jojola 1998, 173). Nor has this literal orientalization gone out of fashion. One of the recurring themes in Angélico Chávez's *My Penitente Land* (originally published in 1974 and still very much in print) is that landscape similarities between ancient Palestine and New Mexico worked to ensure that Hispano spirituality bore a striking resemblance to the religion of Abraham and Moses.

Most often, however, Anglo orientalization of the Southwest has been implicit rather than explicit. Pueblo culture, for example, has been orientalized in Anglo discourse in the same way that Middle Eastern cultures were orientalized: through the use of images and emphases that depict Pueblo culture as simultaneously exotic, timeless, and—especially—feminine. For Barbara Babcock (1990; 1997), the Anglo feminization of Pueblo culture, in particular, explains why the study of Pueblo pottery (which is made by women) has generated more scholarly literature than any other aspect of Pueblo culture; why pottery has been the primary Pueblo trade item; why María Martinez of San Ildefonso Pueblo became the most well-known Pueblo artist; and why "olla maiden" images, that is, depictions of traditionally dressed Pueblo women who are either making or carrying an *olla* (water jug), have long been the master symbol of Pueblo culture in Anglo-American popular culture.

Recognizing that Anglo audiences *like* stories that depict Pueblo culture as implicitly feminine helps to explain some otherwise puzzling features of scholarly works about New Mexico that meet with success among Anglo audiences. Consider, for example, Ramón Gutiérrez's *When Jesus Came, the Corn Mothers Went Away* (1991). Taken at face value, the title of this very popular book is problematic. After all, "Corn Mothers" is clearly a reference to Pueblo religion, so the title suggests that the book is going to be about how a male-centered Christianity displaced a nurturant, female-centered indigenous religion. In fact, Gutiérrez has relatively little to say about Pueblo religion, and what he does say certainly does not suggest that Christianity displaced traditional religion in the pueblos.[1] On the contrary, the bulk of his book is concerned with the ways in which marriage, sexuality, and power shaped the relationship(s) of Hispano and Pueblo populations of colonial New Mexico, and with the internal organization of Hispano society itself. So why—whether at Gutiérrez's own instigation or at the instigation of one of his editors at Stanford University Press—did the "Corn Mothers" reference come to figure so prominently in the book's title?[2] The answer, I suggest, is that because Gutiérrez's book is saturated with stories of Hispano males copulating with Pueblo females (sometimes with their permission, most often without), it is a book that contributes to the feminization of Pueblo culture that has been a staple of Southwestern historiography for more than a century. Given this, the title quite neatly and concisely presages what is to come by setting up those correlated contrasts (Jesus:Corn-Mothers::male:female::European:Pueblo) upon which the (appealing) construction of Pueblo culture as feminine depends.

At the most general level, I grant, the lesson to be learned from all this boils down to the admittedly banal conclusion that Anglo audiences prefer stories about subaltern groups that implicitly suggest the superiority of Anglo culture. In the case of the Pueblos, this gives an edge to those scholarly stories—like the one told by Gutiérrez and others over the past century and a half—that feminize an exotic Pueblo Other. Similarly, in the case of Hispanic Catholicism in the United States generally, I suspect this argument helps to explain the current popularity of scholarly accounts that depict Hispanic Catholicism as having a "matriarchal core" in contradistinction to the patriarchal emphasis that pervades the Catholicism favored by Anglo Catholics (see Díaz-Stevens 1993; Díaz-Stevens and Stevens-Arroyo 1998).

In the specific case of Hispano Catholics in New Mexico, however, the orientalizing predisposition that pervades Anglo discourse about subaltern groups (both in New Mexico and elsewhere) runs into a problem. On the one hand, it leads to a historiographical emphasis on the Penitentes, since this is an obvious way of representing Hispano culture as exotic and thus as qualitatively different from Anglo culture. On the other hand, as we have seen throughout this book, the Penitentes were pervaded by a number of undeniably "masculine" emphases. This means that an emphasis on the Penitentes, which is the one thing that most allows the Anglo imagination to construct Hispano culture as exotic, simultaneously prevents feminization. As a result, and unlike what is true in the case of Anglo discourse about New Mexico's Pueblo populations (and Anglo discourse about the Middle East), the *inferiority* of Hispano culture must be established in some other way—at least if the result is going to be a story popular with Anglo audiences. As we have already seen at several points in this book, the usual way of doing this is to construct the Penitentes as *premodern,* that is, as representing the survival of customs and beliefs that predated the rise of the modern in the West.

The premodernism of the Penitentes can be romanticized, as when commentators like Alice Corbin Henderson derive the Penitentes from medieval traditions that may be charming but that in the end must pass out of existence in the modern world. Penitente premodernism can also be demonized, as when Protestant commentators like the Reverend Darley see the Penitentes as representing the worst extremes of superstition and barbarism. Finally, it can be essentialized, as when scholars like William Wroth and others see the Penitentes as deriving from traditions of Spanish religiosity that predate the Council of Trent and that have remained constant and invariant over the intervening centuries. Still, no matter what version of this story you tell, the implicit superiority of "modern" Anglos over "premodern" Hispanos is a given.

❧ Hispano Preferences

If Anglo audiences prefer stories that construct the Penitentes as exotic and premodern, what about Hispano/Hispanic audiences? In this case, there seem to be two preferred stories. The first suggests that the Penitentes provided Hispanos with a source of social solidarity that could be used for building a distinctively Hispano social identity. Ray John de Aragón, for example, says that "many of the customs and practices of the Penitentes have already disappeared irretrievably. This is truly unfortunate, in my view, since I strongly believe pride in the cultural heritage of New Mexico will help us forge ahead into the future. Los Hermanos de la Luz stood for faith, family, community, and cultural pride" (1998, 233).

More recently, Alberto López Pulido (2000) has developed what is probably the most sophisticated version of this first story. He suggests that the emphasis on flagellation in most existing accounts about the Penitentes obscures the fact that the core elements in Penitente spirituality are prayer, charity, and setting a good example. These particular elements, he argues, ensure that Penitente spirituality works to sacralize everyday activities. The net result is that Penitente spirituality is a form of "practical Christianity" that promotes an "interdependence between the spiritual and material

worlds" (68) and so creates "a realm of human experiences where social relations are interdependent and emotional, and a sense of obligation is actively present" (69). Given all this, he argues, Penitentes spirituality "of-
fers its followers a wellspring of strength, consolation, and at times, even
resistance to forces that seek to change it" and thus works to "establish and
preserve the collective memory and historical identity" (74) of the Hispano
community in New Mexico.

Unfortunately, virtually all of the evidence that López Pulido presents
in support of his vision of Penitente spirituality is drawn from interviews
done in the 1990s with contemporary Penitente members. In other words,
while his account may be an accurate description of what the Penitentes
have *become* in recent decades, especially as young males associated with
the revived *santero* tradition have entered the Brotherhood, there is no basis
(as yet) for saying that it reflects the worldview of Penitente members in
the nineteenth and early twentieth centuries.

A second story preferred by Hispano authors and Hispano audiences,
and one that is by no means inconsistent with the first, constructs the Penitentes as a lay organization that worked to preserve age-old and impeccably Catholic traditions at a time when the clergy was unable or unwilling
to do so. Thus, for example, in an article written a few years before his
book, López Pulido (1997, 381) suggested that the Penitentes demonstrate
"the ecclesiastical importance of the laity in the Roman Catholic tradition.
As Cardinal John Henry Newman has taught us that during critical mo-
ments in the history of the Church when the hierarchy failed to uphold the
traditions of the Apostles, the laity served as a witness for maintaining or-
thodoxy and keeping the Christian faith alive." Generally, this story seems
to have a special appeal for writers and audiences concerned with cele-
brating the presence in the United States of distinctively Hispanic Catholic
traditions that have historically been overlooked by the American hierarchy. María Díaz-Stevens and Anthony M. Stevens-Arroyo (1998, 117), for example, celebrate the Penitentes as a "lay reaction and defense of Catholic
values" in a situation where clerical leadership was lacking.

This second story, of course, runs afoul of several empirical patterns
that have already been mentioned in this book (e.g., that the Penitentes
emerged first in areas *staffed,* not abandoned, by clergy; that Penitente
membership increased, not decreased, as clergy became more plentiful;
and so on). But then, in some ways that is the point: the stories we tell
about the past are often appealing not because of, but rather in spite of, the
evidence. In any event, common to both this second story and the first is

the suggestion that the Penitentes represent something of which Hispano Catholics can be proud, not ashamed—and this clearly contributes to the appeal these stories have for Hispano/Hispanic authors and audiences.

Although there is nothing in my argument that precludes the suggestion that the Penitentes functioned to promote social solidarity in Hispano villages or served as the basis for the development of a distinctively Hispano identity, I *have* suggested that Penitente membership shaped the personalities of Hispano males in a way that made Anglo oppression of the Hispano population of New Mexico a more efficient and more effective process than it might otherwise have been. This is a fairly startling negation of the stories preferred by Hispano/Hispanic audiences, and the political consequences of that fact need to be confronted.

⸎ The Political Value of Subaltern Historiography

Looking back on *Orientalism* with the perspective of hindsight, Edward Said (1994, 332) suggests that it was one of several books published in the late 1970s and early 1980s that "undermine[d] the naive belief in the certain positivity and unchanging historicity of a culture, a self, a national identity." True enough, but it is also the case, as Said himself notes (335), that *Orientalism* was widely seen as giving voice to subaltern populations (notably the Arabic peoples of the Middle East) whose views were often not represented in discussions of their own culture. What Said was doing, in other words, or at least what he was seen as doing, was undermining a purely Western view of Middle Eastern culture. But what happens when the view being eroded is one held by the subaltern population being studied? What happens, in other words, when the "culture, self, and national identity" whose historicity is being challenged are central to the political claims of activists and scholars speaking on behalf of some particular subaltern group? This question has been at the center of an often-acrimonious debate conducted over the past decade or so; and during the course of that debate, a number of scholars have mounted a serious challenge to the model of "disinterested scholarship" that has long held sway in Western academic circles.

One of the books Said identifies (332) as having been similar in its theoretical intent to *Orientalism* is Eric Hobsbawn and Terence Ranger's *The Invention of Tradition* (1983). Although the different essays in this book dealt with a variety of topics, they all in some way made the claim that many "traditions" are not traditional at all but rather are cultural inventions that have emerged in the relatively recent past. David Cannadine (1983), for example, argued that many of the traditions associated with the British monarchy only came into existence during the nineteenth and twentieth centuries; while Hugh Trevor-Roper (1983) argued that kilts and clan tartans, far from being part of an archaic Highland heritage, were popularized only in the eighteenth and nineteenth centuries. Likely because the essays in the Hobsbawn/Ranger book dealt with European materials, the essays in that book did not generate much controversy.

On the other hand, an emphasis on the "invention of tradition" also emerged in anthropology, especially in connection with the study of Pacific Island and Native American societies, and here there *was* controversy. Jocelyn Linnekin (1983), for example, argued that many of the traditions being revived by nationalist groups in Hawaii were derived from the often-mistaken presumption that current practices in rural communities were accurate reflections of practices that had existed in the distant past. Alan Hanson (1989) suggested that many Maori institutions accepted as traditional by Maori activists in New Zealand were in fact inventions concocted in the nineteenth century by *European* scholars anxious to establish points of similarity between European culture and Maori culture. Somewhat more generally, Roger Keesing (1989) argued that visions of the precolonial past being embraced by a variety of Pacific peoples had often incorporated distinctively Western categories of thought. In the Americas, Sam Gill (1987) argued that the "Mother Earth" cult that now figures so prominently in Native American spirituality had not existed in the indigenous societies of North America and had, in fact, been an invention of non-Indian commentators writing in the nineteenth century.

In these (anthropological) cases, activists and scholars from the populations being studied reacted with hostility and outrage to the suggestion that their traditions had been "invented." Some critics objected to the patronizing implication that indigenous populations lacked the ability to develop traditions on their own and thus had had to borrow their traditions from European sources. A more common criticism, however, was that those arguing for "invented tradition" had ignored the conclusions reached by indigenous scholars. The Hawaiian scholar Haunani-Kay Trask (1991, 160) suggested that people like Roger Keesing were a type of *"maha'oi haole,* that is, rude, intrusive white people who go where they do not belong," and who "hasn't bothered to read our Native nationalists and scholars, including those, like myself, who have been very critical of these same *haole* academics." Russell Means criticizes Gill for "never having checked out the accuracy of his interpretations with any Indian academics" with the result that his (Gill's) work "isn't just shoddy scholarship, it's culture imperialism" (cited in Jaimes 1988, 25). Ward Churchill (1998, 112–15) chides Gill for deriving some of his data from contemporary Indian informants but not accepting their own interpretations of that data, and then goes on to cite an "Osage/Cherokee theologian" who compares Gill's work to works that deny the Holocaust.[3]

Implicit in all these critiques is the contention that there is a privileged relationship between indigenous scholars and the indigenous populations they study, and that this privileged relationship should be recognized by Western academics and Western academic institutions. Such a contention, of course, negates a fundamental premise of the "scientific method" as it is understood by most Western scholars, which is that truth claims should be evaluated by putting them through a process of peer review that takes into account matters of evidence and argumentation but *not* the status of the person making the claim. Indeed, for someone like Sam Gill (1994, 972), the suggestion that "one race, ethnicity or gender is somehow privileged in any area of academic study is racism and refutes important gains that have been made in this century." Unfortunately, while I suspect that many academics would agree with Gill here, and while I would certainly have agreed with it myself at one point, such a response overlooks issues that cannot be overlooked.

First, although the scientific enterprise is supposed to be an impersonal process that evaluates all truth claims using the same set of standards, a number of commentators—feminist commentators in particular[4]—have demonstrated (convincingly, I think) that the scientific method as actually *used* by its practitioners is not brought to bear with equal force on all hypotheses. On the contrary, some hypotheses have always had a much better chance of "making it through" the process of verification than others and thus a better chance of being accepted as knowledge—and one of the key determinants of success is whether or not the hypothesis or idea is consistent with prevailing cultural biases. In other words, Gill's remarks notwithstanding, investigators whose work is congruent with hegemonic (Western) values *are*, at least on average, more likely to meet with success in the academic world than investigators from subaltern groups whose work is not congruent with those values.

Also ignored in any peremptory dismissal of the claim that the conclusions reached by indigenous scholars should be privileged in studying indigenous populations is the political context in which this claim is being made. What is at stake here, as several commentators (Briggs 1996; Metz

1998; Deloria 1998) is *discursive authority*, that is, the ability of activists and scholars from subaltern populations to speak authoritatively on matters of concern to those populations. In particular, subaltern populations are often locked in a struggle with powerful groups over entitlements to land and other scarce resources. In such a situation, stories about the past that stress the continuity of long-established traditions can be a powerful political tool that gives legitimacy to subaltern demands. This means that any body of scholarship that erodes the authoritativeness of subaltern voices in matters relating to their own past, no matter how well-intentioned, simultaneously erodes their authority to make claims in the present. This is why the members of a subaltern group will quite naturally work for the right to articulate the stories they prefer, and this is why they will protest loudly when their preferred stories are challenged by nonindigenous academics.

In the New Mexico context, such protests were clearly in evidence several decades ago when Angélico Chávez (1967; 1974, 182–83) suggested that the real leader of the Pueblo Revolt had not been the San Juan Indian leader Popé (as suggested by all conventional histories) but rather Domingo Naranjo. Naranjo's father, Chávez argued, had been a black manservant brought into New Mexico by one of Oñate's soldiers; his mother had been a Tlascaltec Indian from Mexico, also brought into the colony as a servant. Naranjo, in Chávez's reconstruction, had withdrawn from Spanish society and become a powerful shaman at Taos Pueblo, and it was from here that he had planned the great revolt. Angélico Chávez's revisionism brought a strong rebuke from Pueblo scholars, who found his hypothesis not simply wrong but offensive, since it suggested that the Pueblos could not have planned and carried out the revolt without outside help (see Simmons 2000, 20–21).

The protests elicited by Chávez's work (which, in the end, never did gain much support in academic circles), however, were nothing compared to the furore that erupted over Ramón Gutiérrez's already-mentioned *When Jesus Came, the Corn Mothers Went Away*. While the North American academic mainstream showered Gutiérrez's book with an almost embarrassingly large number of awards,[5] the reaction from Pueblo scholars and Pueblo populations was quite dramatically different. Gutiérrez's book, for example, was hotly denounced at two well-attended public meetings held in 1993 in Albuquerque (Rodríguez 1995, 892). A collection of written commentaries by twelve different authors, most of whom were Pueblo, was complied by the Native American Studies Center at the University of New Mexico and published in *The American Indian Culture and Research Journal*

(1993, 17:3, 141–77), and criticisms continue to be published (see Miller 1998, 104–6). Although his critics leveled a number of charges against Gutiérrez and his book, two in particular were made over and over again.

First, Gutiérrez was criticized for his depiction of Pueblo sexuality at the time of European contact, and in particular for suggesting that Pueblo notions of reciprocity predisposed Pueblo women to offer themselves sexually to Spanish males in order to achieve some material benefit. Such a claim was seen, not just as historically incorrect, but as deeply insulting to Pueblo people in the present if only because, as Susan Miller (1998, 104) suggests, it presented the Pueblos as "a set of aboriginal Gomorrahs peopled by naked, screwing women and men." Second, Gutiérrez was criticized for ignoring (read: not agreeing with) the conclusions about Pueblo culture in the past that have been reached by Pueblo scholars themselves.

Implicit in both of these criticisms is the view, similar to the one encountered in indigenous objections to "invention-of-tradition" studies, that there is a privileged link between contemporary Pueblo populations and Pueblo populations in the past and that this privileged link should be recognized and respected by non-Pueblo scholars. Some critics were willing to be quite explicit about this contention. Penny Bird, a resident of Santo Domingo Pueblo, for example, says: "Indeed, our lifeways are changing, but there are certain things that continue, and the philosophical foundations of our community continue. *I do not recognize any authority from any culture except ours for a discussion of these foundations*" (1993, 170; emphasis added).

Ted Jojola (1993), from Isleta Pueblo, went even further. After reviewing Federal legislation that has given Native Americans legal control over matters relating to their artifacts, graves, languages, and religion, he suggests that such legislation should serve as the "foundation for the development of a patent on culture and historical interpretation" (142). The suggestion, in other words, seems to be that Pueblo intellectuals be given a *legal right* to have their interpretations predominate in matters of Pueblo history.

Here again, such concerns cannot be dismissed lightly. The Pueblo Indian populations of New Mexico, like other indigenous populations in the Pacific or elsewhere in the Americas, are locked in a continuing struggle with powerful interests over access to scarce resources like land and water. Anything that undermines the credibility of Pueblo scholars and activists—and this includes scholarly challenges to the vision of the past that Pueblo populations prefer and on the basis of which they make claims in the present—makes it that much less likely that they will prevail in this struggle. Little wonder, then, that Pueblo scholars and activists have claimed the same right to tell their *own* stories about their *own* past that has been claimed by indigenous scholars and activists in other parts of the world.

The Hispano population of New Mexico is also locked in a continuing struggle with powerful Anglo (and sometimes Pueblo) interests over scarce resources, so here too it is only to be expected that any challenge to the stories preferred by Hispano audiences will provoke objections. I suspect, for example, that many Hispanos might take offense at the suggestion made in the last chapter that Penitente ritual allowed for the gratification of homosexual desire. Though I was careful to indicate that by "homosexual desire" I meant something very general and diffuse, and that I was very specifically *not* referring to sexual acts involving phallic penetration, such qualifications are likely to get lost. The only thing that many readers will hear is that Hispano males were homosexual—so it seems entirely possible that my argument will be seen as working to discredit Hispano traditions in the eyes of a general public that still disapproves of homosexuality. Similarly, I suspect that many readers will take my suggestion that Penitente membership fostered a personality type that legitimized the U.S. legal system as nothing more than a "blame the victim" strategy that makes Hispanos responsible for their own dispossession and thus works to absolve the American government of guilt.

The argument I have advanced is also likely to be rejected by anyone who embraces Penitente tradition as the basis for building a politically useful Hispano-Catholic identity. During the 1970s and 1980s, for example, Hispano opposition to tourist-related development in the Taos area was associated with a religious revival in San Francisco de Asís parish at Ranchos de Taos. This revival involved—among other things—restoration and annual maintenance of the church's adobe exterior by community labor[6] as well as a revival of interest in the Penitente Brotherhood (Rodríguez 1990, 550). Even now, a very bloody Penitente crucifix hangs on the wall just to the right of the main altar in this small church. How will the suggestion that the Penitentes functioned to make Anglo oppression of the Hispano population a more efficient and effective process sit with the Hispano Catholics who attend services at this church on a regular basis and who regularly confront that very visible emblem of the Penitentes (not to mention those who are members of the Brotherhood)? Not well, I suspect.

❧ Destabilizing Stereotypes

I would nevertheless defend the story I have told on the grounds that it shatters many of the stereotypes about Hispano society on which Anglo rationalizations of Hispano oppression depend—and that shattering such stereotypes is a necessary precondition for establishing a political climate in which the wrongs done to the Hispano population can be redressed. At one level, this book should be seen as a continuation of that positive revaluation of Hispano society in the pre-annexation period that was initiated in the 1990s by scholars like Ross Frank. Thus, I have suggested that the Penitentes were a creative response to the strains and stresses on Hispano social organization caused by the economic changes taking place in the late 1700s, and also that what was happening in New Mexico during the early 1900s, before the collision with Anglo culture, bears a strong resemblance to the sort of modernization that had occurred in Counter-Reformation Europe three centuries earlier.

The pre-annexation Hispano society that emerges in this story, then, is not the stagnant society whose members passively cling to age-old traditions so long favored by Anglo historians, nor is it the society characterized by exotic and dramatically "different" practices that figures so prominently in orientalizing discourse about the Southwest. On the contrary, it was a society whose members responded to change *with* change and who, in particular, embraced unfamiliar forms of piety in order to safeguard forms of social organization that were important to them. In short, pre-annexation Hispano society was a dynamic society, and one that certainly did not depend on Anglo influence to induce change. It was not nearly as different or exotic as most Anglos like to believe. The value of such a view is that it undermines the suggestion that annexation (and Anglo influence generally) was ultimately beneficial because it brought economic development and a transition to modernity. On the contrary, the story told here suggests that annexation can be seen as an event that *cut short* a decades-old process of indigenous change that was transforming, and in its own way modernizing, Hispano society in New Mexico. I take it as self-evident that any argument that makes it more difficult to see annexation as generally beneficial simultaneously makes it easier for Anglo publics to appreciate the wrongs that flowed from annexation, and in particular, to appreciate the tragic human consequences of Hispano dispossession.

৵ As a final thought, I would add that the story I have told is also valuable because it raises questions about pre-annexation Hispano society that hint at a previously unacknowledged complexity. What still needs to be explained, for example, is *why* (to once again cite La Chispa, the sorceress we encountered in Chapter 2) New Mexico was for so long a land where the saints were deaf, and a land that the Mother of God never saw fit to visit in the way she visited other Catholic lands. What also needs to be explained is why certain of the religious innovations that emerged in the early 1800s (like the Penitentes) proved to be especially popular with Hispanos, while others (like devotion to Our Lord of Esquipulas) did not. Hispano Catholics, in short, may not be who we thought they were, but we are still a long way from knowing how they thought and acted over the past several centuries.

NOTES

Introduction

1. The term *Hispano* will be used throughout this book to refer both to those Spanish-speaking settlers who established themselves in the upper Rio Grande area in northern New Mexico and southern Colorado during the colonial period and who shared a common culture that was Spanish in origin, and to those Spanish-speaking residents of New Mexico in the postcolonial period who saw themselves as descended from those early settlers and as sharing their cultural traditions. On the use of this term and its relation to other terms (Hispanic, Mexican-American, Chicano, Latino, etc.), see S. Rodríguez (1987, 391); Carrillo (1997, 25–26), Wilson (1997, 148–49), Bright (1998, 605).

1. Penitente Historiography and Its Problems

1. Padre Martínez was an important figure in New Mexico history, and there is much evidence that this early letter notwithstanding, he became a strong supporter of the Penitente movement; see Chapter 4.

2. Cather's depiction of both Lamy/Latour and Padre Martínez of Taos will be discussed at length in Chapter 4.

3. For more on the community functions performed by the Penitentes, see Kutsche and Gallegos (1979).

4. In describing Penitente practice, I have relied heavily on Weigle (1976a), which remains the most comprehensive account of the Penitentes yet written. Other works consulted include Córdova (1972), Cassidy (1936), Woodward (1935), and Wroth (1991). Unless otherwise noted, any interpretations offered are my own.

5. For versions of El Veradero Jesús, which is a prayer that is also found in non-Penitente areas like Texas and Mexico, see Steele and Rivera (1985, 184–90)

6. This letter is one of several found in a box entitled "De Witt Clinton Peters letters to his family, 1854–1869," BANC MSS P-E 236.

7. Franciscan robes in New Mexico were light blue.

8. The Stations of the Cross, a popular devotion that emerged in certain areas of Europe during the late fifteenth century, had become popular throughout the Catholic world by the late seventeenth century and had always been promoted most of all by the Franciscans. For a more detailed account of this devotion, see Carroll (1989, 41–56).

9. For a history of the Tenebrae service, see Thurston (1904, 238–73; 1913).

10. A "third order" was a group of laity associated with some particular religious order. Third order members were not required to live communally, but they were permitted (at least on occasion) to wear the habit of that order and to participate in charitable works conducted by that order. Although most of the mendicant groups (including the Dominicans, Servites, and Carmelites) had third orders, the most well-known third order has always been the Franciscan Third Order.

2. The Golden Age that Wasn't

1. This disjunction between the Hispano population and the Franciscans lasted until 1929, when Manuel Ezequiel Chavez entered the order, taking the name Fray Angélico Chávez, and in so doing became the first native-born Franciscan in the history of New Mexico (T. Chavez 1996).

2. Bishop Martín de Elizacoechea visited New Mexico in 1737. As far as I know, a report of his visitation has not as yet come to light. Some time ago, Adams (1954, 16n) suggested that it might have been among the papers sent back to Spain in the years 1738–43.

3. A similar rumor had circulated in Spain during the fifteenth century. In that case, it was the *converso* population (Christians who had themselves or whose ancestors had converted from Judaism) who were supposed to have made plans to slaughter the local Christian (non-*converso*) population on Corpus Christi (see Baer 1992, 2:339). In that case, as in New Mexico during the eighteenth century, the rumored uprising never did take place.

4. A 1957 survey of household heads living in rural Cuba, for example, found that only about half had ever laid eyes on a priest and fewer than ten percent had ever had contact with a priest (Crahan 1987, 4).

5. A number of scholars have hypothesized that there was a strong crypto-Jewish presence in New Mexico and other areas of the Southwest during the colonial period (see, for example, Nidel 1984; Hordes, 1991; 1996). Could this explain the patterns being reviewed in this chapter? Possibly, but it seems unwise to suggest this until the evidence in support of this hypothesis becomes clearer. In almost all cases, for example, the scholars arguing for a strong crypto-Jewish presence in the colonial Southwest (Arizona, New Mexico, and Texas) point mainly to the customs and behaviors that "survive" in contemporary Hispanic families and that seem similar to Jewish practices. In some cases, however, their similarity to Jewish practices is achieved only by ignoring significant differences; in others, it is possible that the Hispanic practices in question are the remnants of missionizing by an Adventist (Protestant) church earlier in this century (see Neulander 1996). For an overview of the debate surrounding the "crypto-Jews-in-New-Mexico" hypothesis, see Carroll (2002).

6. On the use of the "Indies right here" metaphor among missionaries in Italy and Spain, see Prosperi (1980).

7. For accounts of the Spanish assault at Acoma and its aftermath, which included the amputations mentioned in the Introduction, see Hammond (1927, 120–21); Knaut (1995, 36–46).

8. I know of only one other case of an apparition that was supposedly experienced by a Spanish settler in New Mexico during the colonial period, and it involves Nues-

tra Señora de la Macana. As we shall see later in this chapter, there are grounds for doubting both the original account of this apparition and the claim that the apparition was even known to Hispano settlers.

9. For a discussion of the "shepherd" theme in European apparition traditions, see Lafaye (1976, 219-20); Carroll (1986, 134f); Zimdars-Swartz (1991, 38). In the nineteenth and twentieth centuries, well-known instances of the Virgin Mary appearing to shepherds would include the apparition of Mary to two young shepherds at LaSallete, France, in 1846 and the apparitions of Mary to three young shepherds at Fatima, Portugal, in 1917.

10. See Vargas Uguarte (1956) for some of the most well-known Marian apparitions in the Spanish Americas.

11. For a discussion of why the official church found it advantageous to approve of image cults during the Counter-Reformation, see Carroll (1996, 49–76).

12. Historical studies of ex-voto traditions at particular sanctuaries in European locations routinely find that such traditions almost always start with relatively expensive gifts (e.g., jewelry) made by local elites to some particular cult, and that this pattern of gift-giving is then adopted—using less expensive gifts, like the painted ex-voto discussed later in this chapter—by the local populace generally. The data from New Mexico, then, suggest that ex-voto use began the same way it began at other locations, with local elites donating relatively expensive gifts to particular cults, but that it never developed the popular tradition that emerged elsewhere.

13. In 1992 "La Conquistadora" was officially renamed "Our Lady of Peace" by archdiocesan authorities in order to avoid connotations of cultural domination (see Wilson 1997, 230). The older usage, however, is still in common use. In any event, I have chosen to use "La Conquistadora" in order to tie my discussion as clearly as possible to the preexisting scholarly literature relating to this cult.

14. At first glance Nuestra Señora de Belén, whose image Domínguez encountered at Picurís Pueblo, might seem to be an exception here, given that "Belén" is a community just south of Tomé. In fact, Nuestra Señora de Belén is simply "Our Lady of Bethlehem," a Marian title that appears in several European and Spanish colonial locations during the early modern period; and the community at Belén (New Mexico) was named in honor of this Madonna (see McDonald 1998). In other words, Nuestra Señora de Belén (just like Nuestra Señora de la Luz, Nuestra Señora del Pilar, etc.) was the focus of a cult that had developed outside New Mexico.

15. For an overview of the Iconoclast Controversy, see Carroll (1996, 49–52).

16. Dunne (1944) provides an English-language account of the Tepehuanes rebellion in 1616 and the subsequent emergence of the Zape cult.

17. In contrast to many other Pueblo communities, Xongopavi (the modern Shongopavi) and most other Hopi settlements rejected even the facade of Catholicism, both before and after the Pueblo Revolt (see Brew 1979).

18. A photographic copy of Montalvo's booklet is available in the Archives of the Archdiocese of Santa Fe; however, it does not appear in the microfilm edition of those archives. For more on the bibliographic history of this booklet, see Angélico Chávez (1959, 92). Chávez, I might note, built a very entertaining novel around the bare bones of the Macana story as outlined in Montalvo's booklet (see A. Chávez 1960).

19. This version appears as Document 10 in Papeles de Jesuitas (BANC M-M 193). De-

spite being identified as a Jesuit document in this collection, it was, as Angélico Chávez (1959, 83) long ago pointed out, almost certainly authored by a Franciscan associated with the Convento Grande in Mexico City.

20. Bernardo Abeyta was also a key figure in the early history of the Penitente movement; his simultaneous involvement with the Penitentes and the sanctuary at Chimayó will be discussed in more detail in Chapter 4.

21. See the various letters in Folder #17, Miscellaneous Church Records, Documents 2–9, New Mexico State Archives and Records Center, Santa Fe; see also AHAD 223: 381.

22. For some excellent color plates depicting representative examples of painted ex-voto, see Rodríguez Becerra and Vázquez Soto (1980); Faranda (1993); D'Antonio (1979).

23. On the tin *retablo* tradition in Mexico, see Gibbs (1954), Giffords (1991; 1992); Cerda (1993).

24. For a particularly good selection of color plates showing some of these Mexican ex-voto, see Giffords (1992); Luna (2000).

25. For an overview of the literature on New Mexican *santos,* see Boyd (1998); L. Frank (1992); Wroth (1982; 1991).

26. Wilder (1976) presents a concise overview of the artistic emphases that define *santero* art, and my summary follows his comments; see also Wroth (1988); L. Frank (1992).

3. Awash in a (Very Small) Sea of Crimson Blood

1. What Villagrá is referring to here is likely some version of an Altar of Repose. This was a special altar, often decorated with lights, canopies, and flowers, in which a host consecrated on Holy Thursday (usually at a different altar) was deposited and where it remained until Good Friday. The use of such altars in this way seems to date from the late fifteenth century (Meehan 1913), which means that the ritual described by Villagrá would have been about century old at the time it was performed by Oñate and his group.

2. Reprinted with the kind permission of the University of New Mexico Press; see Villagrá in the Bibliography for full bibliographic details.

3. For a more detailed account of the various activities that constituted these penitential missions, see Carroll (1996, 83–86); Rienzo (1980).

4. Ritualized bathing in rivers on selected occasions, but most notably on June 24, the Feast of St. John the Baptist, was a practice that had existed in a number of European countries for centuries. It was the association of this ritual with the summer solstice that made the practice seem pagan to the rationalist reformers of the European Enlightenment.

5. Given that this paragraph comes after the paragraphs describing what is to be done during Lent and during Holy Week, "Fridays of the Holy Spirit" here is most likely a reference to the Fridays of Paschal-tide, the fifty-day period that runs from Easter to Pentecost.

4. Suffering Fathers and the Crisis of Patriarchal Authority in Late Colonial New Mexico

1. For examples of Penitente *santos* depicting Nuestro Padre Jesús Nazareno, see Wroth (1982; 1991) and Larry Frank (1992).

2. The usual interpretation given to these sprouting plumes by art historians (see, e.g., González Gómez and Roda Peña 1992, 31) is that they originated in an attempt to capture a cruciform nimbus (halo) in sculpted form.

3. The reference is to the "three falls" that Christ is supposed to have experienced while carrying his cross to Calvary. While these falls are not mentioned in any of the Gospel accounts of the passion, a popular tradition suggesting that Christ had fallen three times under the weight of the cross emerged in the Middle Ages and quickly became part of Christian tradition. These beliefs were subsequently incorporated into the Stations of the Cross, a devotion that emerged in the late fifteenth century and that was popularized most of all by the Franciscans. On the history of the Stations of the Cross, see Carroll (1989, 41–56).

4. "Ecce Homo" comes from the Gospel of John, which puts these words (which mean "Behold the man") into Pilate's mouth as he exhibits Christ to the assembled crowd.

5. For a detailed account of the biases that define the Black Legend and how they have shaped Anglo historiography over the past several centuries, see D. Weber (1988, 153–67; 1992); Gibson (1971); Powell (1971). The Black Legend will be discussed in more detail later in this chapter.

6. Cipriani (1981) traces the white tunics worn in most Pugliese communities to (1) the symbolism associated with white in the Judeo-Christian tradition (e.g., the whiteness of the sacrificial lamb), and (2) the fact that Luke's account of Jesus' encounter with Herod suggests that Herod dressed Christ in a white tunic before sending him back to Pilate. At least with regard to the second point, English-speakers may be puzzled. Cipriani says that the text of Luke 23:11 reads "Ed Erode . . . facendogli indossare un veste bianco, poi lo rimandò a Pilato" (And Herod . . . caused him to be dressed in a white garment, then sent him back to Pilate). English Bibles, however, suggest something a bit different. The King James Version, for example, says "And Herod arrayed him in a gorgeous robe, and sent him back to Pilate." The Revised Standard Version reads much the same, only substituting "gorgeous apparel" for "gorgeous robe."

7. For more on the ideal settlement pattern as envisioned in the Laws of the Indies, see Jones (1996, 6–8); Van Ness (1991, 27–33).

8. There is some evidence that the original layout of the settlement at Santa Fe conformed more to the Laws of the Indies ideal than would come to be the case at the time of the Domínguez visit (Ellis 1976).

9. This incident is described in Swadesh (1974, 35).

10. The stability of the Pueblo population in the late eighteenth century, however, had been preceded by a dramatic decline caused mainly by the introduction of European diseases and subsequent epidemics. There is evidence, for example, that by the time of the Pueblo Revolt in 1680, the Pueblo population had been reduced by 80 percent from what it had been at the time of European contact (Reff 1995).

11. The particular reforms reviewed in the last chapter, aimed at eliminating emotional excess from religious ritual and bringing religion more under the control of the state, were a part of the Bourbon Reforms.

12. Raids by nomadic Indians on Hispano settlements would intensify again in the decades following Mexican Independence in 1821; for speculation on why, see David Weber (1981).

13. For some reason, the text of Gutiérrez's 1991 book says, "The expansion of the day laborers category both in relative size and proportion also occurred in Santa Cruz during this period" (323), despite the fact that his tabular data (on 322) provides no evidence for such an increase in the case of Santa Cruz.

14. For the details of Kutsche's argument here, see his original article.

15. In what follows, unless otherwise noted, I am relying on the reconstructions of Hispano settlement patterns that have been developed by Van Ness (1979; 1987; 1991) and Gamble (1988).

16. Swadesh (1974, 22), for example, points out that dispersed settlement allowed Hispano settlers to raise and sell the semi-domesticated tobacco called *punche* without having to pay the taxes levied by the colonial government.

17. See Carlson (1990) for an especially clear discussion, with aerial photographs, of the ways in which irrigation canals and agricultural strips were laid out in relation to one another and in relation to features of the local landscape.

18. For biographical information on Abeyta, see Steele and Rivera (1985, 16–19, 32–33); de Borhegyi (1953, 90–95).

19. Solórzano (1914) lists thirty-nine different satellite churches dedicated to Our Lord of Esquipulas in Guatemala, Honduras, Nicaragua, Costa Rica, and Mexico. Charles Carrillo (1999, 52) notes, in particular, that a cult organized around Our Lord of Esquipulas had existed at the church of San Juan de Dios in Durango since at least the early 1700s.

20. Fray Sebastián Alvarez's 1813 letter to diocesan authorities at Durango is Document #2 in Folder #17, Miscellaneous Church Records, New Mexico State Records Center and Archives, Santa Fe. Interestingly, I think, while Abeyta's original petition had spoken only of fostering a devotion to "Our God and Redeemer . . . under his advocation as Esquipulas," Alvarez makes explicit reference to *"la milagrosa Imagen del Señor de Esquipulas"* venerated in Abeyta's private chapel. Similarly, the letter approving construction of the chapel from Francisco Fernández Valentin (who was vicar general of the Vacant See of Durango at the time) makes reference to *"la Milagrosa Imagen del Señor vajo la advocación de Esquipulas"* (see Document #8 in Folder 17, above). It seems possible, in other words, that it was Church leaders like Alvarez and Valentin, rather than Abeyta himself, who were trying to establish in New Mexico the sort of cult organized around a miraculous image that was common in Mexico and elsewhere. This in turn raises the possibility that Abeyta's concern may have been more with the rituals and beliefs surrounding devotion to Our Lord of Esquipulas than with the concrete image itself.

21. See Chapter 2, note 21.

5. Padre Martínez of Taos and the Meaning of Discipline

1. I should note, however, that although it is routine in Cather studies to say that Latour is based on Lamy, Thomas Steele (2000) has pointed out that in many ways Cather's Latour is quite different from the historical Lamy.

2. As mentioned in Chapter 1, the Vicariate of Santa Fe was created in 1850; it became a diocese in 1853 and an archdiocese in 1875.

3. See, for example, Angélico Chávez (1981), Vigil (1975), and the various essays in Mares (1988a).

4. I recognize that Martínez's modern defenders usually bristle at the term "schism," pointing out that, since Padre Martínez at no point denied the authority of the papacy, his activities were not truly schismatic (see A. Chávez 1981, 146–47). Even so, the term is a convenient label for designating the services Martínez provided for Catholics at Taos that were outside the control of Bishop Lamy.

5. This comment was originally published in Spanish. A week later, on May 31, 1856, the *Gazette* reprinted the letter in English; the text here is from the English-language version.

6. For a nuanced and very detailed account of how scholars in various national traditions did and did not use the term *Counter-Reformation,* see O'Malley (2000, 16–42).

7. The studies by De Rosa and his students have generally not been translated into English. For an overview of some of these studies, see Carroll (1992, 94–104; 1996, 6–10).

8. Santiago Valdez had been a student in Martínez's coeducational school at Taos and came to be adopted by Martínez as a son.

9. Angélico Chávez (1981, 62) reports that all copies of the original (Spanish-language) version of Martínez's autobiographical account have been lost, with the result that the translation by Romero is all that we now have.

10. As Martínez y Alíre (1998) points out, the law ending compulsory tithing was one of a series of measures, all promoted by the liberal government in power at the time, that were designed to curb the economic and political power of the Church.

6. The Penitentes and the Rise of the Modern in New Mexico

1. On the administrative structure of *cofradías* in Spain, see Foster (1953); Webster (1998, 36–38); Ulierte Ruiz (1991, 161–74). For the administrative structure of *cofradías* in Mexico and Peru during the colonial period, see Taylor (1996, 301–24); Bechtloff (1996 [1992], 81–158); Lavrin (1988); Meyers (1988); Celestino and Meyers (1988); Reverter-Pezet (1985).

2. Sponsorship of a particular devotion by some particular individual in the community, often someone who was willing to defray the costs of that devotion, was common in Mexico and known as a *mayordomía* (see Taylor 1996, 321–22).

3. When Loyola died in 1556, there were twelve Jesuit provinces: Italy (except for Rome), Sicily, Upper Germany, Lower Germany, France, Aragon, Castile, Andalucía, Portugal, Brazil, India and Ethiopia (cf. O'Malley 1993, 54).

4. On the administrative structure of the mendicant orders, see Iriarte (1983); Hinnebusch (1965).

5. The Jesuits had been expelled from Spain and the Spanish colonies, including Mexico, in 1767.

6. Briggs (1988, 36–39) provides a good account of how the incorporation of common lands into the Santa Fe National Forest affected the economy of one particular community, Córdova.

7. Stories that Connect to Guilt and Rage

1. The easy fit between Robert Paul's argument and the social disciplining tradition is most clearly seen, I think, in an article that Paul (1998) published shortly after the publication of his 1996 book. Although he still does not deal with the rise of the state in the early modern period, he does argue—borrowing heavily from the work of Nor-

bert Elias—that the "conscientious personality" fostered by Christian ideology and Christian ritual greatly aided the rise of the centralized Roman state, which in turn was one of the reasons why Christianity flourished in the Roman Empire.

2. For a more detailed discussion of this change in Saint Sebastian's iconography, as well as several examples of how Renaissance artists depicted the saint, see Rinaldi (1979); Marshall (1994).

3. Lewes (1995) provides a concise overview of the various processes that Freud saw as predisposing males toward a homosexual object choice.

Epilogue. The Stories We Tell about Subaltern Groups

1. As far as I know, Kessell (1993, 365) was the only reviewer who called attention to the fact that the title of Gutiérrez's book made little sense, given the book's content.

2. There was no reference to "Jesus" or "Corn mothers," I might add, in the title of Gutiérrez's 1980 Ph.D. dissertation, which was the basis for his book.

3. For a more detailed overview of the hostile reactions to these early "invention of tradition" studies in anthropology, see Briggs (1996).

4. For an overview of these feminist critiques of science, see the literature review in Carroll (1998).

5. The prizes and awards won by Gutiérrez's book include: the Herbert Eugene Bolton Memorial Prize from the Conference on Latin American History; the Frederick Jackson Turner award and the James Rawley Award, both from the Organization of American Historians; the Hubert Herring Award from the Pacific Coast Council on Latin American Studies; and the Spain and America in the Quincentennial of the Discovery Award from Spain's Ministry of Culture.

6. San Francisco de Asís Church at Rancho de Taos is the church immortalized in the well-known painting by Georgia O'Keeffe.

BIBLIOGRAPHY

Abbreviations

AGI   Archivo General de Indias, Sevilla, sección quinta, Audiencia de Guadalajara; cited by folder number

AHAD   Archivos Históricos del Arzobispado de Durango (microfilm edition, Rio Grande Historical Collections, New Mexico State University Library, Las Cruces, Ms 355); cited by reel: frame number

BANC   The Bancroft Library, University of California, Berkeley; cited by manuscript number.

MANM   Mexican Archives of New Mexico (microfilm edition); cited by reel: frame number

RITCH   Ritch papers concerning the history of New Mexico, 1839–ca. 1885 (microfilm edition); cited by reel number, item call number, and (if available) page number

Adams, Eleanor B., ed. 1954. *Bishop Tamaron's Visitation of New Mexico, 1760.* Albuquerque: Historical Society of New Mexico Publications in History.

Adams, Eleanor B., and Fray Angélico Chávez, eds. 1956. *The Missions of New Mexico, 1776: A Description by Fray Francisco Atanasio Dominguez with Other Contemporary Documents.* Albuquerque: University of New Mexico Press.

Ahlborn, Richard. 1986. *The Penitente Moradas of Abiquiú.* Washington, D.C.: Smithsonian Institution Press.

Alberigo, Giuseppe. 1966. "Prospettive nuove sul Concilio di Trento." *Critica Storica* 5:267–82.

Alcocer, José Antonio. 1958. *Bosquejo de la Historia de Colegio de Nuestra Señora de Guadalupe y sus misiones.* Mexico City: Editorial Porrua, S.A.

Alpert, Michael. 1997. "Did Spanish Crypto-Jews Desecrate Christian Sacred Images and Why? The Case of the Cristo de la Paciencia (1629–32), the Romance of 1717, and the Events of November 1714 in the Calle del Lobo." In *Faith and Fanaticism: Religious Fervour in Early Modern Spain,* ed. Lesley Twomey, 85–94. Aldershot, U.K.: Ashgate.

BIBLIOGRAPHY

Aragón, Ray John de. 1978. *Padre Martínez and Bishop Lamy.* Las Vegas, N.M.: Pan-American Publishing Company.

———. 1988. "Padre Antonio José Martínez: The Man and the Myth." In *Padre Martínez: New Perspectives from Taos,* ed. E. A. Mares, 125–50. Taos, N.M.: Millicent Rogers Museum.

———. 1998. *Hermanos de la Luz: Brothers of the Light.* Santa Fe, N.M.: Heartsfire Books.

Aranda, Charles. 1974. *The Penitente Papers.* Albuquerque, N.M.: author.

Arias de Saavedra, Inmaculada, and Miguel Luis López Muñoz. 1998. "Cofradías y gremios de Navarra en la época de Carlos III." *Hispania Sacra* 50: 677–95.

Babcock, Barbara. 1990. "A New Mexican Rebecca: Imaging Pueblo Women." *Journal of the Southwest* 32 (4): 400–446.

———. 1997. "Mudwomen and Whitemen: A Meditation on Pueblo Potteries and the Politics of Representation." In *The Material Culture of Gender/The Gender of Material Culture,* ed. Katharine Martinez and Kenneth Ames. Winterthur, Del.: Henry Francis du Pont Winterthur Museum.

Baer, Yitzhak. 1992. *A History of the Jews in Christian Spain.* 2 vols. Philadelphia: Jewish Publication Society.

Bancroft, Hubert Howe. 1888. *History of the Pacific States of North America.* Vol. 12, *Arizona and New Mexico.* San Francisco: The History Company, Publishers.

Bechtloff, Dagmar. 1996 [1992]. *Las cofradías en Michoacán durante la época de la Colonia.* Zinacantepec, México: El Colegio de Michoacán.

Belzen, Jacob A., ed. 2001. Psychohistory in the Psychology of Religion: Interdisciplinary Studies. Amsterdam: Editions Rodopi B. V.

Benavides, Fray Alonso de. 1916 [1630]. *The Memorial of Fray Alonso de Benavides 1630,* ed. F. W. Hodge and C. F. Lummis, trans. Mrs. E. E. Ayer. Chicago: Privately printed.

———. 1945 [1634]. *Fray Alsonso de Benavides' Revised Memorial of 1634,* ed. F. W. Hodge, G. P. Hammond, and A. Rey. Albuquerque: University of New Mexico Press.

Bennassar, Bartolomé. 1979. *The Spanish Character: Attitudes and Mentalities from the Sixteenth to the Nineteenth Century.* Berkeley: University of California Press.

Berceo, Gonzalo de. 1997. *Miracles of Our Lady,* trans. R. T. Mount and A. G. Cash. Lexington: University Press of Kentucky.

Bermejo y Carballo, José. 1882. *Glorias religiosas de Sevilla, or Noticia histórico-descriptiva de todas las cofradías de penitencia, sangre y luz fundadas en esta cuidad.* Sevilla: Imprenta y Librería del Salvador.

Bernardi, Claudio. 2000. "Corpus Domini: Ritual Metamorphoses and Social Changes in Sixteenth- and seventeenth-century Genoa." In *The Politics of Ritual Kinship,* ed. N. Terpstra, 228–42. Cambridge: Cambridge University Press.

Beshoar, Barron B. 1949. "Western Trails to Calvary." *Brand Book* 5 (April): 1–19.

Bibby, Reginald, W. E. Hewitt, and Wade Roof. 1998. "Religion and Identity: The Canadian, American, and Brazilian Cases." *International Journal of Comparative Sociology* 39 (2): 237–50.

Bird, Penny. 1993. "Commentary on *When Jesus Came, the Corn Mothers Went Away: Marriage, Sex and Power in New Mexico, 1500–1846,* by Ramón A. Gutiérrez." *American Indian Culture and Research Journal* 17 (3): 169–71.

Bireley, Robert. 1999. *The Refashioning of Catholicism, 1450–1700: A Reassessment of the Counter Reformation.* Washington, D.C.: Catholic University of America Press.

Birner, Fred. 2000. "José Francisco Vigil: Southern Colorado Santero (1855–1928)." *Tradición Revista* 5 (4): 36–41.

Bizzocchi, Roberto. 1994. "Chiesa, religione, Stato agli inizi dell'età moderna." In *Origini dello Stato: processi di formazione statale in Italia fra medioevo ed età moderna*, ed. G. Chittolini, A. Molho, and P. Schiera, 493–513. Bologna: Il Mulino.

Bloom, Lansing B., ed. 1936. "Bourke on the Southwest: X." *New Mexico Historical Review* 11 (3): 217–82.

Bodine, John J. 1968. "The Tri-ethnic Trap." In *Spanish-speaking People in the United States*, ed. June Helm, 145–53. Seattle: University of Washington Press.

Bolton, Herbert E. 1921. *The Spanish Borderlands: A Chronicle of Old Florida and the Southwest*. New Haven: Yale University Press.

Bordes, Maurice. 1978. "Contribution a l'étude des confréries de pénitents a Nice aux XVII-XVIII siècles." *Annales du Midi* 90: 377–88.

Borromeo, Agostino. 1997. "I vescovi italiani e l'applicazione del concilio di Trento." In *I tempi del Concilio: Religione, cultura e società nell'Europa tridentina*, ed. C. Mozzarelli and D. Zardin, 253–69. Roma: Bulzoni editore.

Bossy, John. 1994. "The German Reformation after Moeller." *Journal of Ecclesiastical History* 45 (4): 673–84.

Boyd, E. 1974. *Popular Arts of Spanish New Mexico*. Santa Fe, N.M.: Museum of New Mexico Press.

———. 1998. *Saints and Saint Makers of New Mexico*. Rev. and ed., Robin Farwell Gavin. Foreword by Donna Pierce. Santa Fe, N.M.: Western Edge Press.

Brading, D. A. 1983. "Tridentine Catholicism and Enlightened Despotism in Bourbon Mexico." *Journal of Latin American Studies* 15: 1–22.

———. 1994. *Church and State in Bourbon Mexico: The Diocese of Michoacán 1749–1810*. Cambridge: Cambridge University Press.

Brew, J. O. 1979. "Hopi Prehistory and History to 1850." In *Handbook of North American Indians*. Vol. 9, *Southwest*, ed. Alfonso Ortiz, 514–23. Washington, D.C.: Smithsonian Institution Press.

Bridgers, Lynn. 1997. *Death's Deceiver: The Life of Joseph P. Machebeuf*. Albuquerque: University of New Mexico Press.

Briggs, Charles L. 1988. *Competence in Performance: The Creativity of Tradition in Mexican Verbal Art*. Philadelphia: University of Pennsylvania Press.

———. 1996. "The Politics of Discursive Authority in Research on the "Invention of Tradition." *Cultural Anthropology* 11 (4): 435–69.

Bright, Brenda. 1998. "'Heart Like a Car': Hispano/Chicano Culture in Northern New Mexico." *American Ethnologist* 25 (4): 583–609.

Brinton, Henry. 1968. *The Context of the Reformation*. London: Hutchinson Educational.

Brown, Lorin [Lorenzo de Córdova]. 1978. *Hispano Folklife of New Mexico: The Lorin W. Brown Federal Writers' Project Manuscripts*, ed. Charles L. Briggs and Marta Weigle. Albuquerque: University of New Mexico Press.

Brugge, David M. 1968. "Navajos in the Catholic Church Records of New Mexico, 1694–1875." Window Rock, Ariz.: Parks and Recreation Department, the Navajo Tribe.

Candelaria, Juan. 1929. "Information Communicated by Juan Candelaria, Resident of this Villa de San Francisco Xavier de Albuquerque, born 1692–age 84." *New Mexico Historical Review* 4: 274–97.

Cannadine, David. 1983. "The Context, Performance and Meaning of Ritual: The British Monarchy and the 'Invention of Tradition,' ca. 1820–1977. In *The Invention of Tradition*, ed. Eric Hobsbawn and Terence Ranger, 101–64. Cambridge: Cambridge University Press.

Carlson, Alvar W. 1990. *The Spanish-American Homeland: Four Centuries in New Mexico's Río Arriba*. Baltimore: Johns Hopkins University Press.

Carrera Stampa, Manuel. 1954. *Los Gremios Mexicanos: La organización gremial en Nueva España 1521–1861*. México, D.F.: E.D.I.A.P.S.A.

Carrillo, Charles. 1997. *Hispanic New Mexican Pottery: Evidence of Craft Specialization, 1790–1890*. Albuquerque, N.M.: LTD Press.

———. 1999. "Our Lord of Esquipulas in New Mexico." *Tradición Revista* 4 (2): 50–54.

Carroll, H. Bailey, and J. Villasana Haggard. 1942. *Three New Mexico Chronicles*. Albuquerque, N.M.: Quivira Society.

Carroll, Michael P. 1977. "Leach, Genesis and Structural Analysis: A Critical Evaluation." *American Ethnologist* 4 (Nov): 663–77.

———. 1986. *The Cult of the Virgin Mary*. Princeton: Princeton University Press.

———. 1987. "Moses and Monotheism Revisited: Freud's Personal Myth?" *American Imago* 44 (1): 15–35.

———. 1988. "Moses and Monotheism and the Psychoanalytic Study of Early Christian Mythology." *Journal of Psychohistory* 15 (3): 295–310.

———. 1989. *Catholic Cults and Devotions*. Montreal: McGill-Queen's University Press.

———. 1992. *Madonnas That Maim: Popular Catholicism in Italy Since the Fifteenth Century*. Johns Hopkins University Press.

———. 1996. *Veiled Threats: The Logic of Popular Catholicism in Italy*. Baltimore: Johns Hopkins University Press.

———. 1998. "But Fingerprints Don't Lie, Eh? Prevailing Gender Ideologies and Scientific Knowledge." *Psychology of Women Quarterly* 22: 739–49.

———. 1999. *Irish Pilgrimage: Holy Wells and Popular Catholic Devotion*. Baltimore: Johns Hopkins University Press.

———. 2002. "The Debate Over a Crypto-Jewish Presence in New Mexico: The Role of Ethnographic Allegory and Orientalism." *Sociology of Religion* 63 (1): 1–19.

Casagrande, Giovanna. 2000. "Confraternities and Lay Female Religiosity in Late Medieval and Renaissance Umbria." In *The Politics of Ritual Kinship*, ed. N. Terpstra, 48–65. Cambridge: Cambridge University Press.

Cassidy, Ina Sizer. 1936. "The Penitentes of New Mexico." The Federal Writer's Project of New Mexico, WPA 5-5-32 #13; on file at the Angélico Chávez History Library and Archives, Palace of the Governors, Santa Fe. Ritual collected by Aurora Lucero White.

Cather, Willa. 1999 [1927]. *Death Comes for the Archbishop*. Lincoln: University of Nebraska Press.

Celestino, Olinda, and Albert Meyers. 1988. "The Socio-economic Dynamics of the Confraternal Endowment in Colonial Peru." In *Manipulating the Saints: Religious Brotherhoods and Social Integration in Postconquest Latin America*, ed. Albert Meyers and Diane Elizabeth Hopkins, 101–27. Hamburg, Germany: Wayasbah.

Cerda, Luis. 1993. Review of *The Art of Private Devotion*. *Hispanic American Historical Review* 73 (1): 125–26.

BIBLIOGRAPHY

Cervantes, Miguel de. 1981 [1605]. *Don Quixote,* ed. J. R. Jones. New York: Norton.

Chávez, Fray Angélico. 1948a. "El Vicario Don Santiago Roybal." *El Palacio* 55: 231–52.

———. 1948b. "Nuestra Señora del Rosario La Conquistadora." *New Mexico Historical Review* 23: 93–128, 177–216.

Chávez, [Fray] Angélico. 1954. "The Penitentes of New Mexico." *New Mexico Historical Review* 29 (54): 97–123.

———. 1957. *Archives of the Archdiocese of Santa Fe, 1678–1900.* Washington, D.C.: Academy of Franciscan History.

———. 1959. "Nuestra Señora de la Macana." *New Mexico Historical Review* 34 (2): 81–97.

———. 1960. *The Lady from Toledo.* Fresno, Calif.: Academy Guild Press.

———. 1967. "Pohé-Yemo's Representative and the Pueblo Revolt of 1680." *New Mexico Historical Review* 42 (2): 85–126.

———. 1974. *My Penitente Land.* Albuquerque: University of New Mexico Press.

———. 1981. *But Time and Chance: The Story of Padre Martínez of Taos, 1793–1867.* Santa Fe, N.M.: Sunstone Press.

Chávez, Thomas E. 1996. "In Memoriam: Fray Angélico Chávez (Manual Ezequiel Chávez), 1910–1996." *Colonial Latin American Historical Review* 5 (Summer): 256–60.

Christian, William A. 1981. *Local Religion in Sixteenth-century Spain.* Princeton: Princeton University Press.

Churchill, Ward. 1998. *Fantasies of the Master Race: Literature, Cinema, and the Colonization of American Indians.* San Francisco: City Lights Books.

Cipriani, Roberto. 1981. "Riti e simboli della settimana santa in Capitanata: Il Cristo rosso di Cerignola." In *Rappresentazioni arcaiche della tradizione popolari,* Atti del VI Convegno di Studio. Viterbo, Italy: Centro di Studi sul teatro medioevale e rinascimentale.

Cochrane, Eric. 1970. "New Light on Post-Tridentine Italy: A Note on Recent Counter-Reformation Scholarship." *Catholic Historical Review* 56 (2): 291–319.

———. 1988. "Tridentine Reform." In *Italy, 1530–1630,* 106–64. London: Longman.

Congregación de Nuestra Señora de la Luz, Santa Fe, New Mexico. 1766. *Constituciones de la Congregación de Nuestra Señora de la Luz, erigida en la Villa de Santa Fe, Capital de la Provincia de la Nueva Mexico, y aprobada del Illmó. Señor D. Pedro Tamaron, Obispo de Durango.* Mexico: Phelipe de Zuñiga.

Connolly, S. J. 1982. *Priests and People in Pre-Famine Ireland.* New York: St. Martin's Press.

Córdova, Lorenzo de [Lorin W. Brown]. 1972. *Echoes of the Flute.* Santa Fe, N.M.: Ancient City Press.

Crahan, Margaret. 1987. "Religion and Revolution: Cuba and Nicaragua." Working papers of the Latin American program of the Woodrow Wilson International Center for Scholars, number 174. Washington, D.C.

Cross, F. L. 1957. *The Oxford Dictionary of the Christian Church.* Oxford: Oxford University Press.

Cutter, Charles. 1994. "Community and the Law in Northern New Spain." *Americas* 50 (April): 467–80.

———. 1995. *The Legal Culture of Northern New Spain, 1700–1810.* Albuquerque: University of New Mexico Press.

D'Antonio, Nino. 1979. *Gli ex voto dipinti e il rituale dei fujenti a Madonna dell'Arco.* Cava dei Tirreni, Italy: De Mauro Editore.

Darley, Alexander. 1893. *The Passionists of the Southwest, or The Holy Brotherhood*. Pueblo, Colo.: n.p.

De Aragón, Ray John. 1998. *Hermanos de la Luz: Brothers of the Light*. Santa Fe, N.M.: Heartsfire Books.

de Borhegyi, Stephen F. 1953. "The Miraculous Shrines of Our Lord of Esquipulas in Guatemala and Chimayó, New Mexico." *El Palacio* 60 (3): 83–111.

———. 1954. "The Cult of Our Lord of Esquipulas in Middle America and New Mexico." *El Palacio* 61 (12): 387–401.

Deloria, Vine, Jr. 1998. "Comfortable Fictions and the Struggle for Turf." In *Natives and Academics*, ed. Devon A. Mihesuah, 65–81. Lincoln: University of Nebraska Press.

Delumeau, Jean. 1977 [1971]. *Catholicism between Luther and Voltaire: A New View of the Counter-Reformation*. London: Burns and Oates.

Díaz-Stevens, Ana María. 1993. "The Saving Grace: The Matriarchal Core of Latino Catholicism." *Latino Studies Journal* 4 (3): 60–78.

Díaz-Stevens, Ana María, and Anthony M. Stevens-Arroyo. 1998. *Recognizing the Latino Resurgence in U.S. Religion: The Emmaus Paradigm*. Boulder, Colo.: Westview Press.

Di Palo, Francesco. 1992. *Stabat Mater Dolorosa: La settimana santa in Puglia*. Brindisi, Italy: Schena Editore.

Domínguez, Fray Francisco Atanasio. 1956 [1776]; see Adams, Eleanor B., and Angélico Chávez. 1956.

Dozier, Edward. 1958. "Spanish-Catholic Influences on Rio Grande Pueblo Religion." *American Anthropologist* 60: 441–48.

———. 1961. "Rio Grande Pueblos." In *Perspectives in American Indian culture change*, ed. Edward Spicer, 94–186. Chicago: University of Chicago Press.

———. 1964. "The Pueblo Indians of the Southwest." *Current Anthropology* 5 (2): 79–97.

Dunne, Peter Masten. 1944. *Pioneer Jesuits in Northern Mexico*. Berkeley: University of California Press.

Durán, Tobías. 1984. "We Come as Friends: The Social and Historical Context of Nineteenth Century New Mexico." Southwest Hispanic Research Institute, Working paper #106.

Durand, Jorge, and Douglas S. Massey. 1995. *Miracles on the Border: Retablos of Mexican Migrants to the United States*. Tucson: University of Arizona Press.

Ebright, Malcolm. 1989. "Introduction." In *Spanish and Mexican Land Grants and the Law*, ed. M. Ebright, 3–11. Manhattan, Kans.: Sunflower University Press.

———. 1994. *Land Grants and Lawsuits in Northern New Mexico*. Albuquerque: University of New Mexico Press.

Edmonson, Munro S. 1957. *Los Manitos: A Study of Institutional Values*. New Orleans: Middle American Research Institute, Tulane University.

Egan, Martha J. 1993. *Relicarios: Devotional Miniatures from the Americas*. Santa Fe: Museum of New Mexico Press.

Eggan, Fred. 1979. "Pueblos: Introduction." In *Handbook of North American Indians*, Vol. 9, *Southwest*, ed. Alfonso Ortiz, 224–35. Washington, D.C.: Smithsonian Institution.

Elias, Norbert. 1978 [1939]. *The Civilizing Process*. Translated by Edmund Jephcott. New York: Urizen Books.

Ellis, Bruce T. 1976. "Santa Fe's Seventeenth Century Plaza, Parish Church, and Convent Reconsidered." In *Collected Papers in Honor of Marjorie Ferguson Lambert*, ed. A. H. Schroeder, 183–98. Albuquerque: Archeological Society of New Mexico.

Emory, W. H. 1848. *Notes of a Military Reconnaissance from Fort Leavenworth in Missouri to San Diego in California*. Washington, D.C.: Wendell and Van Benthuysen, Printers.

Espinosa, J. Manuel. 1993. "The Origin of the Penitentes of New Mexico: Separating Fact from Fiction." *Catholic Historical Review* 74 (3): 454–77.

Esquibel, José Antonio. 1998. "Sacramental Records and the Preservation of New Mexico Family Genealogies from the Colonial Era to the Present" In *Seeds of Struggle/Harvest of Faith*, ed. Thomas J. Steele, S.J., Paul Rhetts, and Barbe Awalt, 27–42. Albuquerque: LPD Press.

Fanning, William H. W. 1913. "Societies, Secret." In *The Catholic Encyclopedia*, 14:71–74. New York: Encyclopedia Press.

Faranda, Franco. 1993. *Per grazia ricevuta: Dipinti votivi in Diocesi di Imola*. Imola, Italy: Editrice NDM.

Fenlon, Dermot. 1972. *Heresy and Obedience in Tridentine Italy: Cardinal Pole and the Counter Reformation*. Cambridge: Cambridge University Press.

Febvre, Lucien. 1973 [1929]. "The Origins of the French Reformation: A Badly-put Question?" In his *A New Kind of History*, ed. Peter Burke, 44–107. London: Routledge and Kegan Paul.

Florencia, Francisco de, and Juan Antonio de Oviedo. 1755. *Zodiaco Mariano*. Mexico: En la Nueva Imprenta del Real, y mas Antiguo Colegio de San Ildefonso.

Flynn, Maureen. 1999. "Baroque Piety and Spanish Confraternities." In *Confraternities and Catholic Reform in Italy, France and Spain*, ed. John Patrick Donnelly, S.J., and Michael W. Mahher, S.J, 233–45. Kirksville, Mo.: Thomas Jefferson University Press.

Fontaine, Michelle M. 1999. "A House Divided: The Compagnia de Santa Maria dei Battuti in Modena on the Eve of Catholic Reform." In *Confraternities and Catholic Reform in Italy, France and Spain*, ed. John Patrick Donnelly, S.J., and Michael W. Maher, S.J., 55–73. Kirksville, Mo.: Thomas Jefferson University Press.

Fontana, Bernard L. 1983. "Nuestra Señora de Valvanera in the Southwest." In *Hispanic Arts and Ethnohistory in the Southwest*, ed. Marta Weigle, 80-92. Santa Fe, N.M.: Ancient City Press.

Foster, George. 1953. "Cofradía and Compadrazgo in Spain and Spanish America." *Southwestern Journal of Anthropology* 9 (1): 1–28.

Foucault, Michel. 1990 [1976]. *The History of Sexuality*, Vol. 1: *An Introduction*. New York: Vintage Books.

Fragnito, Gigliola. 1994. "Istituzioni ecclesiastiche e costruzione dello Stato: riflessioni e spunti." In *Origini dello Stato: Processi di formazione statale in Italia fra medioevo ed età moderna*, ed. G. Chittolini, A. Molho, and P. Schiera, 531–51. Bologna, Italy: Il Mulino.

Francis, E. K. 1956. "Padre Martínez: A New Mexican myth." *New Mexico Historical Review* 31 (October): 265–89.

Frank, Larry. 1992. *New Kingdom of the Saints: Religious Art of New Mexico 1780–1907*. Santa Fe, N.M.: Red Crane Books.

Frank, Ross. 1992. "From Settler to Citizen: Economic Development and Cultural

Change in Late Colonial New Mexico, 1750–1820." Ph.D. diss., University of California, Berkeley.

———. 1996. "Economic Growth and the Creation of the Vecino Homeland in New Mexico, 1780–1820." *Revista de Indias* 56 (208): 743–82.

Freud, Sigmund. 1913. *Totem and Taboo.* In *The Standard Edition of the Complete Psychological Works of Sigmund Freud* [hereafter SE], 13: 1–161. Edited and translated by James Strachey. 24 vols. London: Hogarth.

———. 1922. "Some Neurotic Mechanisms in Jealousy, Paranoia and Homosexuality." *SE* 18: 221–32.

———. 1939. *Moses and Monotheism: Three Essays. SE* 23: 1–138.

Gallegos, José Ignacio. 1969. *Historia de la Iglesia en Durango.* México: Editorial Jus.

Gamble, Judith Louise. 1988. "Living with the Land: The Spanish Roots of Eighteenth-Century Land Use Patterns in Northern New Mexico." Ph.D. diss., University of Colorado, Boulder.

García Ayluardo, Clara. 1994. "A World of Images: Cult, Ritual and Society in Colonial Mexico City." In *Rituals of Rule, Rituals of Resistance: Public Celebrations and Popular Culture in Mexico,* ed. W. Beezley, C. Martin, and W. French, 77–93. Wilmington, Del.: SR Books.

García Gutiérrez, Pedro, and Agustín Martínez Carbajo. 1994. *Iglesias de Sevilla.* Madrid: Avapiés.

Gibbs, Jerome. 1954. "The Retablo Ex-voto in Mexican Churches." *El Palacio* 61 (12): 402–7.

Gibson, Charles. 1971. *The Black Legend: Anti-Spanish Attitudes in the Old World and the New.* New York: Alfred A. Knopf.

Giffords, Gloria Fraser. 1991. *The Art of Private Devotion: Retablo Painting of Mexico.* Fort Worth, Tex.: InterCultura.

———. 1992. *Mexican Folk Retablos.* Rev. ed. Albuquerque: University of New Mexico Press.

Gill, Sam. 1987. *Mother Earth: An American Story.* Chicago: University of Chicago Press.

———. 1994. "The Academic Study of Religion." *Journal of the American Academy of Religion* 62 (4): 965–75.

Gómez, José. 1986. *Diario curioso y cuaderno de las cosas memorables en México durante el gobierno de Revillagigedo (1789-1794).* México: Universidad Nacional Autónoma de México.

Gonzales, Manuel G. 1999. *Mexicanos: A History of Mexicans in the United States.* Bloomington: Indiana University Press.

González de León, Félix. 1852. *Historia crítica y descriptiva de las cofradías de penitencia, sangre y luz, fundadas en la ciudad de Sevilla.* Sevilla: D. Antonia Alavarez.

González Gómez, Juan Miguel, and José Roda Peña. 1992. *Imaginería procesional de la semana santa de Sevilla.* Sevilla: Universidad de Sevilla Secretariado de Publicaciones.

Greenleaf, Richard E. 1985. "The Inquisition in Eighteenth-century New Mexico." *New Mexico Historical Review* 60 (1): 29–80.

Gregg, Josiah. 1954 [1843]. *Commerce of the Prairies.* Norman: University of Oklahoma Press.

Gutiérrez, Ramón A. 1980. "Marriage, Sex and the Family: Social Change in Colonial New Mexico, 1690–1846." Ph.D. diss., University of Wisconsin, Madison.

———. 1991. *When Jesus Came, the Corn Mothers Went Away*. Stanford: Stanford University Press.

———. 1995. "El Santuario de Chimayó: A Synthetic Shrine in New Mexico." In *Feasts and Celebration in North American Ethnic Communities*, ed. Ramón Gutiérrez and Genevieve Fabre. Albuquerque: University of New Mexico Press.

Hackett, Charles W., ed. 1931. *Pichardo's Treatise on the Limits of Louisiana and Texas*. 4 vols. Austin: University of Texas Press.

———, ed. 1937. *Historical Documents Relating to New Mexico, Nueva Vizcaya, and Approaches Thereto, to 1773*. 3 vols. Washington, D.C.: Carnegie Institution.

———. 1970. *Revolt of the Pueblo Indians of New Mexico and Otermín's Attempted Reconquest 1680–1682*. 2 vols. Albuquerque: University of New Mexico Press.

Hall, G. Emlen. 2000. "Tularosa and the Dismantling of New Mexico Community Ditches." *New Mexico Historical Review* 75 (1): 77–106.

Hall, Thomas D. 1989. *Social Change in the Southwest, 1350–1880*. Lawrence: University of Kansas Press.

Hall, Douglas Kent. 1995. *New Mexico: Voices in an Ancient Landscape*. New York : H. Holt.

Hammond, George P. 1927. *Don Juan de Oñate and the Founding of New Mexico*. Santa Fe, N.M.: El Palacio Press.

Hammond, George P., and Agapito Rey. 1953. *Don Juan de Oñate, Colonizer of New Mexico 1595–1628*. Albuquerque: University of New Mexico Press.

Hanson, Alan. 1989. "The Making of the Maori: Culture Invention and Its Logic." *American Anthropologist* 91: 890–902.

Harris, Michael. 1927. "Willa Cather's Masterpiece." *Commonweal* 6 (September 28): 490–92.

Harline, Craig. 1990. "Official Religion-Popular Religion in Recent Historiography of the Catholic Reformation." *Archive for Reformation History* 81: 239–62.

Henderson, Alice Corbin. 1998 [1937]. *Brothers of Light: The Penitentes of the Southwest*. New York: Harcourt, Brace and Company. Reprint, Las Cruces, N.M.: Yucca Tree Press.

Henderson, John. 1978. "The Flagellant Movement and Flagellant Confraternities in Central Italy, 1260–1400." In *Religious Motivation and Biographical and Sociological Problems for the Church Historian*, ed. Derek Baker, 147–60. Oxford: Basil Blackwell.

Hernández, Francisco Martín. 1979. "La formación del clero en los siglos XVII y XVIII." In *Historia de la Iglesia in España IV: La Iglesia en la España de los siglos XVII y XVIII*, Antonio Mestre Sanchis, 523–82. Madrid: Biblioteca de Autores Cristianos.

Hernandez, Juan. 1963. "Cactus Whips and Wooden Crosses." *Journal of American Folklore* 76 (April): 216–24.

Hinnebusch, William A. 1965. *The History of the Dominican Order: Origins and Growth to 1500*, vol. 1. Staten Island, N.Y.: Alba House.

Hinsley Jr., Curtis M. 1990. "Authoring Authenticity." *Journal of the Southwest* 32 (4): 462–78.

Hobsbawn, Eric, and Terence Ranger, eds. 1983. *The Invention of Tradition*. Cambridge: Cambridge University Press.

Hodge, Frederick Webb, George P. Hammond, and Agapito Rey, eds. 1945. *Fray Alonso de Benavides' Revised Memorial of 1634*. Albuquerque: University of New Mexico Press.

Hopcroft, Rosemary. 1994. "The Origins of Regular Open-field Systems in Pre-industrial Europe." *Journal of European Economic History* 23 (3): 363–77.

Hordes, Stanley M. 1991. "The Inquisition and the Crypto-Jewish Community in Colonial New Spain and New Mexico." In *Cultural Encounters: The Impact of the Inquisition in Spain and the New World,* ed. M. E. Perry and A. J. Cruz, 207–17. Berkeley: University of California Press.

———. 1996. "The Sephardic Legacy in New Mexico: A History of the Crypto-Jews." *Journal of the West* 35 (4): 82–90.

Horka-Follick, Lorayne. 1969. *Los Hermanos Penitentes: A Vestige of Medievalism in the Southwestern United States.* New York: Tower Publications.

Howlett, Rev. W. J. 1908. *Life of the Right Reverend Joseph P. Machebeuf, D.D.* Pueblo, Colo.: Franklin Press Company.

Hsia, R. Po-Chia. 1989. *Social Discipline in the Reformation: Central Europe 1550–1750.* London: Routledge.

———. 1998. *The World of Catholic Renewal 1540–1770.* Cambridge: Cambridge University Press.

Hudon, William V. 1989. "Two Instructions to Preachers from the Tridentine Reformation." *Sixteenth Century Journal* 20 (3): 457–70.

———. 1996. "Review Essay: Religion and Society in Early Modern Italy—Old Questions, New Insights." *American Historical Review* 101 (June): 783–804.

Iriarte, Fr. Lazaro. 1983. *Franciscan History.* Chicago: Franciscan Herald Press.

Ivey, James E. 1998. "The Architectural Background of the New Mexico Missions." In *Seeds of Struggle/Harvest of Faith,* ed. Thomas J. Steele, S.J., Paul Rhetts, and Barbe Awalt, 43–52. Albuquerque: LPD Press.

Jaimes, M. Annette. 1988. "On "Mother Earth"—An Interview with Russell Means." *Bloomsbury Review* 8 (3): 25–26.

Jaramillo, Cleofas. 1941. *Shadows of the Past.* Santa Fe, N.M.: Ancient City Press.

Jojola, Ted. 1993. "Commentary on *When Jesus Came, the Corn Mothers Went Away: Marriage, Sex and Power in New Mexico, 1500–1846,* by Ramón A. Gutiérrez." *American Indian Culture and Research Journal* 17 (3): 141–43.

———. 1998. "On Revision and Revisionism: American Indian Representations in New Mexico." In *Natives and Academics,* ed. Devon A. Mihesuah, 172–80. Lincoln: University of Nebraska Press.

Jones, Oakah L. 1996. *Los Paisanos: Spanish Settlers on the Northern Frontier of New Spain.* Norman: University of Oklahoma Press.

Kamen, Henry. 1993. *The Phoenix and the Flame: Catalonia and the Counter Reformation.* New Haven: Yale University Press.

Keesing, Roger. 1989. "Creating the Past: Custom and Identity in the Contemporary Pacific." *Contemporary Pacific* 1 (1): 19–41.

Kelly, Henry W. 1941. "Franciscan Missions of New Mexico 1740–1760." *Historical Society of New Mexico Publications in History* 10 (April): 1–94. Reprinted in *The Spanish Missions of New Mexico,* ed. John Kessell and Rick Hendricks. New York: Garland Publishers, 1991.

Kessell, John L. 1980. *The Missions of New Mexico Since 1776.* Albuquerque: University of New Mexico Press.

———. 1990. "Bolton's Coronado." *Journal of the Southwest* 32 (1): 83–96.

————. 1993. Review of *When Jesus Came, the Corn Mothers Went Away*, by Ramón Gutiérrez." *Pacific Historical Review* 62 (3): 363–64.

King, Lesley S. 1999. *Frommer's New Mexico*. New York: Macmillan.

Knaut, Andrew L. 1995. *The Pueblo Revolt of 1680*. Norman: University of Oklahoma Press.

Knight, Christina. 1999. *Fodor's 2000: New Mexico*. New York: Fodor's Travel Publications.

Knowlton, Clark S. 1973. "Causes of Land Loss among the Spanish-Americans in Northern New Mexico." In *The Chicanos: Life and Struggles of the Mexican Minority in the United States*, ed. Gilberto López y Rivas, 111–21. New York: Monthly Review Press.

Kubler, George. 1940. *The Religious Architecture of New Mexico in the Colonial Period and since the American Occupation*. Colorado Springs, Colo.: Taylor Museum.

Kutsche, Paul. 1979. "Introduction: Atomism, Factionalism and Flexibility." In *The Survival of Spanish American Villages*, ed. Paul Kutsche, 7–19. Colorado Springs: Colorado College.

Kutsche, Paul, and Dennis Gallegos. 1979. "Community Functions of the Cofradía de Nuestro Padre Jesús Nazareno." In *The Survival of Spanish American Villages*, ed. Paul Kutsche, 91–98. Colorado Springs: Colorado College.

Lafaye, Jacques. 1976. *Quetzalcóatl and Guadalupe*. Chicago: University of Chicago Press.

Lancelloti, Arturo. 1951. *Feste tradizionali*. Milano: Società Editrice Libraria.

Larkin, Brian. 1999. "The Splendor of Worship: Baroque Catholicism, Religious Reform, and Last Wills and Testaments in Eighteenth-Century Mexico City." *Colonial Latin American Review* 8 (4): 405–42.

Larson, Robert W. 1975. "The White Caps of New Mexico: A Study of Ethnic Militancy in the Southwest." *Pacific Historical Review* 44 (2): 171–86.

Lavrin, Asunción. 1988. "Diversity and Disparity: Rural and Urban Confraternities in Eighteenth-century Mexico." In *Manipulating the Saints: Religious Brotherhoods and Social Integration in Postconquest Latin America*, ed. Albert Meyers and Diane Elizabeth Hopkins, 67–100. Hamburg, Germany: Wayasbah.

Lea, Aurora Lucero-White. 1953. *Literary Folklore of the Hispanic Southwest*. San Antonio, Tex.: Naylor.

Lévi-Strauss, Claude. 1963. "The Structural Study of Myth." In his *Structural Anthropology*, 206–31. New York: Basic Books.

Lewes, Kenneth. 1995. "Psychoanalysis and Male Homosexuality." In *The Psychology of Sexual Orientation, Behavior and Identity: A Handbook*, ed. L. Diamant and R. McAnulty, 104–20. Westport, Conn.: Greenwood Press.

Linnekin, Jocelyn. 1983. "Defining Tradition: Variations on the Hawaiian Identity." *American Ethnologist* 10 (2): 241–52.

Livingstone, Elizabeth, ed. 1977. *The Concise Oxford Dictionary of the Christian Church*, 2d ed. Oxford: Oxford University Press.

Llompart, Gabriel. 1969. "Desfile iconográfico de penitentes españoles (siglos XVI al XX)." *Revista de dialectología populares* 25: 31–51.

Lombardi Satriani, Luigi M. 1981. "La teatralizzatione del sangue." In *Rappresentazioni arcaiche della tradizione popolare*, Atti de VI Convegno di Studio, 27–31 maggio 1981. Viterbo, Italy: Union Printing.

López-Gastón, José R. 1985. *Tradición hispanica de Nuevo México*. México: Editorial Progreso, S.A.

López Pérez, Manuel, ed. 1984. *Semana Santa en Jaén*. Cordoba: Publicaciones del Monte de Piedad y Caja de Ahorros de Cordoba.

López Pulido, Alberto. 1997. "Lyrics of the Penitentes: The Contribution of Los Hermanos Penitentes to Roman Catholicism in New Mexico." In *Seeds of Struggle/Harvest of Faith*, ed. Thomas J. Steele, S.J., Paul Rhetts, and Barbe Awalt, 373–84. Albuquerque: LPD Press.

———. 2000. *The Sacred World of the Penitentes*. Washington, D.C.: Smithsonian Institution Press.

Lummis, Charles F. 1952 [1895]. *The Land of Poco Tiempo*. Albuquerque: University of New Mexico Press.

Luna, Sandra. 2000. *Retablos y ex votos*. Mexico City: Museo Franz Mayer.

Mares, E. A., ed. 1988a. *Padre Martínez: New Perspectives from Taos*. Taos, N.M.: Millicent Rogers Museum.

———. 1988b. "The Many Faces of Padre Antonio José Martínez: A Historiographic Essay." In *Padre Martínez: New Perspectives from Taos*, ed. E. A. Mares, 18–47. Taos, N.M.: Millicent Rogers Museum.

Marshall, Louise. 1994. "Manipulating the Sacred: Image and Plague in Renaissance Italy." *Renaissance Quarterly* 42 (3): 485–532.

Martin, A. Lynn. 1988. *The Jesuit Mind: The Mentality of an Elite in Early Modern France*. Ithaca: Cornell University Press.

Martínez y Alíre, Rev. Jerome J. 1998. "The Influence of the Roman Catholic Church in New Mexico under Mexican Administration: 1821–1848. In *Seeds of Struggle/Harvest of Faith*, ed. Thomas J. Steele, S.J., Paul Rhetts, and Barbe Awalt, 329–43. Albuquerque: LPD Press.

McDonald, Margaret Espinosa. 1998. "The Community Influence and Cultural Power of Nuestra Señora de Belén." In *Seeds of Struggle/Harvest of Faith*, ed. Thomas J. Steele, S.J., Paul Rhetts, and Barbe Awalt, 195–206. Albuquerque: LPD Press.

McKevitt, Gerald, S.J. 1992. "Italian Jesuits in New Mexico: A Report by Donato M. Gasparri, 1867–1869. *New Mexico Historical Review* 67 (4): 357–92.

Meehan, Andrew. 1913. "Repose, Altar of." In *The Catholic Encyclopedia*, 12:776. New York: Encyclopedia Press.

Megged, Amos. 1996. *Exporting the Catholic Reformation: Local Religion in Early-Colonial Mexico*. Leiden: E.J. Brill.

Metz, Brent. 1998. "Without Nation, Without Community: The Growth of Maya Nationalism Among Ch'orti's of Eastern Guatemala." *Journal of Anthropological Research* 54 (3): 325–49.

Meyers, Albert. 1988. "Religious Brotherhoods in Latin America." In *Manipulating the Saints: Religious Brotherhood and Social Integration in Postconquest Latin America*, ed. A. Meyers and D. Hopkins, 1–21. Hamburg, Germany: Wayasbah.

Miele, Michele. 1998. "Pietà popolare e classi dirigenti nel culto alla Madonna dell'Arco degli ultimi decenni del Cinquecento." In *Scrivere de santi*, ed. Gennaro Luongo, 363–79. Rome: Viella.

Miller, Susan A. 1998. "Licensed Trafficking and Ethnogenetic Engineering." In *Natives and Academics*, ed. Devon A. Mihesuah, 100–110. Lincoln: University of Nebraska Press.

Mills, George, and Richard Grove. 1956. *Lucifer and the Crucifer: The Enigma of the Penitentes*. Colorado Springs, Colo.: Taylor Museum.

Mitchell, Timothy. 1990. *Passional Culture: Emotion, Religion and Society in Southern Spain*. Philadelphia: University of Pennsylvania Press.

Mocho, Jill. 1997. *Murder and Justice in Frontier New Mexico, 1821–1846*. Albuquerque: University of New Mexico Press.

Montalvo, Fray Felipe. 1755. *Novena a la Puríssima Madre de Dios, y Virgen Immaculada Maria, en su santissima imagen, que con titulo de Ntra. Señora de la Macana se venera en el Convento de N.S.P. San Francisco de Mexico: con una breve relación de la misma sacratísima imagen*. Mexico City.

Montanari, Daniele. 1987. *Disciplinamento in terra veneta: La diocesi di Brescia nella seconda metà del XVI secolo*. Bologna: Società editrice il Mulino.

Montoto, Santiago. 1976 [1946]. *Cofradías Sevillanas*. Introduction and notes by Enrique Esquivias Franco. Sevilla: Secretariado de Publicaciones de la Universidad de Sevilla.

Morales, Francisco, O.F.M. 1973. *Ethnic and Social Background of the Franciscan Friars in Seventeenth Century Mexico*. Washington, D.C.: Academy of American Franciscan History.

Moreno Navarro, Isidoro. 1982. *La Semana Santa de Sevilla: conformación, mixtificación y significaciones*. Sevilla: Servicio de Publicaciones del Ayuntamiento de Sevilla, 1982.

———. 1983. *La cofradías de Sevilla en cromo-litografía*. Sevilla: Gráficas del Sur.

Morfi, Juan Agustín de. 1935. *Viaje de indios y diario del Nuevo México*, con una introducción biobibliográfica y acotaciones por Vito Alessio Robles. México: Antigua librería Robredo de J. Porrua e hijos.

———. 1977. *Father Juan Agustín de Morfi's Account of Disorders in New Mexico 1778*. Trans. and ed. Marc Simmons. Albuquerque: Historical Society of New Mexico.

Mullet, Michael. 1984. *The Counter-Reformation*. London: Methuen.

Murphy, John J. 2000. "Historical Essay" and "Explanatory Notes." In *Death Comes for the Archbishop*, Willa Cather, 325–71, 381–512. Lincoln: University of Nebraska Press.

Neulander, Judith. 1996. "The New Mexican Crypto-Jewish Canon: Choosing to Be 'Chosen' in Millennial Tradition." *Jewish Folklore and Ethnology Review* 18 (1–2): 19–58.

Nidel, David S. 1984. "Modern Descendants of Conversos in New Mexico." *Western States Jewish History* 16: 249–62.

Nolan, Mary Lee, and Sidney Nolan. 1989. *Christian Pilgrimage in Modern Western Europe*. Chapel Hill: University of North Carolina Press.

Norget, Kristin. 1999. "Progressive Theology and Popular Religiosity in Oaxaca, Mexico." In *Latin American Religion in Motion*, ed. Christian Smith and Joshua Prokopy, 91–110. New York: Routledge.

Norris, Jim. 1994. "The Franciscans in New Mexico, 1692–1754: Towards a New Assessment." *Americas* 51 (2): 151–71.

Nostrand, Richard L. 1992. *The Hispano Homeland*. Norman: University of Oklahoma Press.

Nunn, Tey Marianna. 1993. "Santo Niño de Atocha: Development, Dispersal and Devotion of a New World Image." M.A. thesis, University of New Mexico, Albuquerque.

Olin, John C. 1990. *Catholic Reform from Cardinal Ximenes to the Council of Trent, 1495–1563*. New York: Fordham University Press.

BIBLIOGRAPHY

O'Malley, John W. 1991. "Was Ignatius Loyola a Church Reformer? How to Look at Early Modern Catholicism." *Catholic Historical Review* 77: 177–93.

———. 1993. *The First Jesuits*. Cambridge: Harvard University Press.

———. 1996. "Jesuits." In *The Oxford Encyclopedia of the Reformation*, ed. Hans J. Hillerband, 333–38. Oxford: Oxford University Press.

———. 2000. *Trent and All That*. Cambridge: Harvard University Press.

Orlandi, Giuseppe. 1994. "La missione popolare in età moderna." In *Storia dell'Italia religiosa II: L'età moderna*, ed. Gabriele De Rosa and Tullio Gregory, 419–52. Bari, Italy: Giuseppe Laterza & Figli.

Ortiz, Simon. 1993. "Commentary on *When Jesus Came, the Corn Mothers Went Away: Marriage, Sex and Power in New Mexico, 1500–1846*, by Ramón A. Gutiérrez." *American Indian Culture and Research Journal* 17 (3): 150–53.

Ortiz Echagüe, José. 1950. *España mística*. 2d. ed. Madrid: Mayfe.

Parmentier, Richard J. 1997. "The Pueblo Mythological Triangle: Poseyemu, Montezuma, and Jesus in the Pueblos." In *Handbook of North American Indians*, vol. 9, *Southwest*, ed. Alfonso Ortiz, 609–22. Washington, D.C.: Smithsonian Institution Press.

Paul, Robert A. 1996. *Moses and Civilization: The Meaning Behind Freud's Myth*. New Haven: Yale University Press.

———. 1998. "The Genealogy of Civilization." *American Anthropologist* 100 (2): 387–96.

———. 1999. "The Male Negative Oedipus Complex in Cross-cultural Perspective." *Journal for the Psychoanalysis of Culture and Society* 4 (1): 31–38.

Peterson, Karen. 1992. "New Faces of the Penitentes." *El Palacio* 97 (2): 16–20, 52.

Pollen, J. H. 1913. "Counter-Reformation." In *The Catholic Encyclopedia*, 4:437–45. New York: Encyclopedia Press.

Poole, Stafford. 1997. *Our Lady of Guadalupe: The Origins and Sources of a Mexican National Symbol, 1531–1797*. Tucson: University of Arizona Press.

Poska, Allyson M. 1998. *Regulating the People: The Catholic Reformation in Seventeenth-century Spain*. Leiden: Brill.

Powell, Philip Wayne. 1971. *Tree of Hate: Propaganda and Prejudices affecting United States Relations with the Hispanic World*. New York: Basic Books.

Prodi, Paolo. 1985. "Riforma interiore e disciplinamento sociale in San Carlo Borromeo." *Intersezioni* 5 (2): 273–85.

———. 1989. "Controriforma e/o riforma cattolica: superamento di vecchi dilemmi nei nuovi panorami storiografici." *Romische historische mitteilungen* 31: 227–37.

———. 1994. *Disciplina dell'anima, disciplina del corpo e disciplina della società tra medioevo ed età moderna*. Bologna: Società editrice il Mulino.

Prosperi, Adriano. 1980. "'Otras Indias': missonari della controriforma tra contadine e selvaggi." In *Scienze, credenze occulte, livelli di cultura, Convegno Internazionale di Studi (Firenze, 26–30 giugno 1980)*, 205–33. Firenze: Leo S. Olschki editore.

———. 1994. "Riforma cattolica, controriforma, disciplinamento sociale." In *Storia dell'Italia religiosa-II: L'età moderna*, ed. Gabriele De Rosa and Tullio Gregory, 3–48. Bari, Italy: Editori Laterza.

Rada, Manuel de Jesús. 1829. "Proposición hecha al Soberano Congreso General de la Unión por el Diputado del Territorio de Nuevo México." MANM 9: 507–10.

Reff, Daniel. 1995. "The Predicament of Culture and Spanish Missionary Accounts of the Tepehuan and Pueblo Revolts." *Ethnohistory* 42 (1): 63–90.

Reinhard, Wolfgang. 1989. "Reformation, Counter-Reformation and the Early Modern State: A Reassessment." *Catholic Historical Review* 75 (July): 383–404.

Reséndez, Andrés. 1999. "National Identity on a Shifting Border: Texas and New Mexico in the Age of Transition, 1821–1848." *Journal of American History* 86 (2): 668–88.

Reverter-Pezet, Guillermo. 1985. *Las cofradías en el Virreynato del Perú.* Lima, Peru: G. G. Reverter-Pezet.

Rienzo, Maria Gabriella. 1980. "Il processo di cristianizzazione e le missioni popolari nel Mezzogiorno. Aspetti istituzioni e socio-religiosi." In *Per la storia sociale e religiosa del Mezzogiorno d'Italia,* ed. Giuseppe Galasso and Carlo Russo, vol. 1. Naples: Guida editori.

Rinaldi, Stefania Mason. 1979. "Le immagini della peste nella cultura figurativa veneziana." In *Venezia e la peste, Comune de Venezia,* 209–24. Venezia: Marsilio Editori.

Rodríguez, Sylvia. 1987. "Land, Water and Ethnic Identity in Taos." In *Land, Water and Culture: New Perspectives on Hispanic Land Grants,* ed. Charles L. Briggs and John R. Van Ness, 313–403. Albuquerque: University of New Mexico.

———. 1990. "Ethnic Reconstruction in Contemporary Taos." *Journal of the Southwest* 32 (4): 541–55.

———. 1992. "The Hispano Homeland Debate Revisited." *Perspectives in Mexican American Studies* 3: 95–113.

———. 1994. "The Tourist Gaze, Gentrification, and the Commodification of Subjectivity in Taos." In *Essays on the Changing Images of the Southwest,* ed. R. Francaviglia and D. Narrett, 105–26. College Station: Published for the University of Texas at Arlington by Texas A&M University Press.

———. 1995. "Subaltern Historiography on the Rio Grande: On Gutiérrez's *When Jesus Came, the Corn Mothers Went Away.*" *American Ethnologist* 21 (4): 892–99.

Rodríguez Becerra, Salvador, and José María Vázquez Soto. 1980. *Exvotos de Andalucía: milagros y promesas en la religiosidad popular.* Seville: Argantonio, Ediciones andaluzas.

Romero, Cecil V. 1928. "Apologia of Presbyter Antonio J. Martínez." *New Mexico Historical Review* 3 (Oct): 325–46.

Rosenbaum, Robert. 1981. *Mexicano Resistance in the Southwest.* Austin: University of Texas Press.

Rusconi, Roberto. 1992. "Gli ordini religiosi maschili dalla Controriforma alle soppressioni settecentesche: cultura, predicazione, missioni." In *Clero e società nell'Italia moderna,* ed. Mario Rosa, 207–74. Bari: Editori Laterza.

Said, Edward. 1994 [1978]. *Orientalism.* New York: Vintage Books.

Sallnow, Michael J. 1987. *Pilgrims of the Andes: Regional Cults in Cusco.* Washington, D.C.: Smithsonian Institution Press.

Salpointe, J. B. 1898. *Soldiers of the Cross.* Banning, Calif.: St. Boniface's Industrial School.

Sánchez, Juan M. 1909. *Doctrina Cristiana del P. Jerónimo de Ripalda é intento bibliográfico de la misma, años 1591-1900.* Madrid: Imprenta Alemana.

Sánchez, George I. 1996 [1940]. *Forgotten People: A Study of New Mexicans.* Albuquerque: University of New Mexico Press.

Sánchez, Pedro. 1978 [1906]. *Recollections of the Life of the Priest Don Antonio José Martínez,* trans. Ray John de Aragón. Santa Fe, N.M.: Lightening Tree.

Sánchez Herrero, José. 1999. "Crisis y permanencia: religiosidad de las cofradías de Semana Santa de Sevilla, 1750-1874." In *Las cofradías de Sevilla en el siglo de la crisis*, ed. León Carlos Álvarez Santalo et al., 35–84. Sevilla: Universidad de Sevilla.

Schlesinger, Andrew B. 1971. "Las Gorras Blancas, 1889–1891." *Journal of Mexican American History* 1 (Spring): 87–143.

Schroeder, H. J. 1950. *Canons and Decrees of the Council of Trent*. St. Louis, Mo.: B. Herder.

Shalkop, Robert. 1967. *Wooden Saints: The Santos of New Mexico*. Colorado Springs, Colo.: Taylor Museum.

Simmons, Marc. 1968. *Spanish Government in New Mexico*. Albuquerque: University of New Mexico Press.

———. 1969. "Settlement Patterns and Village Plans in Colonial New Mexico." *Journal of the West* 8 (1–4): 7–21.

———, ed. 1977. *Father Juan Agustín de Morfi's Account of Disorders in New Mexico 1778*. Isleta Pueblo, N.M.: Historical Society of New Mexico.

———. 1983. "Colonial New Mexico and Mexico: The Historical Relationship." In *Colonial Frontiers*, ed. Christine Mather, 71–89. Santa Fe, N.M.: Ancient City Press.

———. 1991. *Coronado's Land: Daily Life in Colonial New Mexico*. Albuquerque: University of New Mexico Press.

———. 2000. "Fray Angélico Chávez: The Making of a Maverick Historian." In *Fray Angélico Chávez: Poet, Priest and Artist*, ed. Ellen McCracken, 11–23. Albuquerque: University of New Mexico Press.

Simmons, Virginia McConnell. 1999. *The San Luis Valley: Land of the Six-armed Cross*, 2d ed. Niwot, Colo.: University Press of Colorado.

Snow, David H. 1979. "Rural Hispanic Community Organization in Northern New Mexico: An Historical Perspective." In *The Survival of Spanish American Villages*, ed. Paul Kutsche, 45–52. Colorado Springs: Colorado College.

Solano, Francisco de, and Pilar Ponce, eds. 1988. *Cuestionarios para la formación de las relaciones geográficas de Indias, siglos XVI/XIX*. Madrid: Consejo Superior de Investigaciones Científicas.

Solórzano, Juan Paz. 1914. *Historia del Señor Crucificado de Esquipulas*. Guatemala: Arenales Hijos.

Sprott, Robert. 1984. "Making Up What Is Lacking: Towards an Interpretation of the Penitentes." *Working Paper #110, Southwest Hispanic Research Institute*. Albuquerque: University of New Mexico.

Stanford, Lois. 1998. "Persistence in Religious Faith and Practice: Traditional Holy Week Observances in Soccoro, Texas." *Catholic Southwest* 9: 75–98.

Stark, Louisa R. 1971. "The Origin of the Penitente Death Cart." *Journal of American Folklore* 84: 304–10.

Steele, Thomas J., S.J. 1974. *Santos and Saints: Essays and Handbook*. Albuquerque, N.M.: Calvin Horn.

———. 1978. "The Spanish Passion Play in New Mexico and Colorado." *New Mexico Historical Review* 53 (3): 239–59.

———. 1988. "The View from the Rectory." In *Padre Martínez: New Perspectives from Taos*, ed. E. A. Mares, 71–102. Taos, N.M.: Millicent Rogers Museum.

————. 1992. "Foreword." In Larry Frank, *New Kingdom of the Saints: Religious Art of New Mexico 1780–1907.* Santa Fe, N.M.: Red Crane Books.

————. 1993a. "Cofradía." In his *Folk and Church in New Mexico,* 1–20. Colorado Springs, Colo.: Hulbert Center for Southwest Studies.

————. 1993b. "Cleansing the Air: The Fatal Vigil at Llano de Santa Bárbara." In his *Folk and Church in New Mexico,* 21–29. Colorado Springs, Colo.: Hulbert Center for Southwest Studies.

————. 1993c. "The Padre's Will, 1859, or The Little World of Don Tomás Abeyta." In his *Folk and Church in New Mexico,* 48–57. Colorado Springs, Colo.: Hulbert Center for Southwest Studies.

————. *Santos and Saints: The Religious Folk Art of Hispanic New Mexico.* Santa Fe, N.M.: Ancient City Press.

————. 1995. "Albuquerque in 1821: Padre Leyva's Descriptions." *New Mexico Historical Review* 70 (2): 159–78.

————. 1997a. "Significant Santos from the Regis Collection." In *The Regis Santos: Thirty Years of Collecting, 1966–1996,* ed. Thomas J. Steele, Barbe Awalt, and Paul Rhetts, 17–64. Albuquerque: LPD Press.

————. 1997b. *New Mexican Spanish Religious Oratory, 1800–1900.* Albuquerque: University of New Mexico Press.

————. 1998a. "Family Spirituality in Traditional Hispanic New Mexico." In *Our Saints among Us/Nuestros santos entre nosotros: 400 years of New Mexican Devotional Art,* ed. Barbe Awalt and Paul Rhetts, 23–30. Albuquerque: LPD Press.

————. 1998b. "Foreword." In Alice Corbin Henderson, *Brothers of Light: The Penitentes of the Southwest,* vii–xii. Las Cruces, N.M.: Yucca Tree Press.

————, ed. and trans. 2002. *Archbishop Lamy: In His Own Words.* Albuquerque, N.M.: LPD Press.

Steele, Thomas J., S.J., and Rowena A. Rivera. 1985. *Penitente Self-government.* Santa Fe, N.M.: Ancient City Press.

Swadesh, Frances Leon. 1974. *Los primeros pobladores: Hispanic Americans of the Ute frontier.* Notre Dame: University of Notre Dame Press.

Taylor, William B. 1996. *Magistrates of the Sacred: Priests and Parishioners in Eighteenth-century Mexico.* Stanford: Stanford University Press.

Taves, Ann. 1986. *The Household of Faith.* Notre Dame: University of Notre Dame Press.

Teja, Jesús Frank de la. 2001. "St. James at the Fair: Religious Ceremony, Civic Boosterism, and Commercial Development on the Colonial Mexican Frontier." *Americas* 57 (3): 395–417.

Terpstra, Nicholas. 1990. "Women in the Brotherhoods: Gender, Class and Politics in Renaissance Bolognese Confraternities." *Renaissance and Reformation* 26 (3): 193–211.

Tjarks, Alicia. 1978. "Demographic, Ethnic, and Occupational Structure of New Mexico, 1790." *Americas* 35: 45–88.

Thomas, Alfred B. 1969. *Forgotten Frontiers: A Study of the Spanish Indian Policy of Don Juan Bautista de Anza, Governor of New Mexico 1777–1787.* Norman: University of Oklahoma Press.

Thurston, Herbert. 1904. *Lent and Holy Week: Chapters on Catholic Observance and Ritual.* New York: Longmans, Green and Co.

————. 1913. "Tenebrae." In *The Catholic Encyclopedia*, 14:506. New York: Encyclopedia Press.

————. 1933. "The False Visionaries of Lourdes." *Month* 3 (October): 289–301.

Torquemada, Juan de. 1986. *Monarquía indiana*. 3 vols. Mexico City: Editorial Porrúa.

Trask, Haunani-Kay. 1991. "Natives and Anthropologists: The Colonial Struggle." *Contemporary Pacific* 3 (1): 159–77.

Trevor-Roper, Hugh. 1983. "The Invention of Tradition: the Highland Tradition of Scotland." In *The Invention of Tradition*, ed. Eric Hobsbawn and Terence Ranger, 15–41. Cambridge: Cambridge University Press.

Trexler, Richard. 1995. *Sex and Conquest: Gendered Violence, Political Order and the European Conquest of the Americas*. Ithaca: Cornell University Press.

Ulierte Ruiz, Telesforo. 1991. *Orígenes de la cofradía de Nuestro Padre Jesús Nazareno*. Alcaudete, Jaén: Cofradía de Nuestro Padre Jesús Nazareno.

Valle, Rafael Heliodoro. 1946. *Santiago en America*. México: Editorial Santiago.

Van Ness, John. 1979. "Hispanic Village Organization in Northern New Mexico: Corporate Community Structure in Historical and Comparative Perspective." In *The Survival of Spanish American Villages*, ed. Paul Kutsche, 21–44. Colorado Springs, Colo.: Colorado College.

————. 1987. "Hispanic Land Grants: Ecology and Subsistence in the Uplands of Northern New Mexico and Southern Colorado." In *Land, Water and Culture: New Perspectives on Hispanic Land Grants*, ed. Charles L. Briggs and John R. Van Ness, 141–214. Albuquerque: University of New Mexico.

————. 1991. *Hispanos in Northern New Mexico: The Development of Corporate Community and Multicommunity*. New York: AMS Press.

Vargas Ugarte, Rubén, S.J. 1956. *Historia del culto de María en Iberoamérica y de sus imágenes y santuarios más celebrados*. 2 vols. Madrid.

Varjabedian, Craig, and Michael Wallis. 1994. *En Divina Luz: the Penitente Moradas of New Mexico*. Albuquerque: University of New Mexico Press.

Venegas, Miguel. 1839. *Manualito de parrocos, para los auto[s] del ministerio mas precisos, y auxiliar a los enfermos*. Tomada del de Juan Francisco López. Nuevo Mexico: Imprenta del Presbítero Antonio José Martínez a cargo de J. M. Baca.

Vetancurt, Agustin. 1971 [1698]. *Teatro mexicano*. Mexico City: Editorial Porrúa.

Vigil, Ralph. 1975. "Willa Cather and Historical Reality." *New Mexico Historical Review* 50: 123–38.

Villacastín, Tomás de. [1618] 1976. *A manuall of devout meditations and exercises, instructing how to pray mentally, drawne for the most part, out of the Spiritual Exercise of B. F. Ignatius*. Reprint, Ilkley (Yorkshire): Scholar Press, 1976.

————. 1797. *Jaculatorias arregladas a las meditaciones del Tomás de Villacastin, dispuestas por un indigno discipulo de la Santa Escuela de Christo del Convento del Espíritu Santo de la Ciudad de México*. Mexico City: Mariano de Zúñiga y Ontiveros.

Villagrá, Gaspar Pérez de. 1992. *Historia de la Nueva México, 1610*. Trans. and ed. Miguel Encinias, Alfred Rodríguez, and Joseph P. Sánchez. Albuquerque: University of New Mexico Press.

Vismara Chiappa, Paola. 1982. "Forme della pietà barocca nelle compagne lombarde tra sei e settecento." In *Economia, istituzioni, cultura in Lombardia nell'età di Maria Teresa*, ed. Aldo Rotelli and Gennaro Barbarisi. Milano: Società Editrice Il Mulino.

Vollmar, E. R. 1954. "Religious Processions and Penitente Activities at Conejos, 1874." *Colorado Magazine* 31 (1): 172–79.

Wagner, Henry. 1937. "New Mexico Spanish Press." *New Mexico Historical Review* 12 (January): 1–40.

Ward, Albert E. 1999. "Documenting an Eighteenth-Century Italian Medal from Central New Mexico." *Kiva* 65 (2): 167–79.

Warren, Nancy Hunter. 1987. *Villages of Hispanic New Mexico.* Santa Fe: School of American Research Press.

Weber, David J. 1975. "El gobierno territorial de Nuevo México-la exposición del Padre Martinez de 1831." *Historia Mexicana* 25 (2): 302–15.

———. 1981. "American Westward Expansion and the Breakdown of Relations between Pobladores and 'Indios Bárbaros' on Mexico's Far Northern Frontier, 1821–1846." *New Mexico Historical Review* 56 (July): 221–38.

———. 1988. *Myth and the History of the Hispanic Southwest.* Albuquerque: University of New Mexico Press.

———. 1992. "The Spanish Legacy in North America and the Historical Imagination." *Western Historical Quarterly* 23 (1): 4–24.

Weber, Max. 1958. *From Max Weber: Essays in Sociology,* ed. H. H. Gerth and C. Wright Mills. New York: Oxford University Press.

Webster, Susan Verdi. 1998. *Art and Ritual in Golden-Age Spain.* Princeton: Princeton University Press.

Weigle, Marta. 1976a. *Brothers of Light, Brothers of Blood.* Albuquerque: University of New Mexico Press.

———. 1976b. *A Penitente Bibliography.* Albuquerque: University of New Mexico Press.

———. 1994. "On Coyotes and Crosses: That Which Is Wild and Wooden of the Twentieth-Century Southwest." In *Essays on the Changing Images of the Southwest,* ed. R. Francaviglia and D. Narrett, 72–104. College Station: Published for the University of Texas at Arlington by Texas A&M University Press.

Weigle, Marta, and Barbara A. Babcock. 1996. "Introduction." In *The Great Southwest of the Fred Harvey Company and the Santa Fe Railway,* ed. M. Weigle and B. A. Babcock, 1–8. Phoenix, Ariz.: Heard Museum.

Weinstein, Donald. 1970. *Savonarola and Florence: Prophecy and Patriotism in the Renaissance.* Princeton: Princeton University Press, 1970.

Weissman, Ronald F. E. 1982. *Ritual Brotherhood in Renaissance Florence.* New York: Academic Press.

Wilder, Mitchell A. 1976 [1943]. *Santos: The Religious Folk Art of New Mexico.* New York: Hacker Art Books.

Wilson, Chris. 1997. *The Myth of Santa Fe: Creating a Modern Regional Tradition.* Albuquerque: University of New Mexico Press.

Woodress, James. 1987. *Willa Cather, A Literary Life.* Lincoln: University of Nebraska Press.

Woodward, Dorothy. 1935. "The Penitentes of New Mexico." Ph.D. diss., Yale University.

Wright, Robert Wright. 1998. "How Many Are 'a Few'? Catholic Clergy in Northern New Mexico, 1780–1851." In *Seeds of Struggle/Harvest of Faith,* ed. Thomas J. Steele, S.J., Paul Rhetts, and Barbe Awalt, 219–61. Albuquerque: LPD Press.

BIBLIOGRAPHY

Wroth, William. 1979. "The Flowering and Decline of the New Mexican Santero: 1780–1900." In *New Spain's Far Northern Frontier,* ed. David J. Weber, 273–82. Albuquerque: University of New Mexico Press.

———. 1982. *Christian Images in Hispanic New Mexico.* Colorado Springs, Colo.: Taylor Museum.

———. 1988. "New Mexican Santos and the Preservation of Religious Tradition." *El Palacio* 94 (1): 4–17.

———. 1991. *Images of Penance, Images of Mercy.* Colorado Springs, Colo.: Taylor Museum.

Zardin, Danilo. 1987. "Le confraternite in Italia settentrionale fra XV e XVIII secolo." *Società e storia* 35: 81–137

———. 2000. "Relaunching Confraternities in the Tridentine Era: Shaping Consciences and Christianizing Society in Milan and Lombardy." In *The Politics of Ritual Kinship,* ed. N. Terpstra, 190–209. Cambridge: Cambridge University Press.

Zarri, Gabriella, ed. 1996. *Donna, disciplina, creanza cristiana dal XV al XVII secolo: studi e testi a stampa.* Rome: Edizioni di storia e letteratura.

———. 1996. "Donna, disciplina, creanza cristiana: un percorso di ricerca." In *Donna, disciplina, creanza cristiana dal XV al XVII secolo: studi e testi a stampa,* ed. Gabriella Zarri, 7–19. Rome: Edizioni di storia e letteratura.

Zimdars-Swartz, Sandra L. 1991. *Encountering Mary: From La Salette to Medjugorje.* Princeton: Princeton University Press.

INDEX